The Third Revolution

Also by Richard Koch

Wake Up and Shake Up Your Company (with Andrew Campbell) – Pitman Publishing

The Successful New Boss's First 100 Days – Pitman Publishing

The Investor's Guide to Selecting Shares That Perform – Financial Times/Pitman Publishing

The Financial Times Guide to Management and Finance – Financial Times/Pitman Publishing

The A–Z of Management and Finance – Financial Times/Pitman Publishing

The Financial Times Guide to Strategy – Financial Times/Pitman Publishing

Managing Without Management (with Ian Godden) – Nicholas Brealey

Breakup! (with David Sadtler and Andrew Campbell) – Capstone

The 80/20 Principle – Nicholas Brealey

Moses on Leadership (with Andrew Campbell) – Capstone

The Third Revolution

*Creating Unprecedented Wealth and Happiness
for Everyone in the New Millennium*

Richard Koch

CAPSTONE

First Published 1998
Capstone Publishing Limited
Oxford Centre for Innovation
Mill Street
Oxford OX2 0JX
United Kingdom
http://www.capstone.co.uk

British Library Cataloguing in Publication Data
A CIP catalogue record for this book is available from the British Library

ISBN 1-900961-13-X

Typeset in 11/15 Bembo by
Sparks Computer Solutions, Oxford
http://www.sparks.co.uk
Printed and bound by
T.J. International Ltd, Padstow, Cornwall

This book is printed on acid-free paper

To the memories of

Raymond Howard ('Don') Koch
my father
advocate of education and equality

and

Bryan Dixon Mayson
steadfast friend
humanist and powerhouse for good

who both inspired this book and its ideals

Contents

Preliminaries

This is a book about politics by someone whose trade is business. Those respectful of professional boundaries may find this disturbing, impertinent or even disqualifying. Open-minded readers will soon realize that the boundaries between politics, business, and social issues have been drawn too tightly for society's good. Whether or not I have succeeded in my attempt to critique both politics and business, and provide a better model for both, it should be apparent that someone is going to have to provide such an integration. This book is at least a start.

I am profoundly grateful for all the comments and ideas I received from Andrew Campbell. At an early stage Andrew and I discussed the idea of writing this book together. In the end we simply did not have enough time to see whether our ideas could be successfully melded, but there are many of his original thoughts in the book, including the idea of the Democratic Corporation and some of the thinking behind the Four Principles of Progress. Most useful of all were Andrew's provocations and (often derisive) reactions to draft text. Andrew still does not agree with parts of this manifesto but its debt to him is huge.

I have been greatly helped by many people whose expertise differs from my own. Many thanks in particular to A.F. ('Pat') Thompson of Wadham College, Oxford, for fearless criticism; to Robert A.G. Monks for both praise and dissent; to John Redwood for acid words, courteously and usefully expressed; to Robin Field for literary advice; to Al Ries for his honest disagreement with my main policy prescriptions; to Raymond Ackerman for his wise remarks; to Chris Eyles for his skepticism; and above all to Mark Allin and Richard Burton for their direction, encouragement and editorial skill. My thanks also to the large number of friends and associates who read the draft and helped to improve the contents. Finally, to Lee Dempsey, for all his support throughout the writing.

And, come the revolution, I will know where to send the tumbrils.

Richard Koch

Preface

The first step in the revolution ... is to raise the proletariat to the position of ruling class, to win the battle of democracy ...

In place of the old bourgeois society, with its classes and class antagonisms, we shall have an association, in which the free development of each is the condition for the free development of all.

— Karl Marx and Friedrich Engels [1]

Come senators, congressmen, please lend a hand
And don't criticize what you can't understand
Your sons and your daughters are beyond your command
The old road is rapidly ageing
Please get out the way if you can't lend a hand
'Cos the times, they are a-changing

— Bob Dylan

Summary

- The world has been transformed for the better by two revolutions, capitalism and democracy
- Democracy was expected to abolish capitalism. It nearly did so.
- Today, both capitalism and democracy continue to expand their power. They coexist uneasily. Capitalism and democracy share many attributes, but capitalism continues to have a dark side that can only be extirpated by democratic reform.
- All the left's attempts to reform or replace capitalism have failed, because their intellectual premises were wrong. The intentions, however, were and remain valid. The intellectual bankruptcies of socialism and social democracy have created a void.
- A breakthrough is possible only by fusing capitalism and democracy. Democracy must embrace the market mechanism in a totally new way in order to abolish capitalism as we know it, to democratize capitalism.
- This third revolution can unite and give moral purpose to developed societies and, within the next century, banish war, hunger and oppression from the face of the earth.

To anyone in 1750, our world is utopia. The world has far more people, living at a far higher average standard, than the observer of 1750 would have believed possible. To say then that within two and a half centuries most people in America, Europe and East Asia would not only have ample food, but also that they would live like kings, would have invited derision. To have gone on to say that kings would have little or no power, and that democracy would have swept the world, would have invited instant consignment to the madhouse.

Yet less than a hundred years later, in 1848, a document sizzling with insight and power explained why the world was being transformed and how democracy could transform the daily lives of millions. For the subsequent 100 years, the *Communist Manifesto* was the best short guide to both the past and the future.

The authors of the guide, Karl Marx and Friedrich Engels, referred to two revolutions that would utterly change human history. Though they did not call it either 'the first revolution' or 'capitalism', they pointed to the transformation from feudalism to capitalism wrought by 'modern industry' and its protagonists, 'the bourgeoisie' (also called 'capitalists'): [2]

> *Modern industry has established the world market, for which the discovery of America paved the way. This market has given an immense development to commerce, to navigation, to communication by land. This development has, in turn, reacted on the extension of industry; and in proportion as industry, commerce, navigation, railways extended, in the same proportion the bourgeoisie developed, increased its capital, and pushed into the background every class handed down from the Middle Ages ...*
>
> *The bourgeoisie ... has been the first to show what man's activity can bring about. It has accomplished wonders far surpassing Egyptian pyramids, Roman aqueducts, and Gothic cathedrals ...*
>
> *... In place of the old local and national seclusion and self-sufficiency, we have intercourse in every direction, universal inter-dependence of nations ...*
>
> *The bourgeoisie, by the rapid improvement of all instruments of production, by the immensely facilitated means of communication, draws all,*

*even the most barbarian, nations into civilization ... It creates a world
after its own image.*

*The bourgeoisie has subjected the country to the rule of the towns ...
and has thus rescued a considerable part of the population from the idiocy
of rural life ...*

*The bourgeoisie, during its rule of scarce one hundred years, has cre-
ated more massive and more colossal productive forces than have all pre-
ceding generations altogether. Subjection of Nature's forces to man, machinery, application of chemistry to industry and agriculture, steam-navi-
gation, railways, clearing of whole continents for cultivation, canalization
of rivers, whole populations conjured out of the ground – what earlier
century had even a presentiment that such productive forces slumbered in
the lap of social labour?*

Yet despite these accomplishments, the same revolution (later dubbed capitalism) led to human oppression: [3]

*The bourgeoisie, wherever it has got the upper hand, has put an end to all
feudal, patriarchal, idyllic relations. It has pitilessly torn asunder the motley
feudal ties that bound man to his 'natural superiors', and has left remaining no other nexus between man and man than naked self-interest, than
callous 'cash payment'. It has drowned the most heavenly ecstasies of
religious fervour, of chivalrous enthusiasm, of philistine sentimentalism,
into the icy waters of egotistical calculation ... for [feudal] exploitation,
veiled by religious and political illusions, it has substituted naked, shame-
less, direct, brutal exploitation.*

Fortunately, Marx and Engels implied, we were not yet at the end of history.
There was a second revolution riding to the rescue – democracy. 'The march
of modern history' would use political means to create a superior economic
and social world: [4]

*... the first step in the revolution by the working class, is to raise the
proletariat to the position of working class, to win the battle of democracy.*

> *The proletariat will use its political supremacy to wrest, by degrees, all capital from the bourgeoisie, to centralize all instruments of production in the hands of the State, i.e. of the proletariat organized as the ruling class; and to increase the total of productive forces as rapidly as possible.*

Marx and Engels looked forward to a world where peace and prosperity would rule, where exploitation and war would be obsolete [5]:

> *National differences and antagonisms between peoples are daily more and more vanishing, owing to the development of the bourgeoisie, to freedom of commerce, to the world market, to uniformity in the mode of production and in the conditions of life corresponding thereto.*
>
> *The supremacy of the proletariat will cause them to vanish still further. ...*
>
> *In proportion as the exploitation of one individual by another is put an end to, the exploitation of one nation by another will also be put an end to ... the hostility of one nation to another will come to an end.*

Even with our hindsight, the *Communist Manifesto* remains illuminating. Democracy did indeed triumph, though by no means as quickly as Marx and Engels expected. 'Democracy' did not overthrow capitalism, though it came a great deal closer than we now realize. Our generation sees capitalism triumphant and rampant, but in the 1930s and early 1940s capitalism was on its knees, and could quite plausibly have disappeared for ever, to near-universal relief. 'Democracy' did respond to a strong instinct to create a better system than capitalism, to evolve a political and economic system that would serve ordinary people, usually ending up with a negation of both capitalism and democracy – socialism, communism, fascism, Nazism – systems that, by the early 1940s, looked virtually certain to dominate the future.

Against the odds, capitalism and democracy have both prospered, and, on balance, done tremendous good. They have created the modern world. Let's trace very briefly the history of the two revolutions.

What is capitalism?

1 **Capitalism is an economic system where money is the universal common denominator and the measure of value.** Exchanges of money are the principal way in which resources are allocated and transferred from one application to another.

2 **Under capitalism, production is organized for profit.** A capitalist enterprise must either be cash positive, or operate at a profit (the promise of cash to come), or be expected to become profitable and cash positive in the future – or it must close down. As James Burnham observed:

What decides whether a shoe factory can keep going is not whether the owner likes to make shoes or whether people are going barefoot ... or whether workers need wages but whether the product can be sold on the market at a profit, however modest.

Capitalism is characterized by frequent and often rapid shifts in the composition of producing units. New firms are always being created and existing firms, whether they are young or old, may die. In this way, capitalism reallocates resources from the unproductive to the productive.

3 **Capitalism uses the skill of entrepreneurs to shift resources from lower to higher value applications**

In aiming to make a profit, capitalist enterprise aims to use resources in a way that adds to society's resources. The profit system naturally uses resources tomorrow better than they are used today.

4 **Capitalism operates via markets.** For each economic transaction, there are buyers and sellers. Markets work best when there are many buyers and sellers, so that no individual buyer or seller can rig the market.

There are different types of market. There is a market for goods and services. The buyers are consumers or other customers (including producer units) and the sellers are producer units.

There is a market for capital. The buyers are producer units and the sellers are owners of capital, otherwise known as investors, either individual capitalists or investment institutions.

There is a market for entrepreneurs. The buyers are investors and the sellers are individual entrepreneurs.

There is a market for labor. The buyers are producer units and the sellers are individual workers, otherwise known as employees.

Under capitalism, no-one organizes the system or the market. The capitalist system is not controlled by anyone, not by capitalists, nor by anyone else. The system is spontaneous and anarchic.

5 **The price mechanism** is central to capitalism. Each market always has a price. The price regulates supply and demand and provides constant information to buyers and sellers. Prices rise when there are more buyers than sellers at the initial price; they rise until the number of buyers and sellers is identical. Prices fall when there are more sellers than buyers, until the number of each is equalized. The movement of prices shifts the allocation of resources and stocks to provide what customers want within the constraint of what is, or could become, available.

When prices are immobile, rigged by producers or customers acting in concert, 'sticky' (that is, slow to reflect shifts in supply and demand), or otherwise unresponsive to market pressures, a capitalist system may still operate but it will be inefficient. Beyond a certain point, if the price mechanism fails to operate tolerably freely, the capitalist system will stop working.

6 **Capitalism is a system of private and individual, rather than collective, enterprise.** Though individuals may band together to pool capital or for other purposes, the individuals ultimately control their own destiny. The state may regulate industry and enforce laws, but must do so equitably and without favoring any individual enterprise. Nor may the state own business enterprises. Any interference or ownership by the state that conflicts with these requirements creates a non-capitalist system. Under capitalism, decisions on what should be produced are made through the free market, and therefore ultimately by sovereign consumers with purchasing power; there are no political or administrative decisions on what to produce or how.

7 **Capitalism is based on specialization and the single-purpose corporation.** A capitalist enterprise always exists to meet a specific economic need. Over time, capitalism leads to a progressively greater profusion and specialization of producer units. Though the owners of enterprise may diversify, each individual producing unit owned will have a special purpose with its own specific market and customers.

8 **Capitalist enterprises are required to compete against other capitalist enterprises.** Without effective competition, capitalism does not operate well: producers gain an unfair advantage over consumers. In practice, where there is no competition, producers consume more resources than they should; they become fat and happy.

Capitalist enterprise – the owners and managers of individual capitalist enterprises – often seek to avoid competition, by fair means and foul. No capitalist system will operate well over the long haul if competition can be avoided or evaded. Free markets tend to correct the failure to compete, because sooner or later profitable opportunities can usually be created for new players to smash monopolies. Nonetheless, the state has an important role in helping to speed up this process, by requiring monopolies to be dismantled.

9 **Capitalism is inherently dynamic and expansive.** Individual businesses tend to want to expand, to make more money and to stamp their personality more firmly on the world. There are no limits to expansion provided there is enough capital and talent to drive the process. Talent and capital are attracted to success. To torment Oscar Wilde, nothing expands like success.

10 **Capitalism is inherently international.** Any individual producing unit with a defined field of expertise and goods or services for which there is a ready and expanding market will tend to seek the widest possible geographical market. Any owner of capital will want the highest possible return, regardless of national boundaries. Capitalist society is the first to have a world view. In practice, capitalism has been the first system to lead to organizations often owned and operated by people from different nations. Capitalism has shrunk and homogenized the world. Under capitalism, nations have a greater economic interest in collaborating, within free markets, than in conquering each other.

11 **Capitalism is based on useful knowledge.** Capitalism uses, multiplies and cross-pollinates knowledge and skill in order to lower the cost or increase the performance of goods and services and hence to increase the returns to capital. The explosion of knowledge and the explosion of capital in the modern world are inextricably combined. No other economic system has the same vested interest in, or track record in producing, useful knowledge.

12 **Capitalism is not a fixed system.** Capitalism is an economic system that is compatible with many different ways of organizing society. It is compatible with personal freedom and with tyranny; with hierarchical and democratic polities; and with relatively equal or extremely unequal distributions of wealth. It is compatible with either exploitation or protection of the mass of people in society. There have been many different types of capitalism in the world at different times and in different places, and there will be many new and different forms in the future.

Even in the economic sphere, capitalism can work in many different ways. It can work mainly through one-person or small businesses, or mainly through vast corporations, or anything in between. Laws, institutions and customs can favor producers or consumers. The proportions of wealth taken by capitalists, by workers, by entrepreneurs, or by managers can vary dramatically.

The past or present shape of capitalism is not a blueprint for its future.

These characteristics of capitalism allow for great heterogeneity and evolution. The best short guide, however, to whether a system is or is not capitalist are these two rules: Capitalism is centered around markets that no-one controls; and capitalism requires that all important decisions on the allocation of resources are taken by a very large number of individuals rather than by an elite or the state.

The first revolution – modern capitalism

If capitalism means the financing of trade and the accumulation of capital through money-lending and what we would today call venture capital, then most important sea-ports throughout history have been locii of capitalism. The ancient Phoenicians, Greeks and Romans contained important classes of sea-going merchants. We know for sure that capitalism of this type was alive and well in late 14th century Florence. In the 15th century there was an enormous expansion of trade. International fairs took place in Antwerp, Frankfurt, Lyons and Piacenza. In the 17th century, Amsterdam joined in. A century later London established its dominance in trade [6].

Industrial capitalism has a shorter, but not negligible, pre-history. In 1619, a poet recorded (with a probable high degree of romancing) the factory of Jack of Newbury, said to employ 600 workers on 200 looms in Henry VIII's time. The 18th century saw a fantastic expansion of manufacturing in many countries, with the world's industrial centers being China and India. In 1730, Mr Wang of Hangchow employed tens of thousands of textile workers: 4000 weavers and several times that number of spinners [7].

Yet, it is probably correct to date the 'take-off' of industrial capitalism in mid-to-late 18th century Britain. (Historians have struggled to explain quite why Britain, less advanced industrially than China or India, was the 'airport' for industrial take-off. One correct though far from complete explanation is that labor was too cheap in Asia to reward technological innovation; it was worth substituting capital for labor in Britain, where labor was costlier.) From then on, capitalism emerged from the fringes of society to take first one country and then another by storm. By the mid-19th century, as Marx and Engels noted, capitalism had transformed not just Britain's economy, but also its landscape, geography, social structure, and, to a limited but irreversible degree, its politics. It was already clear that the British model of economic development represented a higher stage of history.

Later that century, America became a capitalist country, followed by Germany, and at a distance and more slowly, other European countries including Russia. Wherever capitalism struck, it transformed society, and this is the unique character of modern capitalism – first, changing the economy and social structures of each country where it took root, and then creating a world society of capitalist nations.

Capitalism only became dominant in the 20th century, and then only after a titanic struggle. In 1917, Russia, not yet firmly in the capitalist world, opted out. Shortly after the Nazis consolidated their power in 1933 Germany, too, exited the capitalist world, taking with it, in short order, the European countries it conquered. By 1940, the United States and Britain were the only large capitalist economies on earth.

After 1945, capitalism made a storming come-back. All developed countries became capitalist. Equally, all countries that adopted capitalism became developed. Japan became one of the world's top economies, with GDP per head second only to Switzerland. In the past ten years, the East Asian 'tiger' economies and some in Latin America have grown at rates unprecedented in economic history, at 6–10% per annum; and the statistics show that Singapore, with a doubling of per capita wealth between 1990 and 1997, briefly overtook the US on that measure [8].

Substantial and sustained economic growth is a modern phenomenon, a product of capitalism [9]. Before 1800, it did not exist. Since then, economic growth under capitalism has averaged 2–3 per cent per annum, and growth in hourly productivity and incomes per head have averaged 3–4 per cent. A 3 per cent increase means that wealth doubles every 23 years, and that over 100 years there is an increase of *20 times*. This is how large population growth can co-exist with the abolition of poverty, how working hours can be cut and the dignity of each individual be respected.

Capitalism and marketism

The power of markets can be deployed without the historical apparatus and paraphernalia of capitalism. A very significant and dynamic part of China's economy, particularly the export sector, is 'marketist' without being 'capitalist' in the sense defined above. The Chinese state is the sponsor and governing body of market enterprise in a way that is totally foreign to traditional capitalism.

'Marketism' may be defined as any economic system that uses the market to allocate resources. This makes 'marketism' the most catholic and comprehensive descriptor. There can therefore be many varieties of marketism: 'capitalist marketism' or simply 'capitalism' could be used to describe historical forms of marketism, where inequality of purchasing power has co-existed with free markets; 'communist marketism' could describe the system in the Chinese free economic zones; and 'democratic marketism' could describe a free market system where the state ensures reasonable equality of purchasing power but leaves markets free to execute virtually all economic transactions.

The real driver of economic progress is free markets rather than capitalism. In the past only capitalism allowed free markets. It is clear that the 21st century will see many forms of effective marketism that are quite distinct from traditional capitalism. Before long, when we mean the free market system, we may speak of marketism rather than capitalism.

These concepts are discussed further in Chapter 5. To avoid confusion, however, outside of Chapter 5, I use the accepted term 'capitalism' to describe the market system.

The power of capitalism

Before we reform capitalism, we had better appreciate its power and glory. Modern capitalism is the most marvellous device ever for multiplying resources. It makes better use of existing resources. It creates altogether new xxii • The Third Revolution

ones. The process of creation and multiplication is tireless and unceasing.

Many writers [10] have tried to explain the power of capitalism; in Chapter 5 I summarize their views and add my own gloss. How does capitalism create such wealth? There are two paramount points. One is that capitalism is the only market-based economic system and that *markets encourage resources to be used more productively, and move resources from low to high value uses* (as defined by those with purchasing power). This is an extremely decentralized system, and, though it is not perfect, it creates continuous improvement, as good practice drives out bad. Where markets reign, there is continuous and pervasive improvement; where they do not, improvement is sporadic and local.

The second key point is that *markets exalt useful knowledge; they make science and technology central to society*. Markets latch on to inventions and adapt and diffuse them rapidly for commercial purposes. Capitalism could not have created the wealth explosion since 1750 without the concomitant knowledge explosion − the steam engine and all its derivatives; modern agriculture and agribusiness; electricity, gas and nuclear power; the internal combustion engine; modern medicine; the computer; integrated circuits; the micro-chip; bio-technology. Attractive as it might be to believe that the knowledge explosion jump-started capitalism rather than the other way round, this argument cannot be sustained [11]. If markets do not dominate society, much technology is surplus to requirements and shelved; otherwise, as the historian Felipe Fernandez-Armesto remarks, 'the Incas would have had the wheel-and-axle and the ancient Greeks steam power' [12].

It is wonderful for humanists to realize, however, that the power driving capitalism is the market mechanism and that the market thrives on decentralized and distributed power, power residing with the lowest unit or level of disaggregation in society, namely the individual. Capitalism has generally been characterized by rule by elites, gross inequality, and social division; but for markets to work well, none of these are mandatory. I show in Chapter 5 that the profit motive and the desire to become rich are just a small part of why markets work so well; while the Policy section (Chapters 7–11) demonstrates how markets can be used to create a *more equal* society.

The second revolution – modern democracy

It could be argued that democracy is older than capitalism, at least 2500 years old. In 507 BC, Cleisthenes the Alcmaenid seized power in Athens, invoking the power of the people and proposing sovereign power for the *Ecclesia*, the Assembly of Citizens that had existed even earlier. Athenian democracy then lasted for 185 years, ensuring equality of all citizens before the law, electing top officials and holding them to account [13].

Quite apart from the imperfections of Athenian democracy – manipulation by the rich and by demagogues, and the existence of slavery – the key point is that it didn't last. The flame flickered briefly in history and was then decisively extinguished or confined to the margins of history. It matters little that, here and there, something that can be described as democracy persisted. Tacitus describes the popular assemblies of Germanic tribes. Historical evidence survives of a *ding* or popular assembly held on the island of Bjorko (Sweden) in the 9th century AD; and thereabouts or soon after there were popular assemblies in Denmark, Iceland and the Isle of Man. Nordic democracy was often spread by Viking conquest, with traces appearing in England, Scotland, Russia and even Poland [14]. Nevertheless, none of these democracies became a dominant model for the world or were ever enjoyed by more than a tiny fraction of the world's people.

Modern democracy is quite different. Since the start of the American Revolution in 1775–6, and the French Revolution of 1789–93, democracy has made a jagged and slow but ultimately successful bid to become the world's dominant political system. With hindsight, the American Revolution established the first real and significant modern democracy. American democracy initially comprised only white, male citizenship, and it was not until 1842, when Rhode Island finally fell into line, that it applied to all states. Yet despite the existence of slavery in southern states (extinguished only after the American Civil War in 1865), and the absence of rights for women, the Declaration of Independence, with its common, equally distributed, 'rights of man', was a new departure.

What is democracy?

Democracy can mean many things. Unless otherwise qualified, when I use the word I refer to a political system that approximates as closely as possible to the following ideal:

1 **Democracy is a political system where the currency – votes – is distributed equally amongst all adult citizens.** Democracy requires universal suffrage. Ideally, each citizen has equal influence in determining the composition and actions of government.
2 **Democracy includes a system of guaranteed and impartial rights for all citizens,** ensuring the rule of law, equal treatment in respect of the law and in the course of daily life, and the protection of minorities and of each individual. Each citizen's life and welfare is as important as that of any other citizen. In this sense, at least, democracy must be egalitarian. It must discourage the division of society into classes with different rights and privileges.
3 **Democracy means rule for the people.** This means that society must be run for the benefit of everyone, not for an elite.
4 **Democracy means rule by the people.** Citizens must be active and interested participants in the governing process, and must recognize civic duties as well as rights. Democracy cannot flourish unless citizens are interested and engaged in the political process. As was recognized in the 19th century, this implies a strong link between democracy and the education of citizens.

   Most democracies are 'representative democracies', where citizens elect representatives who rule. Representative democracy has many virtues and may be inevitable, but care should be taken to avoid elites or pressure groups hijacking government and divorcing ordinary citizens from it. The best forms of democracy supplement representation with more direct democracy: referenda on crucial matters, local democracy, and market-type controls. Direct democracy also has its dangers but it is the lifeblood of true democracy, and, through electronic means, increasingly feasible.
5 **Democracy requires free and open competition for political power.** Democracy is incompatible with one party rule or elections where there is only one candidate. The best forms of democracy make it easy for new parties or individuals unassociated with any party to compete for votes.
6 **Democracy means that the ordinary citizen has control over her life.** Democracy abhors any hierarchical control of the citizen.

To use modern industrial jargon, the citizen is empowered and not supervised. Democracy therefore requires the most extreme form of decentralization of power that is possible and compatible with other democratic principles. Wherever possible, strong central government – the hallmark of undemocratic regimes throughout the ages – is replaced by local government and self-government.

7 **Democracy requires the advancement of positive freedoms for citizens.** At the heart of the democratic ideal is 'life, liberty and the pursuit of happiness'. Democratic society is therefore properly interested in the freedom and quality of life of each and every citizen. Hence it is part of democracy's concern to facilitate as far as possible 'the greatest happiness of the greatest number' and the happiness and liberty of all citizens. Again, however, these steps should be undertaken as far as possible on local and voluntary bases, so that concern for fellow citizens arises organically and is not imposed by central government.

8 **Democracy generates a feeling of community and fraternity and takes care of the common good.** All forms of governance should resonate with symbolic power, derived by standing for all that is best and most noble in community life.

9 **Democracy has an ethical content and encourages virtue and altruism to flourish.** There are many dangers with virtuous democracy, and the second modern experiment in democracy, the French Revolution, fell into nearly all of them, leading to a reign of terror in which prominent revolutionaries all lost their heads. Yet democracy without mission and virtue is like an airport without noise: it may still exist, but it does nothing useful.

Right from the Declaration of Independence, the rhetoric of democracy has set standards and aspirations much higher than democracy could at that time deliver. Yet vision and even hypocrisy have proved useful. Over time, democracy has managed to approximate closer and closer to the ideals proclaimed by earlier democrats. Astonishingly, rhetoric has been a leading indicator of performance.

Democracy should not be a mere balancing of interests, a market in votes, a technocratic and morally neutral piece of machinery. Democracy should involve passion and a sense of purpose, a determination to make the world a better place, and an effort to raise human life above the determination of animal and plant genes to replicate themselves. Democracy should never forget, to paraphrase Ivan Alexander, that it is a noble experiment that nature has not tried.

America's democracy, like the fragile and fleeting democracy of the French Revolution of 1789–93, explicitly saw itself as the harbinger of a new and better model of society. The astute French observer, Alexis de Tocqueville, who visited America in 1831, was one of the first foreigners to declare that American democracy would last and that, sooner or later, the rest of the civilized world would follow suit.

For a long time, American democracy and republicanism were nearly alone. The political philosopher, Francis Fukuyama, counts three liberal democracies in 1790 – Switzerland and France, briefly, as well as the United States; and then five in 1848 (deleting France, and adding Belgium, the Netherlands, and, Great Britain); 13 in 1900; 25 in 1919; only 13 in 1940; and then the great upsurge after World War II – 36 in 1960 and 61 in 1990, not counting the fledgling democracies of central and eastern Europe after the fall of the USSR [15].

Democracy was even slower to establish itself than Fukuyama says. The revolutions of 1848 produced democracies that lasted no more than a year, while Switzerland did not introduce universal male suffrage until 1874, nor Britain until 1884. Democracy was still a dirty word for the ruling elites in all the Great Powers, except America, before the First World War; for example, Benjamin Disraeli, a British Prime Minister who greatly extended the franchise, nevertheless saw the fruits of democracy as depleted treasuries, foolish wars, devalued property and diminished freedom [16].

In short, modern democracy is at the earliest a late-18th century invention, a mid-19th century reality (of large countries) only in the United States, a challenger for power in the other Great Powers only in the late 19th century, and a predominant reality only in our own century. For us, of course, democracy must include full female suffrage, which means that it is a 20th century phenomenon.

I argue (see box) that democracy is not just a set of rules and rights to protect the liberty of citizens, but that it is rule by the people to extend the positive freedoms of all individuals. It is, precisely as Marx and Engels wrote in 1848, an unprecedented attempt to eliminate 'the exploitation of one part of society by the other' and ensure 'the free development of all'.

Democracy has had its teething troubles, its humbug, even its monsters. But the democratic ideals expressed in the American Declaration of Independence

– the right of each individual to 'life, liberty and the pursuit of happiness' – have come to mean just that. Modern developed democracies are quite unlike any other states that have ever existed. They stand for social justice. They seek to create the good life for all citizens, regardless of background. They are pacific and don't try to expand their boundaries. All this is new and worthy of celebration. The ideal pre-dated the reality; but, equally, the reality has come to correspond surprisingly and impressively to the ideal. Democracy has transcended the shackles of nature and history.

Capitalism and democracy: uneasy bedfellows

In 19th century Europe, the struggle for democracy was increasingly associated with that against capitalism. All the varieties of socialism, including but far from confined to communism, held that progress required the overthrow of capitalism and the substitution of new economic rules for society. Nor was this all. In the *Communist Manifesto*, Marx and Engels note that

> ... when the class struggle nears the decisive hour, the process of dissolution ... within the whole range of old society, assumes such a violent, glaring character, that a small section of the ruling class cuts itself adrift, and joins the revolutionary class, the class that holds the future in its hands. Just as therefore at an earlier period, a section of the nobility went over to the bourgeoisie, so now a portion of the bourgeoisie goes over to the proletariat, and in particular, a portion of the bourgeois ideologists ... [17]

And so it came to pass. Towards the end of the 19th century, not only did many middle-class intellectuals join the socialist crusade against capitalism, but also many successful, wealthy capitalists denounced their own system. Chapter 1 tells the exciting story of how, in the first half of our century, the prevalent view that capitalism would not and should not survive very nearly became a self-fulfilling prophecy. The claims of 'democracy' were opposed to those of 'capitalism', and since capitalism represented the interests of a narrow elite, it could hardly be expected to survive.

The battle between democracy and capitalism ended in an outcome that no-one anticipated. *Both* survived. In the last two decades, democracy and capitalism have both extended and deepened their sway so that they are now, respectively, the world's dominant political and economic systems. Yet this is not a stable and harmonious equilibrium. Democracy and capitalism have come to terms with each other but they are bedfellows through force of circumstances rather than choice; the result of a shotgun wedding, not a love affair. The waves of capitalism and democracy have washed past each other without establishing common cause, or even clear agreement on their spheres of influence.

The dark side of capitalism

In the most capitalist economies, and notably the United States, large chunks of people, whole segments of the nation, have been excluded from the rich fruits of capitalism. We see increasing inequality, the collapse of a bright tradition of sturdy individualism into the squalid shadows of dependence, trust between citizens crumbling, the rise of a new underclass and more virulent crime, the weakening of community bonds and the collapse of natural assumptions of common social purpose. Where capitalism is most extensive, it is also most exclusive. The gap between those who are included in capitalism, and those who are excluded, is becoming a chasm.

Japan, the greatest capitalist success story of the post-1945 era, has seen absolutely no growth in profits or the value of its companies for the past seven years. Measured correctly, Japan's magnificent capitalist engine has been making losses. There too, social cohesion, though still strong, is under unprecedented attack.

In many developing countries, children labor for trivial wages in dangerous sweat shops.

In the former Soviet Union, the sense of liberation released by the revolutions of 1989–91 has turned to bewilderment, cynicism, wild exploitation, and gangsterism.

In both the advanced and the advancing world, the triumph of capitalism has turned into a Pyrrhic victory. No-one can escape the global spread of the market system, but everywhere it brings disruption and apparently greater inequality.

The incompatibility between capitalist and democratic values – the same inherent conflict that led most pre-1945 thinkers to the view that capitalism was doomed – has not been resolved; it has merely been swept under the carpet. In February 1997 the conflict re-emerged from a most unlikely quarter, when the billionaire currency speculator, George Soros, wrote in the *Atlantic Monthly*: [18]

> *Although I have made a fortune in the financial markets, I now fear that the untrammeled intensification of laissez-faire capitalism and the spread of market values into all areas of life is endangering our open and democratic society. The main enemy of the open society, I believe, is no longer the communist but the capitalist threat.*

This has shades of the early 20th century, when the 'revolutionary capitalists' like Henry Ford and King Gillette denounced capitalism, and lent great support to the anti-capitalist, pro-democratic cause. Indeed, Mr Soros himself draws an intriguing parallel between the dominance of capitalism at both the start and the end of the 20th century [19]:

> *The present situation is comparable to that at the turn of the past century. It was a golden age of capitalism, characterized by the principle of laissez-faire; so is the present. The earlier period was in some ways more stable. There was an imperial power, England, that was prepared to dispatch gunboats to faraway places because as the main beneficiary of the system it had a vested interest in maintaining that system. Today the United States does not want to be the policeman of the world. The earlier period had the gold standard; today the main currencies float and crush against each other like continental plates. Yet the free-market regime that prevailed a hundred years ago was destroyed by the First World War. Totalitarian ideologies came to the fore, and by the end of the Second World War there was practically no movement of capital between countries. How much more likely the present regime is to break down unless we learn from experience!*

Capitalism versus democracy?

Are capitalism and democracy antagonists? And if so, what can we do about it?

We need an answer that is both balanced and novel. It will not do to pretend, as do the apologists of capitalism, that there is no problem, only a misunderstanding. The New Right claims that capitalism is inherently democratic and that the capitalist system always benefits the poor as well as the rich. Actually, the New Right has some very good arguments, and much of what they say is true; Chapter 5 gives due weight to these elements of truth. Capitalism *is* the best economic system. It *does* help the poor as well as the rich. It *is* congruent with many democratic values; it *does* decentralize and pass authority from central powers to individuals. But, ultimately, it cannot be maintained that current manifestations of capitalism are fair, or conducive to social cohesion; quite simply, they are not. As honest capitalists like George Soros acknowledge, capitalism is running increasingly counter to the values on which open and democratic societies depend. There are many defects in contemporary capitalism, not just social but also economic, including defects that are not often highlighted, ones that flow from the dominance of big business and managers in our society. These defects are dissected in Chapters 4 and 5.

On the other hand, as I show in Chapters 2 and 3, all the left's attempts, throughout this century, to reform or replace capitalism have failed, not least because their intellectual premises were badly flawed. The glorification of big business and the hope that the large corporation could provide a more 'social-ized' form of enterprise, at once efficient and fair, has been a consistent theme of the broad left in the past 100 years. The halo put around big business has never been justified but *has* been very influential; it has done much harm. Other intellectual planks of the left and center – those broadly described as social-democratic – have proved equally fallacious. To name but five products, social-democracy has given us redistribution of incomes, the mega-state dispensing welfare, a large state business sector, a large state education sector, and the attempt to create full employment via so-called Keynesian economic policies. The objective behind all of these policies was worthy – the wish to create a fairer and more democratic society – but all of these policies have failed, and some of them have clearly done more harm than good.

All these policies were related to each other and they all failed because the *principles* and the reasoning behind them were wrong. The common heresy is that big is better; that people of goodwill, managerial experts, can devise outcomes for the population that are better than market solutions; that markets can be cut across with impunity and without creating great waste; and that everyone should mind everyone else's business.

Social democratic policies have been discredited by experience, but it is more difficult to dismantle the social democratic mindset, which has become an accepted and much-loved part of our intellectual furniture. It is much easier to love the warm and fuzzy concepts of co-operative humanity than it is to love the market, even though the latter delivers and the former do not.

What then is the answer? It is not the denial of the radical right, the pretense that capitalism is perfect and there is no problem. Nor is it the social democratic heritage, the ghostly smile on the Cheshire cat that refuses to disappear. We need reform, even revolution, but we need a *new* answer.

The answer is a third revolution, to fuse capitalism and democracy.

A synthesis of capitalism and democracy is necessary to preserve and enhance the power of each to do good for humanity. To achieve democracy's objectives, capitalism must be more fully utilized – but capitalism must also be democratized, so that it operates for the benefit of society as a whole and all its members.

The mistake of social democracy was to believe that non-market intervention, to restrict markets and create non-market systems, could help ordinary people. The mistake of laissez-faire capitalism is to reject social objectives and to regard intervention as undesirable. Democratic capitalism, in contrast to both social democracy and laissez-faire capitalism, uses markets to achieve social objectives. The policy section of this book gives some illustrations of how democratic capitalism might work in practice.

Democratic capitalism is market-based but it is new and quite different from the capitalism of today. It is not capitalism for the few, for financiers, for the upper classes, or for the managers of our corporations. It is capitalism, and capital, for everyone. It completes the process, started more than a century ago, whereby the ownership of the means of production, distribution and exchange passes from the few to the many, from the elite to the people at large. It is capitalism for *all* the people. Chapter 7 shows that though the *objectives* of democratic capitalism are not far removed from those of social democracy, the *principles* that direct the attainment of the objective are sharply differentiated from those of social democracy as well as from those of laissez-faire capitalism.

Democratic capitalism drives forward another process, much less evident and advanced, whereby the *control* of economic and social institutions passes from the few to the many, from managers to workers, from manipulators to individuals, from administrators and do-gooders to the disadvantaged and dependent.

Democratic capitalism requires radical reform of our business institutions. If democratic capitalism is to work, corporations must become democratic, smaller and less diversified. Set up the right way, with the right incentives, market mechanisms can ensure that this happens. Chapter 10 shows how.

Democratic capitalism will also change the role of the state. The good state will be immensely influential, ensuring that capital, education and jobs are provided for everyone and that the common good is nurtured. The state will structure markets and use them for social purposes, but do very little itself. Government mechanisms will become local, decentralized and individualized. The corporate state, the national state, and the civil-service-state will all be dismantled. Chapter 11 outlines the way that the weak state can achieve far more than the strong state ever did. Chapters 8 and 9 discuss, respectively, the redistribution of capital, and new education and employment policies.

The 21st century prize

By the end of the next century, it is possible that war, poverty and social division may have been consigned to the dustbin of history.

We can accomplish all this if every government on earth becomes democratic-capitalist. Economies everywhere would be market-based and inter-dependent. Government would be universally democratic, small, powerful and highly respected. Each country and region would have a strong sense of community identity, of common purpose. Huge increases in wealth would have been generated, and used to create a richer, more diverse yet more united society.

If capitalism and democracy fuse to create the third revolution, all this is possible. No revolution has ever seemed very likely to change the world, until after it had already done so. Yet it is a small step from seeing what capitalism and democracy have already done apart, in conflict or uncomfortable coalition, to seeing a vision of what they could achieve together in perfect harmony.

Endnotes

1 Karl Marx and Friedrich Engels (1848) *Manifesto of the Communist Party*. The version quoted is the 1888 English translation, taken from the Penguin Classic *The Communist Manifesto* (1985) edition, Harmondsworth, pp. 104–5.

2 *Ibid*, pp. 81–5.

3 *Ibid*, p. 82.

4 *Ibid*, p. 104.

5 *Ibid*, p. 102.

6 See Norman Davies (1996) *Europe: A History*, Oxford, Oxford University Press, pp. 442–3.

7 Felipe Fernandez-Armesto (1995) *Millennium*, London, Bantam Press/ Black Swan, p. 359.

8 Charles Hampden-Turner and Fons Trompenaars (1997) *Mastering the Infinite Game*, Oxford, Capstone, pp. 1–3.

9 It does not necessarily follow that because sustained growth only became apparent after capitalism came to dominate society, the growth was caused by capitalism. In theory, the growth and capitalism could both have been caused by a third variable, such as the invention of the steam engine or, more broadly, the knowledge explosion since 1750. It

just so happens that modern capitalism *was* the principal cause both of
the knowledge explosion and of the economic growth (which did indeed result to a considerable extent from the knowledge explosion).
See the next page and also Chapter 6.

10   Interested readers are recommended to read:

Ludwig von Mises (1963) *Human Action*, Chicago, Henry Regnery
Co, third edition.

Joseph A. Schumpeter (1942) *Capitalism, Socialism and Democracy*,
New York, Harper & Row.

Milton Friedman (1962) *Capitalism and Freedom*, Chicago, University of Chicago Press.

Samuel Brittan (1995) *Capitalism with a Human Face*, Aldershot, Edward Elgar.

Lowell Bryan and Diana Farrell (1996) *Market Unbound*, New York,
John Wiley & Sons.

M C O'Dowd (1996) *The O'Dowd Hypothesis* and *The Triumph of
Democratic Capitalism*, Sandton (Johannesburg), FMF Books.

11   See Chapter 5.

12   Felipe Fernandez-Armesto, *op. cit.* (see reference 7 above), p. 370.

13   Norman Davies, *op. cit.* (see reference 6 above), pp. 130–131.

14   *Ibid*, p. 297.

15   Francis Fukuyama (1992) *The End of History and the Last Man*, New
York, Free Press.

16   Felipe Fernandez-Armesto, *op. cit.* (see reference 7 above), p. 343.

17   Karl Marx and Friedrich Engels, *op. cit.* (see reference 1 above), p. 91.

18   George Soros (1997) 'The Capitalist Threat', in *The Atlantic Monthly*,
February 1997, Volume 279, no. 2, pp. 45–55.

19   *Ibid*.

Polemic

Chapter One

When Capitalism Nearly Died

Capitalism is not going to continue … It will disappear in a couple of decades and perhaps in a couple of years

— James Burnham in 1941 [1]

A socialist form of society will inevitably emerge from an equally inevitable decomposition of capitalist society

— Joseph Schumpeter in 1942 [2]

Summary

- As the 1930s progressed, there was an increasingly strong consensus that capitalism was doomed.
- It was believed that the advance of the big business corporation diminished the role of the owner-capitalist and separated ownership from control. Ownership passes to anonymous shareholders, control to management. Capitalism was becoming obsolete.
- The values of capitalism were attacked – often by successful capitalists. Capitalism was materialistic and antisocial; exploited the poor; and induced wasteful competition. Large corporations were better than small ones, and the future belonged to their managers, who would choose to maximize the welfare of society and not profits for the few.
- Capitalist society was being replaced by a new and better form of society. This had already happened in Russia and Germany. The New Deal started this process in America. Some believed that the future lay with socialism, others with managerialism, a new system, neither socialist nor capitalist. Even capitalists knew that their world would not long survive the inevitable trends towards centralized economics and rule for the people.

Less than 60 years ago, most intelligent observers thought that capitalism was on its last legs. A majority of these observers believed that capitalism had outlived its usefulness, and that there was a better system ready to replace it; and that, in large part, a better system *had* already replaced it. A smaller group thought that capitalism *ought* to survive, but was reconciled to its almost inevitable disappearance.

This is an astonishing picture, one that we have forgotten, that has almost been expunged from the history books. Capitalism today is so successful and rampant now that the boot is on the other foot: even those who dislike capitalism can see no practical alternative to it. And yet we do well to remember that capitalism nearly died and to examine why it seemed so weak; and why it bounced back so unexpectedly. In doing so we will discover new truths about our own society and institutions. We shall also learn how easy it is to discover a large part of the truth and draw all the wrong conclusions: a cautionary tale. No-one can travel back to the 1930s and 1940s and still believe that the global triumph of capitalism in the 21st century is as inevitable as nearly everyone today says. If there is one rule of history, it is that the prevailing consensus about the future is always wrong.

The pre-1945 intellectual consensus: capitalism was dying

In the 19th century only socialists confidently predicted the end of capitalism. In the first half of the 20th century, many non-socialists, in fact most thinking people, believed that capitalism could not continue. Let's jump straight back to the 1930s and early 1940s and look at three predictions, all from non-socialists, that represented the intellectual consensus.

First, Adolf A. Berle Jr and Gardiner Means, whose 1932 book, *The Modern Corporation and Private Property*, was one of this century's most influential. Both were American academics, Berle a lawyer and Means a bright young economist. They pointed out that power was passing to large business corporations run by managers rather than entrepreneur-capitalists, and argued that this heralded a change of system:

*Private property, as understood in the capitalist system, is rapidly losing
its original characteristics …*

*Over a decade ago, Walter Rathenau [a German industrialist and
statesman] wrote: 'No-one is a permanent owner … ownership has been
depersonalized … the enterprise becomes transformed into an institution
which resembles the state in character.'*

*The institution … calls for analysis, not in terms of business enter-
prise, but in terms of social organization [3].*

More from Berle and Means soon. Our second witness is James Burnham,
author in 1941 of another hugely original and influential book. Burnham, an
American political philosopher, was accurately described by a contemporary
reviewer as 'an erstwhile Trotskyist … once a romantic optimist … [now] a
romantic pessimist'. His book, which is most enjoyable and mixes brilliant
insight with confident but wrong predictions, was characteristically and im-
modestly called *The Managerial Revolution: What is Happening in the World.*
Burnham makes a compelling case that:

*… capitalism is not going to continue … it will disappear in a couple of
decades and perhaps in a couple of years … [4]*

Our third and final opening testimony is particularly poignant. It comes from
Joseph A Schumpeter (1883–1950), originally a Czech-Austrian who had served
briefly as Austria's finance minister shortly after World War I, who took refuge
in America and had become an acclaimed academic economist by the time he
published his masterly *Capitalism, Socialism and Democracy* in 1942. Schumpeter
was a passionate, but fatalistic, supporter of capitalism, and as certain as Burnham
that capitalism was doomed. He wrote in his Preface:

*… a socialist form of society will inevitably emerge from an equally inevi-
table decomposition of capitalist society … [5]*

Later in the book, he stops to ask:

> *Can capitalism survive? No, I do not think that it can ... One may hate socialism or at least look upon it with cool criticism, and yet foresee its advent ... [6]*

and later on, he again enquires briskly:

> *Can socialism work? Of course it can ... [7]*

Round up the usual suspects

The pre-1945 literature resembles a stripped-down Agatha Christie plot. Capitalism is about to be killed, but it is not clear which assassin will strike the fatal blow. There are three usual suspects: socialism, fascism–Nazism, and managerialism (the first two are familiar; we will define managerialism shortly). There is a consensus, however, on the murder weapon: this is confidently expected to be the modern form of economic organization, the large business corporation. And in all the scenarios, the mega-state lurks menacingly in the background.

Let's elucidate. The thinking is so foreign to our own, yet was so clearly apparent to contemporaries, that we need to take it step by step.

The common theme is the growth of big business and its revolutionary implications. Marx was the first to spot the trend toward big business which, as Schumpeter generously remarks, was a remarkable insight given the economic organization of Marx's day.

In the 1840s, the typical economic unit in England was a small textile factory. The picture in America was similar: in 1832 the McLane Report, covering ten states, showed that in only six industries were there even a small number of firms with more than 50 employees: seven such firms in books and printing, five in cordage, five in shipyards, three in buttons, three in combs and three in glass. As the economic historian, Alfred D. Chandler, reports: 'the overwhelming majority of the enterprises ... had assets of only a few thousand dollars and employed at the most ten or a dozen people ... American manufacturing was still powered almost exclusively by water ... [and] subject to seasonal periods of shutdown because of ice, drought and freshnets.'

Yet Marx foresaw the modern business corporation, heavily capitalized, with huge numbers of workers per enterprise. And so it came to pass. The revolution's main catalyst was the railroad. Railway booms in England and America in the 1840s, 1850s and 1860s transformed society and created the first modern business enterprise. Chandler again:

> ...the operational requirements of the railroads demanded the creation of the first administrative hierarchies in American business ... Ownership and management soon separated. The capital required to build a railroad was far more than that required to purchase a plantation, a textile mill, or even a fleet of ships. Therefore, a single entrepreneur, family, or small group of associates was rarely able to own a railroad. Nor could the many stockholders or their representatives manage it. The administrative tasks were too numerous, too varied and too complex. They required special skills and training which could only be commanded by a full-time salaried manager [8].

But there was more. Everywhere, railroads shrank the country. Travel times plummeted. Fast, all-weather transportation begat the telegraph and a range of mass-production industries including canned food, postal services, mass retailing and eventually mass warfare. And, universally, the average size of business organizations grew, both in terms of capital and employees.

Something else happened, and was noticed. Large organizations were organized on similar lines, with hierarchies of managers increasingly in charge, whether they happened to fall in the private sector or the burgeoning public sector. In 1891 the two largest American employers were the Pennsylvania Railroad, with a payroll over 110,000, and the Post Office with over 95,000 employees. In Europe, state organizations, both national and municipal, became even more important: gas and electricity companies, armies, navies, post offices, telegraph companies, shipping lines, urban transit. Both in the US and Europe, the organizing principles of large organizations were the same whether they were in the private or the public sector.

The similarity was real, but led most observers to two false conclusions – that the modern, large business enterprise was fundamentally different than, and superior to, the small private enterprise company that was typical of Adam Smith's capitalism; and that ultimately it did not matter much whether a large corporation was owned by the state or by private shareholders.

Herein lay the seeds of delusion, delusion that nearly derailed capitalism, delusion that came to become the common intellectual currency of nearly everyone who had power in the inter-war years. The delusion sprouted many branches: that capitalism was a primitive and antisocial system; that individualism was a disorder; that big was better; that competition was wasteful; that the market left too much to chance; that being rich was shameful; that the state was the handmaiden of progress; and that the wave of the future would be created and ridden by the technocrats, the knowledge workers, and the managers in large corporations, who would deserve to inherit the earth. Only the last of these delusions is still widespread.

The revolutionary capitalists: right emotions, wrong ideas

The revolutionary capitalists were dupes, traitors and idealists. Their ideas were generous, but wrong. We were told in the 1840s that 'there is no power on earth like an idea whose time has come'. Ideas sometimes take longer than expected to arrive; nearly a hundred years later, John Maynard Keynes, our century's greatest economist, was writing that 'the power of vested interests is vastly exaggerated compared with the gradual encroachment of ideas'. This faith in intellectual honesty is characteristic of the time, and is amply vindicated by contemporary capitalists who, from about 1880 to 1945, were not afraid to state the truth as they saw it, even if it went against all their family and class interests.

Joseph Schumpeter [9], sitting, as he believed, amidst the ruins of capitalism in 1942, correctly named the most influential subverters of capitalist civilization as the capitalists themselves:

... [the] true pacemakers of socialism were not the intellectuals and the agitators who preached it but the Vanderbilts, Carnegies and Rockefellers.

Though the capitalists were honest, they were also wrong. To take one of Keynes' phrases out of context, the revolutionary capitalists represented 'the dark forces of time and ignorance which envelop our future'. For by the time he wrote the *General Theory* in 1936, Keynes had realized that ideas could be powerful just as easily when they were wrong as when they were right. In a celebrated and pertinent passage, Keynes realized that the key battles of the 1930s were ideological [10]:

> *The ideas of economists and political philosophers, both when they are right and when they are wrong, are more powerful than is commonly understood. Indeed, the world is ruled by little else. Practical men, who believe themselves to be quite exempt from any intellectual influences, are usually the slaves of some defunct economist. Madmen in authority, who hear voices in the air, are distilling their frenzy from some academic scribbler of a few years back ... soon or late, it is ideas, not vested interests, which are dangerous for good or evil.*

Let's examine the convictions of the revolutionary capitalists, and see how they came to hold them. We will find noble elements, nuggets of feeling for their fellow men, nuggets of democratic idealism, swirling amongst the intellectual slime, nuggets that deserve a better home, aspirations that can only be housed constructively within the edifice that we are building, within democratic capitalism. It is a tragedy of immense proportions that the mega-state ideologies of 1917 and 1933, their flames fanned by those who should have known better, claimed the lives of around 100 million people [11], blighted the lives of many millions more, and were only exorcised by terrible world war and the slow but irrefutable demonstration, after 1945, that only the capitalist system could consistently improve the lives of the masses.

The revolutionary capitalists' increasing contempt for capitalism contained five major strands. These five fallacies – pay attention, because we have still not fully extirpated these false and harmful ideas from our own intellectual substrate – were:

1   the desire for wealth and the enjoyment of great wealth are antisocial
2   capitalism does not deliver for the poor; some other system would deliver better
3   capitalism = competition = waste
4   large corporations are better than small ones, and large corporations should serve broad social purposes
5   the future lies with managers and 'managerialism', not with capitalists and their desire to maximize profits.

1   Great wealth is antisocial

Andrew Carnegie, the Scots-born Pittsburgh steel magnate originated what became known (perversely) as the Gospel of Wealth. He preached that 'the millionaire should be ashamed to die rich': he should have given it all away. Henry Ford [12] provided an eloquent echo:

> *We are growing out of this worship of material possessions. It is no longer a distinction to be rich … What we accumulate by way of useless surplus does us no honor.*

Ford also attacks the traditional idea of property, saying that it was wrong for a man to use property as he pleases, to take any number of men into his employ and set them to do 'whatever work seems good to him' and the idea that a dead man's will can bind the living.

Walter Rathenau, a hugely wealthy German industrialist turned statesman, expressed similar views, arguing against inherited wealth, luxury, inequality, and speculation. Writing in 1916, he claimed that 'as a motive force, covetousness has been completely superseded by the sense of responsibility'. He argued for the 'deindividualization of property', a position indistinguishable from socialism. Fundamentally, Rathenau hated materialism.

A revolutionary capitalist for the next century: the curious case of George Soros

George Soros, one of the most successful financial market manipulators of all time, caused outrage in February 1997 when *The Atlantic Monthly* published a long and thoughtful piece by Soros entitled 'The Capitalist Threat'. It was not so much the content as the authorship that sparked liberal indignation. What was a currency speculator – one of a breed that Malaysia's Prime Minister said in September 1997 deserved to be shot – doing lecturing the world on the deficiencies of the system that had made him a billionaire?

In truth, Soros is but the latest revolutionary capitalist to bite the hand that feeds him. He is the linear descendant of the late 19th/early 20th century revolutionary capitalists, men like Andrew Carnegie, Walter Rathenau and Henry Ford, who were hugely successful money makers, fearless critics of the system, and great philanthropists. Soros is all of the above but, unlike his predecessors, he is right. He wants to create a fairer system without rejecting the value that markets bring.

He starts by arguing for the 'open society' that protects the rights of citizens. This is similar to the goal that I argue for in Chapter 7, the society that advances human happiness and liberty. Soros insists that the economic system must be judged against how well it advances the open society. The threat to the open society used to come from the left; now it comes more from *laissez-faire* capitalism:

> *Too much competition and too little cooperation can cause intolerable inequalities and instability ...*
>
> *... laissez-faire capitalism holds that the common good is best served by the uninhibited pursuit of self-interest. Unless it is tempered by the recognition of a common interest that ought to take precedence over particular interests, our present system – which, however imperfect, qualifies as an open society – is liable to break down ...*
>
> *... because communism and even socialism have been thoroughly discredited, I consider the threat from the laissez-faire side more potent ... We are enjoying a truly global market economy in which goods, services, capital, and even people move around quite freely, but we fail to recognize the need to sustain the values and institutions of an open society.*

Soros goes on to argue that contemporary capitalism poses a threat to economic stability, social justice, and international relations.

Market values and materialism, he says, have undermined more basic values. 'The cult of success has replaced a belief in principles. Society has lost its anchor.'

Quite unwarranted assumptions about the perfection of the market have banished arguments for income or wealth redistribution. Social justice has been jettisoned. Inequality increases to the extent where it undermines a cohesive and open society.

Internationally, the wealthy nations have failed to rise to the challenge presented by the fall of communism. Sovereign states have pursued their self-interest, not the common interest. Soros notes that when he mooted a new Marshall Plan at Potsdam in 1989, he was ridiculed. And yet

> ... the system of robber capitalism that has taken hold in Russia is so iniquitous that people may well turn to a charismatic leader promising national revival at the cost of civil liberties ...
>
> an open society is not merely the absence of government intervention and oppression. It is a complicated, sophisticated structure, and deliberate effort is needed to bring it into existence ...
>
> Our global open society lacks the institutions and mechanisms necessary for its preservation.

Soros argues, in effect, that our existing forms of democracy and capitalism are not enough. This defines precisely the need for the third revolution, to derive a form of capitalism that is democratic in its nature and results, and a form of democracy that is at once market-based, internationalist and grounded in humanist values. When the history of the third revolution is written, George Soros will deserve a high place as both ideologist and protagonist.

2   Capitalism does not help the poor

For the revolutionary capitalists, as for Karl Marx and Charles Dickens, it was axiomatic that capitalism could not deliver the maximum potential wealth to the masses and to the poor, and that some other system, organized for that purpose, could do so better. The revolutionary capitalists linked this idea to their faith – correct, as it turned out, but only under the rejected capitalist system – that industrial society could deliver enormously increased future wealth for the masses.

King C. Gillette (1855–1932), the safety razor millionaire, provided a savage critique of capitalism. Writing in 1910, he objected that 'the real purpose of the machine of industry is to supply the necessities of life', something that the capitalism system could not deliver. Henry Ford, a dozen years later, agreed:

> *My effort is in the direction of simplicity. People in general have so little and it costs so much to buy even the barest necessities (let alone that share of the luxuries to which I think everyone is entitled) because nearly everything is much more complex than it needs to be. Our clothing, our food, our household furnishings – all could be much simpler than they are now and at the same time be better-looking.* [13]

3 *Capitalism = competition = waste*

The revolutionary capitalists believed that capitalism could not focus on necessities for the masses because the market system was geared to provide luxuries to the rich; but they coupled this with a critique of competition, which, by having many firms trying to do the same thing, frustrated economies of scale and led to great waste. Competition was also linked to individualism, that is, the selfish satisfaction of individual rather than social purposes.

In King Gillette's fierce words (1910):

> *the disease which sooner or later reaches the heart and brain of a nation and destroys it, is individualism, the individualism which recognizes competition between individuals or nations for individual possessions.* [14]

M.L. Severy [15], while working as Gillette's number two in 1907, wrote:

> *... competition is un-Christian, immoral, corruptive, unjust, inequitable, iniquitous, wasteful, brutal, uncertain, chaotic and inefficient.*

Walter Rathenau [16] in 1916 developed the theme:

> *If we spend two to three billions annually on inebriating drinks, sacrifice*
> *hundreds of billions on tinsel, show and personal adornment, have tens of*
> *thousands of able-bodied salesmen loiter at shop counters … or have hun-*
> *dreds of thousands of them waste time … to battle their competitors …*
> *then we squander national savings, misdirect the entire productive pro-*
> *cess, divert manpower, waste materials, block resources, increase produc-*
> *tion costs and diminish external competitiveness.*

This from the man who was a highly accomplished industrialist and, at the time, successfully directing Germany's industrial war effort – is it any wonder that a year later, having wrested power in Russia, Vladimir Ilyich Lenin energetically set about creating a better system, not based around competition and markets?

Lenin should not be blamed for thinking he was doing the right thing and that a social system would not only be fairer but also much more efficient. (Incidentally, the critique of competition as wasteful seems so obviously correct that it keeps resurfacing: in the 1950s and 1960s in America, just as the capitalism system was delivering unprecedented wealth for ordinary people, it became widespread, especially amongst the young intelligentsia, to attack the consumer society and advertising as wasteful, manipulative and corrupting, exactly the same false arguments as expounded by the revolutionary capitalists 40–50 years earlier.)

4   Large corporations are better and more social

The revolutionary capitalists took up Marx's theory that big business represented the wave of the future, changing and improving industry and society – a theme which, as we shall see soon, was developed even further during the 1930s.

One of the first capitalists to jump on Marx's 'big is better' bandwagon was the Belgian scientist and industrialist Ernest Solvay (1838–1922). Solvay patented the process for making soda ash and turned this into a hugely profitable monopoly. In the 1880s he argued that

> ... the future belongs to big corporations and common-interest organiza-
> tions; it is the price we pay for an assured future. [17]

King Gillette, two decades later, pointed to the emergence of megacorporations and saw their potential to embody social purpose and hence to
replace small–business, individualistic capitalism:

> Economy, stability, and absence of friction are striking characteristics of
> large Corporations ... Look about you. See what individuals are doing
> [bad! Then] look at the United States Steel Corporation, the Railroad
> Corporation, the Standard Oil Company, the Sugar Trust, the Tele-
> phone and Telegraph Monopoly, and the thousands of corporations that
> are binding together in corporate harmony millions and millions of money,
> and thousands upon thousands of individuals, and centralizing intelli-
> gence and power in a matter unknown in any former history of the world
> ...
>   The Standard Oil Company is an example of a rational governmen-
> tal industrial system, if you eliminate stockholders, who are not necessary
> to its operation. [18]

Similarly, Walter Rathenau contrasted small companies – untrustworthy, short-
termist, traders in a bazaar, owned by individuals, families or small groups –
with the new, honest industrialism of large corporations:

> The first small step towards a higher economic morality was that the
> impersonal [large publicly held corporations] proved to be freer of plots and
> false advertising than their ... [small,] closely held equivalents. [19]

5   Managers – the highest form of economic life

Finally, the revolutionary capitalists paved the way for Lenin, Stalin and Hitler
– as well as for the fat cats and honest managers of our own times – by extolling
the managers within large corporations. The managers were not owners, not
capitalists; they were professionals, interested in productivity and efficiency,

and capable of acting in the interests of the many rather than the few. This philosophy, which we call here 'social managerialism', is distinct from the managerialism of our own day in that it explicitly rejected the profit motive and any attempt to pursue what is now called 'shareholder value', that is, the interests of the stockholders.

Social managerialism claimed that the managers in large corporations could and should organize resources 'responsibly', in the interests of society at large, rather than in the interests of individual owners. Social managerialism was always anticapitalist. Beyond this, it was espoused and used by socialists, by fascists and Nazis, and by liberals who struggled (and ultimately failed) to reconcile a large role for the state and a greater degree of economic equality with traditional freedoms. Social managerialism always appeared to start innocuously, by observing and approving the beneficial development of large corporations and their method of working through middle-management professionals. But social managerialism led inexorably to a rejection of the profit motive and ultimately to the state direction of industry.

Walter Rathenau praised executives in large companies because they

> *labour for [the long term] ... if offered the choice between having his salary doubled and becoming one of the directors, a leading officer will prefer responsibility to wealth [20]*

King Gillette, the most extreme of the revolutionary capitalists, saw the megacorporations of the early 20th century as a transition toward a few multinational corporations, and ultimately toward just one World Corporation, which would abolish competition and the profit motive, and where skilled technicians would direct labor in order to maximize productivity. His World Corporation would

> *combine Education, Industry and Government throughout the world in one system, bringing all nations and all peoples into one corporate body, possessing one corporate mind [what today we would call corporate culture] ... regardless of nationality, race, creed, color, age, or sex ... the*

only employer of labor and the only seller of products … Under the World
Corporation farm labor to the number of five million [in the United States
will be] organized into armies, and moved in companies and detachments
under the supervision of skilled agriculturalists … [21]

This was a blueprint for the forced collectivization of Soviet peasants by Lenin
and Stalin as well as for both Soviet and Nazi state direction of all industry and
labor. Though none of the other revolutionary capitalists went as far as Gillette
in saying how managers would develop the large corporation, they all saw it as
a post-capitalist device which could work in close harmony with, or even be
directed by, the state. Lenin's 'state capitalism' was consistent with, and in large
part derived from, the views of Solvay, Gillette, Rathenau and Ford.

The 1930s and early 1940s: high tide of social managerialism

It was left to other thinkers to develop social managerialism, and the assault
upon capitalism, to its logical conclusion. The Wall Street crash of 1929 and
the Great Depression that followed formed the background to what many believed was 'the final crisis of capitalism'. But the arguments and models used to
subvert capitalism and empower the mega-state were not new. They were
simply more sophisticated and powerful versions of the arguments used by
Marx and the revolutionary capitalists, revolving around the new megacorporations and their managers. We can most efficiently and enjoyably trace
these ideas – the ideas that nearly killed capitalism – by reverting to the three
books with whose apocalyptic views we started this chapter.

Berle and Means' classic, *The Modern Corporation and Private Property*, the
first sustained eulogy of social managerialism, showed how American big
business had changed out of all recognition. Two-thirds of big business was
now controlled by managers rather than owners (capitalists). This trend was
both inevitable, because large-scale industry required funds beyond the reach
of single families, however rich, and beneficial, because large corporations

were the most efficient, and because managers were free to direct the enterprise for the benefit of society rather than just for the benefit of capitalists. One of the oddities of the book, from a modern perspective, is the almost mindless praise of big business and oligopoly, and the assumption that the free enterprise system is being replaced with something broader and better.

Berle and Means were in no doubt about the revolutionary nature of the change they documented:

> [we are] in the throes of a revolution in our institution of private property ... American industrial property, through the corporate device [the large managerially controlled corporation] ... [is] being thrown into a collectivist hopper wherein the individual owner [is] steadily being lost in the creation of a series of huge industrial oligopolies ...
>
> These corporations have arisen in field after field as the myriad independent and competing units of private business have given way to the few large groups of the new modern quasi-public corporation. The typical business unit of the 19th century was owned by individuals or small groups; was managed by them or their appointees; and was, in the main, limited in size by the personal wealth of the individuals in control. [22]

They contrast this with the prototype of the modern quasi-public corporation, the American Telephone and Telegraph Company:

> With assets of almost five billion dollars, with 454,000 employees, and stockholders to the number of 567,694, this company may indeed be called an economic empire ... One hundred companies of this size would control the whole of American wealth ... The property owner who invests in a modern corporation ... surrenders his wealth to those in control of the corporation ...[to] become merely a recipient of the wages of capital. [23]

Much of the book is a dry, statistical exposition of the extent to which American industry is under 'management control', where the management can perpetuate itself even though its shareholding is negligible, where, in other words, there is not meaningful capitalist control. Berle and Means compute that of the largest 200 American corporations, at least 58 per cent of them by value, and perhaps as much as 80 per cent, fall under management control, where there is a separation of ownership and control. But the interesting – and tendentious – part of the book is where it draws conceptual conclusions from the indisputable statistics. Though they do not use the words, Berle and Means see the ascendancy of the management-controlled large corporation as ushering in what we would call 'post-capitalist society'. This is how they put it:

> The translation of perhaps two-thirds of the industrial wealth of this country from individual ownership to ownership by the large, publicly financed corporations vitally changes the lives of property owners, the lives of workers, and the methods of property tenure. The divorce of ownership from control ... almost necessarily involves a new form of economic organization of society ... [24]

Here they indulge in some rather unacademic flights of fancy. They jump from dry facts to an imaginative argument, only very loosely tied to any empirical observations, which argues the essence of social managerialism: (a) that large corporations are the highest and best form of economic life; (b) that managers are better stewards than capitalists; (c) that all the traditional capitalist assumptions about the profit motive and its value can be thrown out the window; (d) that the large oligopolistic corporations are not subject to competition and indeed that they should not be; and (e) that these developments create the opportunity to place the economy under social direction, for the benefit of society rather than stockholders.

Follow, if you can, the logic in this progression [25]:

> It is obvious that the corporate system not only tends to be the flower of our industrial organization, but that the public is in a mood to impose on it a steadily growing degree of responsibility for our economic welfare ...
>
> Power over industrial property has been cut off from the beneficial [i.e. personal] ownership of this property ... [this] destroys the very foundation on which the economic order of the past three centuries [private enter-

prise] has rested ... It has been assumed that [the private enterprise profit system] can be relied upon as an effective incentive to the efficient use of any industrial property ...

In the quasi-public corporation, such an assumption no longer holds ... this system [the new non-capitalist corporate system] bids fair to be as all-embracing as was the feudal system ...

Competition has changed in character and the principles applicable to present conditions are radically different [with small scale capitalist business] ... The principles of duopoly have become more important than those of free competition...

Underlying the thinking of economists, lawyers and business men during the last century and a half has been the picture of economic life so skillfully painted by Adam Smith ... yet those terms have ceased to be accurate, and therefore tend to mislead in describing modern enterprise as carried on by the great corporations ...

Today competition in markets dominated by a few great enterprises ... New concepts must be forged ...

Berle and Means argue that if the corporation no longer has to be run to benefit private stockholders – both because in practice the latter have lost power, and because for economic purposes the important thing is to motivate managers – one possibility is that it is run solely for the benefit of the managers. But, they say, there is a third possibility, and one much in tune with the needs of the time: that the corporation should serve society, the public good. In doing so, they would create a new system, neither capitalist nor communist, but a constructive synthesis of both:

Observable throughout the world ... is this insistence that power in economic organization shall be subjected to the same tests of public benefit which have been applied in their turn to power otherwise located. In its most extreme aspect this is exhibited in the communist movement ... In the strictly capitalist countries, and particularly at times of depression, demands are constantly put forward that [managers] ... be made to accept responsibility for the well-being of ... workers, investors, or customers. In a sense the difference in all of these demands lies only in degree ...

The control groups [managers] have ... cleared the way for the claims of a group far wider than either the owners or the control [management]. They have placed the community in a position to demand that the modern corporation serve not alone the owners or the control [management] but all society.

So here we have it. Berle and Means say that the large, managerially controlled corporation is replacing the smaller, capitalist-controlled corporation. The managerially run monopoly or oligopoly is the most efficient organization of industry, and one where the stockholders are increasingly irrelevant. Their first contention was true, the second, their corollary, was false, mere wishful thinking. Means, the bright young economist, implied that the fact of managerial control rendered traditional, pro-capitalist economics irrelevant. Though Means went on until the 1960s trying to flesh out the new economics, and came up with some interesting theories about 'administered prices and wages', he never demonstrated satisfactorily that managerial control of large corporations implied a fundamental discontinuity in, or replacement of, capitalism. But he did not need to. People wanted to believe his argument, and did. Social managerialism, in its non-socialist and non-Nazi forms an empty dogma, was well on the way to becoming, even in America, conventional wisdom.

Now we turn to the man who argued in 1941, with great conviction, eloquence and influence, that managerialism was about to replace both socialism and capitalism.

The managerial revolution

James Burnham's *The Managerial Revolution* is a forgotten classic, a work of penetrating brilliance that even today – when it has been proved hopelessly wrong – vibrates with power and passion. So much of the book is right, and it is so well argued, that it is difficult to spot the precise moment where it veers so badly off the rails. The book writes capitalism's epitaph and, though Burnham hints that he dislikes the managerialism which he says is triumphing, the book was so influential that its predictions were very nearly self-fulfilling.

Burnham states flatly that capitalism is about to end and to be replaced by managerialism: [26]

> ... *capitalist society will be replaced by 'managerial society' ... in fact, the transition from capitalist society to managerial society is already well under way ...*

Burnham argues, in a strikingly original way, that managerialism and not socialism is the real threat to capitalism. He takes the example of Russia, which he says has defected from capitalism but not advanced toward socialism:

> *The determining characteristics of ... socialist society are that it is classless, fully democratic and international ...*
>
> *[Yet Russia shows no progress toward these characteristics ...] The upper 11 per cent or 12 per cent of the Soviet population now receives approximately 50 per cent of the national income. This differentiation is sharper than in the United States ...*
>
> *... the tyranny of the Russian regime is the most extreme that has ever existed in human history, not excepting the regime of Hitler ...*
>
> *Though Russia did not move towards socialism, at the same time it did not move back to capitalism ... the only way out of the theoretical jam is to recognize that the assumption must be dropped, that socialism and capitalism are not the sole alternatives, that Russia's motion has been toward neither capitalism nor socialism, but towards* managerial soci ety*, the type of society now in the process of replacing capitalist society on a world scale.*

Ahead of Peter Drucker, Burnham sketches the role of what Drucker dubbed 'knowledge workers', called in this book 'the highly trained technical workers'. Burnham adds an original twist to the Berle and Means argument about the separation of ownership and control. Whereas Berle and Means had argued that it was socially justifiable to reward managers rather than stockholders, because the managers could affect industrial performance and the stockholders could no longer do so, Burnham argued that the managers would increasingly use their power to arrogate the maximum possible rewards to themselves. We know now that Burnham was right about this:

> *What is occurring in this transition is a drive for social dominance, for power and privilege, for the position of the ruling class, by the social group or class of the* managers ... *This drive will be successful.*

What Burnham got wrong (but only because he incorrectly but not unreasonably – this was 1941 – forecast that Germany would win the world war) was to see the managerial revolution in terms of state socialism. The state would come to own the large business corporations, but the managers would run them for their own principal benefit:

> *The economic framework in which this social dominance of the managers will be assured is based upon the state ownership of the major instruments of production ... there will be no direct property rights in the major instruments of production vested in individuals as individuals...*
>
> *The ideologies expressing the social role and interests and aspirations of the managers ... have not yet been fully worked out ... They are already approximated, however, ... by, for example: Leninism–Stalinism; fascism–Nazism; and, at a more primitive level, by New Dealism and ... technocracy.*

Although some of his insights were outlandish, Burnham carried to its logical conclusion the thinking of Walter Rathenau, Henry Ford, John Maynard Keynes, King Gillette, Ernest Solvay, and Adolf Berle and Gardiner Means. Private enterprise was anachronistic. The future lay with the large, monopolistic or oligopolistic corporation, run by managers and owned by the state. Whether this is called socialism or managerialism, it is clearly not capitalism. And, by the time of World War II, even some capitalists – perhaps even the majority – thought that their game was up.

Joseph Schumpeter: fatalistic capitalist

We shall call as our final witness here an avowed and unrepentant – but pessimistic – capitalist, Joseph A. Schumpeter (1883–1950). We have already quoted his view in 1942 that socialism would replace capitalism. He arrives at this conclusion in a tortuous but fascinating way.

Schumpeter, linking the long line of capitalism's doomsayers from Marx to Burnham, also saw the demise of capitalism as linked to the growth of the managerially controlled large business corporation [27]:

> *The essential point to grasp is that in dealing with capitalism we are dealing with an evolutionary process ... [as] emphasized by Karl Marx ...*
>
> *... a fundamental change is upon the capitalist process ...*

This was, of course, the by-now much-noted separation of ownership from control in large corporations. But Schumpeter's new perspective was to focus, not on the virtues of the new breed of managers, but on the redundancy of the previous engine of capitalism, the class of entrepreneurs [28]:

> *The social function [of the entrepreneur] is already losing importance and is bound to lose it at an accelerating rate ... innovation itself is being reduced to routine. Technological progress is increasingly becoming the business of teams of trained specialists who turn out what is required and make it work in predictable ways. The romance of earlier commercial enterprise is rapidly wearing away ...*
>
> *Thus, economic progress tends to become depersonalized and automatized. Bureau and committee work tends to replace individual action ...*
>
> *Economically and socially, directly and indirectly, the bourgeoisie therefore depends on the entrepreneur and, as a class, will die with him ...*
>
> *Since capitalist enterprise, by its very achievements, tends to automatize progress, we conclude that it tends to make itself superfluous ... The perfectly bureaucratized giant industrial unit not only ousts the small or me-*

*dium-sized firm and 'expropriates' its owners, but also ... the entrepreneur
... and the bourgeoisie as a class which in the process stands to lose not only
its income but also what is infinitely more important, its function.*

So capitalism, a form of civilization based on the entrepreneur, was about to
disappear. And there was an alternative system, which Schumpeter disliked
but thought he could be objective about, ready and willing to take over:

Can socialism work? Of course it can...
 *By socialist society we shall designate an institutional pattern in which
the control over means of production and over production itself is vested
with a central authority ...*
 *... Business excepting the agrarian sector, is controlled [under the so-
cialist future] by a small number of bureaucratized corporations.*

And, in a final passage reminiscent of Burnham (whom he must have read),
Schumpeter argues that the future lies more with socialist managerialism than
with the sort of socialism expected by most socialists:

*... it is only socialism in the sense defined in this book that is so predict-
able. Nothing else is. In particular, there is little reason to believe that
this socialism will mean the advent of the civilization of which orthodox
socialists dream. It is much more likely to present fascist features. That
would be a strange answer to Marx's prayer. But history sometimes in-
dulges in jokes of questionable taste.*

Socialists, managerialists, fatalistic capitalists: all wrong

By 1942, whatever their personal predilections, socialists, fascists, liberals and
even the majority of capitalists had reached a consensus: the future belonged to
the large corporation, to oligopoly, to the managers, and not to anything recognizable as capitalism.

They were all agreed. And they were all wrong. Though they were not wholly wrong – how could they be, having observed the triumph of big business and the breakdown of entrepreneur-owned capitalism, trends that were real and indisputable? – they drew nearly all the wrong conclusions.

Why were they proved wrong? And, even more intriguing, could they have been proved right?

At the objective, economic level, they were wrong because there was and is no better system than capitalism, the market system, the system based on competition, whether of small entrepreneurial or massive managerial corporations. All the talk about running large corporations for the benefit of society rather than stockholders was just so much hot air.

It sounded good – it still sounds good, having in the past few years been warmed up and served as the apparently new idea of stakeholding – but no-one has ever shown how corporations can be run successfully except to do what they have always done: satisfy some customers' needs better than any other corporation and make as large a surplus over the cost of capital as possible. True, there is often a trade-off between short-term profit and long-term profit. True, it is difficult to measure profit or shareholder value objectively. True, it is possible to manipulate reported returns. True, managers and unions can often skim off a large part of the surplus value for themselves, if managers and unions in competing firms do the same. True, managers will often try to avoid or subvert competition. True, corporations will often live off their past, and grow in size and complexity despite progressively subtracting economic value. All true. All useful things to know. But all irrelevant to the main argument.

Capitalism works precisely because, in a market-based economy, no corporation, be it ever so large, can effectively stop progress or competition. Corporations can and do establish monopolies, they can and do abuse their positions, but, over time, they will either reform themselves and deliver value to customers, or someone else will. Capitalism is always stuffed full of inefficiency, so that if you look at a snapshot it is suboptimal. (Complexity theory has recently taught us that optimality *is* suboptimal.) Perfect markets are a convenient fiction, rarely observed. But, over time, capitalism delivers a higher and higher level of production, something that no other system ever has.

It does this, if you like, because of dedication to, and smart commercial use of, science and technology. But capitalism works so well because it also domesticates and makes constructive use of more basic human instincts and energies: greed, the desire to better one's position, the ridiculous urge to become rich, the wish to expand, the urge to power and prestige. When this more ambiguous, slightly darker, side of human nature is suppressed or absent, economic success is less forthcoming.

At one end of the elastic called capitalism is the ambitious (or greedy) person, whether an entrepreneur or a captain of industry. At the other end of the elastic is the sovereign consumer or industrial buyer, taking the best package on offer. In the middle is the mess – industrial structure, competing or colluding competitors, the search for better or cheaper ways to do things, the good and bad things that governments do, bankers, investors, stock analysts, fund managers, venture capitalists, economic fluctuations. But progress is made. Progress is greater when competition and trade are freer. But some form of progress is always made when capitalism is allowed to operate, when businesses great and small are left to make their own decisions, when they have to make a profit to survive.

So the reason the social managerialists were wrong is that the growth of large corporations, and the increasing power of managers, did not fundamentally change the rules of capitalism. Big companies could not stop small companies from existing and competing. Managers still wanted to grow their companies, and to do so they had to make profits. To make profits, they had to take some notice of customers. At the margins, managers might engage in philanthropic acts. Over time, higher standards of civilization could be afforded within corporations. But all this talk about replacing the profit motive with nobler social objectives was nonsense. It could not be done. And it wasn't.

The doomsters' political fallacy

The doomsters also misread the political trends. They were wrong because America won World War II. The Americans preserved western Europe and the United States for capitalism. Nazism vanished. Soviet and then Chinese communism greatly expanded the number of people subject to socialism. First Japan, then most other East Asian countries, transitioned to full-blown capitalism. Under fair competition, the capitalist countries easily outperformed the socialist ones, leading eventually to the suicide, not of capitalism, but of socialism. The story is familiar.

But it could have been different. If Hitler had triumphed, or Hitler and Stalin split Europe, capitalism could have been totally extirpated from Europe. If a new depression had hit America, the New Deal could have assumed a socialist character. If the apparently successful governments of the Old World had rejected the market in favor of the state, how long would the New World have resisted the intellectual fashion? And if all the leading countries of the world had been socialist or national-socialist, would anyone have known that a better alternative existed? And then generations of schoolchildren would have celebrated the insights of Berle and Means, of Burnham, and even of Schumpeter, who knew when to concede capitalism's defeat.

The Duke of Wellington, the English victor of Waterloo against the French army in 1815 remarked that it had been 'a damned close-run thing'. So too with capitalism before 1945. If capitalism had died, ideas, not economics, would have been responsible. Happily, on this occasion, history did not indulge in a joke of questionable taste.

The spirit of the age

Peoples' conclusions derive less from their arguments, than their arguments derive from their conclusions. And their conclusions are inevitably conditioned by the prevailing intellectual consensus. The Spirit of the Age triumphs over the individual's powers of reason and observation.

We can see this clearly from the thinkers of the 1930s and 1940s. Adolf Berle, Gardiner Means, John Maynard Keynes, James Burnham, Joseph Schumpeter – all of these were highly intelligent and idiosyncratic authors. Yet as we examine their arguments, with the benefit of hindsight, we find it difficult to see why such smart people could advance them, and even harder to see why they were accepted so uncritically. The explanation is that they were so congruent with the Spirit of the Age.

Ideas acquire their own momentum and if they are sufficiently pervasive can become self-fulfilling. Sooner or later, ideas that don't work well will be rejected. But as the case of communism shows, bad ideas that reflect the Spirit of the Age can last a very long time and cause a great deal of misery before they die.

We should not imagine that we are exempt from the Spirit of our own Age. If I had lived in the 1920s or 1930s, I am sure that I would have believed in the inevitability of socialism or fascist managerialism. And in the late 1930s or early 1940s, anyone who was not a fanatical fascist, Nazi or socialist would have been crazy not to be a pessimist. The Decline of the West, in Oswald Spengler's gloating title, seemed a foregone conclusion.

As you read this book, ask what near-universal assumptions of our time will seem quaint and curious in the mid-21st century. I will nominate two delusions. One is that our current forms of democracy and capitalism can continue to coexist happily. I do not see how this can be true, given that untrammeled global capitalism leads to greater inequality and irresponsibility as well as greater wealth. Capitalism will need to be reformed or democracy extinguished. The only thing that stops us seeing this truth is that almost no-one believes it is possible to improve on our current economic system. This is the second delusion of our age. The theoretical case for present-day capitalism is as full of holes as the 1930s case against it. When a better system has been invented and proved to work, the capitalist-managerial orthodoxy of the 1980s and 1990s will seem as great a monument to intellectual laziness as the socialist-managerial orthodoxy of the 1930s.

Yet before we move back from the facile assumptions of a forgotten era to those of our own, it is worth examining the means by which the thirties thinkers expected society to be transformed: the large socialized corporation. We'll find more that more than a trace of their discredited theories have lodged themselves, apparently immovably, into our own intellectual furniture.

Endnotes

1   James Burnham (1941) *The Managerial Revolution: What is Happening in the World*, New York, The John Day Company, pp. 29–30.

2   Joseph A. Schumpeter (1942) *Capitalism, Socialism and Democracy*, Preface, New York, Harper & Row, pp. xiii–xiv.

3   Adolf A Berle Jr and Gardiner C Means (1932) *The Modern Corporation and Private Property*, New York, The MacMillan Company, p. 352. The quotation from Walter Rathenau included within this extract is from *Von Kommenden Dingen*, Berlin, 1916 (see Endnote 15 below). Berle and Means attribute the quotation to 1918, no doubt working from an edition of that date.

4   James Burnham, *op. cit.* (see reference 1 above).

5   Joseph A. Schumpeter, *op. cit.* (see reference 2 above).

6   *Ibid*, p. 61.

7   *Ibid*, p. 167.

8   Alfred D. Chandler (1977) *The Visible Hand: The Managerial Revolution in American Business*, Cambridge, MA, The Belknap Press of Harvard University Press, p. 87. The information about the McLane Report and the quotation above from Chandler is from the same book, p. 61.

9   Joseph A. Schumpeter, *op. cit.* (see reference 2 above), p. 134.

10   John Maynard Keynes (1936) *The General Theory of Employment, Interest and Money*.

11   My estimate of around 100 million deaths from the various varieties of socialism is derived as follows: 14.3 million military losses during World War II; 27.1 million civilian deaths in that war; 5.6 million deaths in the Holocaust; and around 54 million people killed in Soviet Russia and the Soviet Union 1917–53, excluding World War II losses. See Norman Davies (1996) *Europe: A History*, Oxford, Oxford University Press, pp. 1328–9.

12 Henry Ford (1922) *My Life and Work*, and Henry Ford (1929) *My Philosophy of Industry*. Quotations taken from Ronnie Lessem (1991) *Ford on Management*, Oxford, Blackwell Publishers Ltd, pp. 10, 141 and 148.

13 *Ibid*.

14 King C. Gillette (1910) *World Corporation*, Boston, MA, New England News Company, pp. 4, 7, 42, 71, 103, 105, 119, 121, 151 and 199.

15 M.L. Severy (1907) *Gillette's Social Redemption*, London, Chatto & Windus, p. 737.

16 Walter Rathenau (1916) *Von Kommenden Dingen*. Quotation is taken from the 1921 translation *In Days To Come*, London, 1921. See pp. 26, 50, 75 and 123.

17 Quoted by Ivan Alexander (1997) *The Civilized Market*, Oxford, Capstone, p. 19. Alexander is quoting from (and providing his own translation of) Solvay's words as recorded in Jacques Bolle (1963) *Solvay 1863–1963*, Brussels, Weissenbruch, pp. 178–9.

18 *Op. cit.* (see reference 13 above).

19 *Op. cit.* (see reference 15 above).

20 *Ibid*.

21 *Op. cit.* (see reference 13 above).

22 *Op. cit.* (see reference 3 above), pp. v (Preface) and 3.

23 *Ibid*, p. 3.

24 *Ibid*, pp. vii–viii (Preface).

25 *Ibid*, pp. viii (Preface), 7–8, 9, 45, 344–7, 350–51, 353 and 355–6.

26 *Op. cit.* (see reference 1 above), p. 29.

27 *Ibid*, pp. 39, 46–49, 71–73.

28 *Op. cit.* (see reference 2 above), pp. 83, 111, 132, 133, 134, 167, 219 and 375.

Chapter Two

The Chimera of the Large Socialized Corporation

It is obvious that the [large] corporate system not only tends to be the flower of our industrial organization, but also that the public is in a mood to impose on it a steadily growing degree of responsibility for our economic welfare ... the [modern large] corporation has changed the nature of profit-seeking enterprise.

— Adolf Berle and Gardiner Means in 1932 [1]

Is in the future trade to govern the state, or the state to govern trade?

— Oswald Spengler [2]

Summary

- The pre-1945 intellectual consensus was that capitalism's demise was linked to the inevitable rise of a new and better type of large business corporation.
- It was believed that state corporations could serve society better and also be more efficient than capitalist corporations.
- It was also believed that a new class of non-state large corporations would emerge that would be quite different and better than traditional capitalist enterprise.
- Big business did indeed flourish. But, unexpectedly, large non-state corporations turned out to be more similar to small non-state corporations than to large state corporations. In all essentials, big business surprisingly resembled small business. It proved impossible to build a superior or different large corporation outside the capitalist system. It was this 'failure', totally unanticipated by anti-capitalist theory, together with the disappointing performance of state industry, that saved capitalism.

The critics' fallacy: big is different

The most basic mistake of all of capitalism's pre-1945 critics was to believe that the evolution towards big business was the key to revolution and progress. From Marx to Burnham, the ousting of capitalism was linked to the emergence of the modern large business corporation. They all believed this changed the game of capitalism.

F. Scott Fitzgerald wrote in *The Rich Boy*: 'Let me tell you about the very rich. They are different from you and me.' Ernest Hemingway was not impressed. 'Yes', he retorted, 'they have more money'.

So with large corporations. Superficially, they *are* different. They, too, have more money, more capital. They obtain it cheaper. Just like rich individuals, they can borrow it more cheaply. They do behave differently from small corporations in many ways, ways that space does not permit us to discuss. But large companies are not a different species. They are still part of the corporate world, still subject to the same laws of economics and capitalism. Like rich people, large corporations have more power than small corporations, and sometimes bend the rules. But large corporations, like small ones, ultimately have to make a profit and generate surplus cash, do things that customers want, compete against other corporations, and, in a civilized society, obey the law. At no stage along the way, from the one person business to the world's largest or richest corporation, does the corporation turn into a different species.

The theorists, from Karl Marx to King Gillette to Walter Rathenau to Gardiner Means to James Burnham, who claimed that large corporations were fundamentally a more evolved and therefore better species, transcending the laws of economics and capitalism – all these eminent and brilliant thinkers were, quite simply, wrong. To varying degrees, these gentlemen constructed elaborate theories about the replacement of traditional capitalism by socialism or social managerialism, based largely on this one fallacy.

What is odder is that they never argued their case closely or carefully. They pointed to the emergence of the modern large business corporation, where ownership had been separated from control. Quite right. But, right up to the

1940s, they then asserted rather than argued from evidence that a different system could be built around the large business corporation, where profit and personal gain would become largely irrelevant. They never showed that this was so, or how the large business corporation could be run differently, in the interests of society. They posited a new system, but never described it or showed how it would work, either theoretically or practically.

The myth of the superior non-capitalist large corporation

Their new system was a chimera. It never existed, and never could. All that existed, and increasingly did as a result of anti-capitalist propaganda, was the state-run corporation and state direction of industry – socialism, fascism, Nazism as systems replacing capitalism, and also, in the countries that still remained 'free' and in part at least capitalist, the experience with a 'mixed economy' or social democracy, where the state controlled or spent a sharply increased proportion of national wealth, both through state corporations and through state social welfare programs.

Because, where large non-state corporations continued to exist in a capitalist or partly capitalist system, these corporations, in defiance of the expectations of the 1920s and 1930s, continued to behave much more like free enterprise small corporations than like their similar-sized state equivalents.

The large free enterprise corporations continued to invest heavily in new technology and physical facilities, they continued to innovate and introduce new products, they struggled to increase the returns to shareholders, they took increasing notice of what customers wanted, they generated large amounts of surplus cash, and then reinvested most of that in their own business or in buying other corporations, and, on the whole, they consistently generated returns well above the cost of capital.

Large or small, the same corporate species

Like individual small businesses, individual large corporations waxed and waned. Like individual small businesses, individual large corporations sometimes went bust, or were 'rescued' by more successful brethren, at the expense of losing their identity.

Like individual small businesses, individual large businesses behaved more or less ethically; broke the law; polluted the environment; exploited or added value to their employees; behaved paternally, or with cold indifference, to both employees and the local community; were more or less responsive to their customers; borrowed money; paid it back; raised money from investors, sometimes never to give it back, sometimes to make the investors rich; developed new products and new techniques; colluded with or declared war on their competitors; set new industry standards or followed, with grumbles, the standards set by others – in these and almost all other respects, companies large and small engaged at the sharp end of capitalism, buying and selling, finding suppliers and customers, usually adding value along the way, usually making progress in myriad directions, always changing under pressure from outside forces, usually making a profit for investors, a good wage for the senior executives, and usually doing, each year, a slightly better job for their customers.

This was and is, and has been for the past quarter millennium, the way of capitalism. It is what free enterprise does as a whole, what companies large and small do individually, what small parts of corporations, individuals or teams, do themselves. The macro picture is an aggregation of many millions of small pictures, a kaleidoscope of pulsating life at the micro level. The picture is messy, confusing, full of inefficiency, always pregnant with opportunity for anyone within the system – investor, entrepreneur, top manager, middle manager, humble employee – to do better, to provide a superior product or service, or to lower the cost of delivering the current one.

Why would anyone want to do this? Sometimes, from love of the customer. Sometimes out of professional pride. Sometimes out of dogged devotion to an idea or pet theory. Often, to make a fortune, to zoom up the zoo, to be promoted, to earn praise and recognition, to prove a point, to beat a rival – motives great and small, worthy and unworthy, but more or less effective in generating action, improvement, and capable, within the capitalist system, of making a difference. Because of competition, better and cheaper products and services tend to prevail.

These mechanisms work in capitalism; and they work, more or less equally well, in small and in large corporations.

Small is better ...

In some ways – responsiveness to customers, spotting niches, economizing on cost, making decisions fast, carrying no passengers, being generally nimble and opportunistic, avoiding the cost and sluggishness inherent in excess complexity and management – the small corporation is at a structural advantage versus its bigger rival.

... and big is better

In other ways the reverse is true – in investing large amounts for the long term, in having access to cheap capital through high stock market ratings and through the banking system, in gaining economies of scale, in developing new technology and systems, in being able to strike out in new directions, in being able to absorb underperforming rivals, in going global, in developing a corporate culture that is bigger than an entrepreneur's or family's values, in instituting a formulaic approach – in all these ways the large corporation has the edge.

... and the market clears

There is no inherent superiority in either approach, in small corporation or large corporation. If the advantages of big corporations outweigh the disadvantages, they will gain market share. If small corporations can do better for customers and investors, they will gain a bigger share of the pie. This is what economists mean when they say: the market clears. What is better economically will become more prevalent. So what has happened in practice in the competition between big and small companies for the larger slice of our economies?

Until about 1980, large corporations grew rather faster than small ones. Since 1980, the reverse has been true. We can all have theories about what will happen in the next century (I believe, for example, that it will be the century of the small but global corporation – but I could be wrong, and for the purposes of our argument here it matters not a whit). It doesn't matter. Small corporations or large will flourish under capitalism according to how well they perform.

What matters is what any type of corporation delivers to society

The proof is in the pudding: the returns to investors; the ability constantly to raise society's wealth; the growth in gross national product per person, despite rising population; the growth in average wages, despite enlarged labor forces. Look at the productivity generated by capitalist or largely capitalist systems – increases in wealth generated exclusively by the private sector, nearly always while also meeting an increased transfer burden of taxation to the state. The money the state has taken from the private sector has perhaps served certain social goals, and in some cases (education, research, infrastructure) helped the economy, but, by taking resources away from the wealth-generating part of the economy, mega-taxation has usually detracted from society's ability to create wealth.

Large free enterprise corporations have delivered. Small free enterprise corporations have delivered. And, as we now know, regardless of what we would want to believe, large state corporations (there are very few small state corporations) have not delivered. So where is the difference? It is not between the first two categories, but between the first two categories on the one hand, and the third category.

According to the pre-1945 critics of capitalism, these state corporations could do as well or better than their free market equivalents. People in power believed this. Lenin believed this. Stalin believed this. Hitler believed this. They all acted energetically on their beliefs. After 1945, first in Europe, but later everywhere around the world (including to some degree the United States, where there is still a large public sector, including for example most airports), whole swathes of productive industry were nationalized. This was no accident, no swing of the political pendulum. It represented the consensus of the time, the consensus that capitalism was fatally flawed and that a better model awaited.

Remember the theory, subscribed to by socialists, by revolutionary capitalists, by President Franklin D. Roosevelt, by all the more-or-less liberal anti-capitalists, and even by mainstream capitalists like John Maynard Keynes, Joseph Schumpeter and the early Peter Drucker, men who should have known better but who succumbed to the spirit of the age. The theory was very simple. It said that large corporations were the wave of the future. That they should be managed by managers, not owners. That they should serve society's interests, not those of the stockholders. That the way to do this was to get rid of the profit motive. That state owned firms were the logical means to this end.

Pay attention! The theory was based on empirical evidence: the growth and evident success of large, managerially led corporations, the increasing requirements of capital, the decline of the entrepreneur in large business. Then, built upon this evidence, were a series of more-or-less logical extensions. No wonder most open-minded people believed the argument.

We know now that the argument was wrong. But we only know this because of experience. State-run large corporations have been a disaster. Large public corporations in the private sector have been successful. So we are no longer interested in the pre-1945 argument, the pre-1945 consensus. Yet *why* was it wrong, not in fact, but in theory? It is important to answer this question, a question that not only has not been satisfactorily answered, but that has rarely been intelligently posed.

Dissecting the anti-capitalist argument

Large corporations represented a new and higher stage of economic development. True up to a point. But large corporations still needed small corporations: as suppliers, customers, and most importantly of all, as ancestors. Every single large corporation before 1945 had originated as a small corporation. If the small corporate sector had not existed, the modern business corporation could never have emerged.

Most fundamentally, however, the argument that large corporations were the future rested on an unspoken, unproven, and untrue assumption: that large corporations were necessarily different from small corporations, qualitatively, as a difference of kind rather than of degree. The same sort of assumption, remember, as that the rich are different from the poor. And the truth is, that under the capitalist system, this assumption was simply not true. Large corporations could and did operate in the capitalist system in a way that was more similar to the way that small free enterprise corporations behaved, than it was to the way that large state corporations operated.

Now, if the argument is posed a different way, as it sometimes was, we can agree that the development of the large business corporation *allowed* the creation of a post-capitalist, an anti-capitalist, corporation: the state corporation. In this sense, large corporations were not the wave of the future. They were the cul-de-sacs of the future, or, from our vantage point, the cul-de-sacs of the past. But the really crucial point, the point still not properly understood, is this – *it was not possible to create a qualitatively different large corporation outside the capitalist system, except via the state corporation.* And, quite clearly, though some of the writers of the 1930s wanted to see large corporations nationalized, others envisaged the evolution of existing free enterprises into socialized corporations different from those of Stalin or Hitler: more socially responsible, stripped of the profit motive and most obligations to shareholders, and yet not organs of the state. It was this dream that proved a total illusion.

And yet the dream refuses to die. It answers a basic need, a sense of decency, of idealism, of discomfort with the market-based operations of capitalism – a wish for economic democracy. So the dream pops up in all sorts of ways: in higher corporate taxation, in greater regulation of business, and in doctrines like stakeholding, which, as we will see, is a simple regression to the errors of the 1930s.

Capitalism's enlightened critics – men like Henry Ford, King Gillette, Walter Rathenau, Adolf Berle and Gardiner Means – made two key errors. First, they thought that is was possible to build a better economic system outside capitalism, around the non-capitalist large corporation. They were wrong.

Second, they assumed that capitalism was incompatible with human decency and democracy. They did not see that to help the poor required giving *more* power to capitalism, while also democratizing it. That democratic capitalism is possible – real capitalism, which allows markets to work their magic, but based on giving real ownership of the means of production, distribution and exchange to the people as individuals rather than to the state.

The friends of capitalism, as well as its enemies, underestimated its flexibility and ability to thrive under quite adverse circumstances. For example, Joseph Schumpeter, writing during World War II, correctly foresaw increasing government intervention and demands on business, but incorrectly held that capitalism would buckle under the strain:

> ... there cannot be any doubt that the present conflagration will – inevitably, everywhere, and independently of the outcome of the war – mean another great stride toward the socialist order ... this time ... the stride will be taken [not only in Europe but] also in the United States ... [3]

Capitalism, Schumpeter thought, would prove too fragile to withstand substantial state activity and higher taxation. Like capitalism's critics, he underestimated the degree to which the system could flourish under adverse circumstances.

Conclusion

Those who found capitalism unsatisfactory hoped and expected that the large business corporation could be 'socialized', whether by the state or by the managers of the corporations behaving differently. The hope was for a new way of organizing the economy that did not rely on entrepreneurs, on the profit motive, and on the market.

Writers of great intellectual power saw the rise of the large corporation. They saw its increasing divorce from the original owner–entrepreneurs. They saw the rise of apparently disinterested professional managers. They then extrapolated these trends to a new world in which corporations would serve society rather than the other way round.

The trend was there. The objective was worthy. All that was missing was the bit in between: a new, non-capitalist model of how to run large corporations. There never was a sensible or coherent model. No-one even attempted it. So we ended up with state corporations that, far from advancing the cause of humanity, clogged up the arteries of commerce wherever they spread. Rarely has such a high price been paid for a missing part of the intellectual blueprint. (In retrospect, the really odd thing is not that the critics of capitalism left this gaping hole in their plans, but that capitalism's defenders failed to notice the hole either.)

Even odder, as we shall see in the next chapter, is the recent resurgence of non-market ideas in a form that has seduced many industrialists, academics and politicians.

Endnotes

1   Adolf A. Berle Jr and Gardiner C. Means (1932) *The Modern Corporation and Private Property*, New York, The MacMillan Company, pp. viii and 7.

2   Quoted in F.A. Hayek (1994) *The Road to Serfdom*, London, Routledge, p.32. The context is interesting. Oswald Spengler asserts:

> the decisive question not only for Germany, but for the world, which must be solved BY Germany FOR the world is: Is in the future trade to govern the state, or the state to govern trade? In the face of this question Prussianism and Socialism are the same ... Prussianism and Socialism combat the England in our midst.

Spengler is saying that English liberalism (capitalism) subordinates the state to trade, whereas both German nationalism and socialism plump for the correct, opposite answer. Hitler's state certainly did govern trade, along with everything else.

The answer that the third revolution gives to Spengler's question is 'Neither!'

3   Joseph A Schumpeter (1942) *Capitalism, Socialism and Democracy*, New
     York, Harper & Row, pp. 374–5.

Chapter Three

The Stakeholding Delusion

The economics of the centre and centre-left today should be geared to the creation of the Stakeholder Economy which involves all of our people, not a privileged few, or even a better off 30 or 40 or 50 per cent ...

... it is surely time to assess how we shift the ... corporate ethos from the company being a mere vehicle for the capital market to be traded, bought and sold as a commodity, towards a vision of the company as a community or partnership in which each employee has a stake, and where a company's responsibilities are more clearly delineated.

— Tony Blair [1]

What is occurring in this transition is a drive for social dominance, for power and privilege, for the position of ruling class, by the social group or class of the MANAGERS ... This drive will be successful.

— James Burnham [2]

Summary

- Social democratic proposals for reforming big business revolve around the idea of 'stakeholding'. The idea is that managers in large corporations should not respond merely to the owners (shareholders) but to others who have a 'stake' in the enterprise, such as employees, suppliers, customers, and the public. The managers are supposed to balance the interests of all these different stakeholders.
- Although the idea of making corporations more accountable to society is laudable, the proponents of stakeholding are barking up the wrong tree. They are proposing to replace the market mechanism with something better. The trouble is, there is nothing better than the market mechanism, and nothing that can even begin to allocate resources as well, to reflect what customers want.
- No sensible stakeholding way to allocate resources has ever been devised. In practice, stakeholding either leads to the state corporation, or to a bastardized market corporation, where managers and/or employees gain power and rewards at the expense of customers and society. The cure is worse than the disease.
- The proponents of stakeholding believe it is a post-1960 invention. In fact, all the essential ideas of stakeholding were enunciated in the 1930s as part of the fog of ideas that nearly choked capitalism.
- The way to make big business work to serve society's interests is to work entirely within the market mechanism, yet to give investors incentives to convert their corporations to democratic corporations.

The intellectual bankruptcy of social democracy – and of much that passes today for state-of-the-art business thinking – cannot be better illustrated than by looking at the idea of corporate 'stakeholding'. Nor can we illustrate much more succinctly the differences between social democracy – with its apparently fresh 1990s ideas in reality plucked, apparently without knowing it, from a body of thinking that arose in the 1930s, and that has been proved wrong in all essentials – and democratic capitalism.

Stakeholder theory relates to how to run big firms

The core of stakeholder theory relates to the way we run our business corporations, so it is concerned with the world of work and the impact of business corporations on wider society. And, though again this is rarely made clear, stakeholder theory really has in mind not the whole business sector, but that of fairly large and generally publicly quoted corporations. There is virtually no discussion in stakeholder theory of the family firm, large or small, or of the small business sector, the entrepreneurial sector of the economy, which is large and growing in its economic importance, and even more important in terms of employment than its contribution to GNP, since small firms have a higher ratio of employees to capital than large firms, and since small firms are creating more jobs than large ones.

The fact that stakeholder theory is confined, for all practical purposes, purely to large business enterprises, in the private sector but publicly quoted, does not mean that it is unimportant. Big business of this type is the dominant social institution in society today. It still accounts, in most capitalist economies, for the majority of non-state economic activity, and in a few countries, including the United States, for an absolute majority of all economic activity. (But I cannot resist commenting, *en passant*, that our infatuation with big business, which dates back to Marx but only reached its peak in the middle half of this century, from 1925 to 1975, is waning and will wane even faster in the next few years. Big business is already losing market share to small and medium size business quite rapidly, and at the fastest rate in our freest and most vibrant capitalist economy, that of the United States. There are important economic and social trends, including the facts that small business is more exciting and attractive to talent and that big business can no longer deliver security, which will accelerate the trend – but this is another story).

John Plender, a leading British financial journalist and broadcaster, gives this sympathetic account in his recent book, *A Stake in the Future: The Stakeholding Solution*: [3]

> *To the extent that stakeholding constitutes an explicit theory, it was initially developed at the level of the firm, not of society or the economy, in the United States in the 1960s. It does not, so far as I have been able to establish, have a single originator or a definitive original statement, but the Stanford Research Institute in California played an important part in fostering the theory ... In essence, the theory is a set of ideas revolving around a critique of the conventional notion of a company as a bundle of property rights in which the various constituents – shareholders, managers, employees, customers and suppliers – conducted their relations through a nexus of private contracts, with the pre-eminent participants, the shareholders, delegating responsibility for running the business to professional managers.*
>
> *Stakeholder theory proposed instead a view of the managerial role which came closer to trusteeship, where the trustees' role was to balance the interests of the various constituencies in the business and to recognize a wider responsibility to society. Its essential insight was that the market liberals' conventional description of corporate life was out of touch with events. In the modern world, large professionally run companies more closely resembled social entities in which investors enjoyed few rights of possession and control, and failed to exercise many of the rights that they did have ... This, indeed, was how many businessmen had long seen things ... the chairman of Standard Oil Company of New Jersey, Frank Abrams, gave an address in 1951 in which he said: 'The job of management is to maintain an equitable and working balance among the claims of the various directly interested groups – stockholders, employees, customers and the public at large.'*

Stakeholder theory: not young, just updated

It is extraordinary that the stakeholder theorists, from the 1960s to the present day, believe that they have invented a new theory. Mr Plender, who asserts that stakeholding theory originated in the US in the 1960s, is a highly experienced and competent journalist. He unearthed the statement quoted above, which contains the heart of the stakeholding case, from Frank Abrams, head of Standard Oil, in *1951*. This should have tipped off Mr Plender. Oil men are not noted for freshly minting academic ideas.

The truth, as we have already seen, is that stakeholding ideas have a long and distinguished intellectual pedigree. The critique of conventional capitalist property relations goes back to the period we can date roughly from 1880 to 1930. The revolutionary capitalists were men like Ernest Solvay, King Gillette, Walter Rathenau and Henry Ford, who were all rich and successful capitalists, but who did not believe that their capitalist system could or should survive. But it was in the 1930s that all the intellectual foundations for stakeholder theory were laid. This is important, because the modern stakeholder theorists have reinvented or appropriated certain parts of the 1930s theory, while leaving other integral parts of the same theory untouched. Although not deliberate, this is significant. The wider and larger theory of the 1930s is more coherent and intellectually impressive. Large-scale practical attempts were made to put it into practice. It worked, after a fashion. But the effects were unfortunate, and in the end, as we shall shortly see, the theory did not work very well. First, let's correct the collective amnesia of the stakeholder movement.

We have referred earlier to the powerful book that appeared in 1932 written by Adolf Berle and Gardiner Means [4]. As we saw earlier, Gardiner and Means, though they were not the first to notice that ownership in large corporations had become separated from control, or that this had come to rest increasingly in the hands of professional managers, nevertheless provided the most conclusive proof that this had happened and ruminated at great length, and in a strikingly original way, on the implications for capitalism and society. They argued that the separation of ownership from control, the fact that those who owned the capital of the corporation did not run it, implied a fundamental and socially beneficial change in, or even replacement of, the capitalist system. Their key argument was that in allowing professional managers to take over the running of companies, the owners or capitalists could no longer expect that the companies would be run in their sole interests. Shareholders and the whole profit system would and should henceforth take a back seat and allow managers to run the corporations in the interests of society. This is the starting-point for the so-called modern doctrine of stakeholding, which clearly dates from 1932 at the latest rather than the 1960s. Berle and Means are quite clear [5]:

> ... the owners of passive property [the shareholders], by surrendering control and responsibility over the active property [the corporation], have surrendered the right that the corporation should be operated in their sole interest.

Berle and Means go on to argue that eliminating this sole interest of shareholders does not imply that the managers in control should be the only beneficiaries of the corporation:

> The control groups [professional management] have, rather, cleared the way for the claims of a group far wider than either the owners or the control [management]. They have placed the community in a position to demand that the modern corporation serve not alone the owners or the control [management] but all society.

But what, Berle and Means go on to ask, did running corporations in the interests of society, rather than just of shareholders and managers, mean in practice? In a crucial passage at the end of their book [6], Berle and Means go on to argue coherently the whole stakeholding concept:

> It remains only for the claims of the community to be put forward with clarity and force ... Should the corporate leaders [top management], for example, set forth a program comprising fair wages, security to employees, reasonable service to the public, and stabilization of property ... the interests of passive property owners [the shareholders] would have to give way

... It is conceivable – indeed it seems almost essential if the corporate system is to survive – that the 'control' [management] of the great corporations should develop into a purely neutral technocracy, balancing a variety of claims by various groups in the community and assigning to each a portion of the income stream on the basis of public policy rather than private cupidity.

In still larger view, the modern corporation [run by managers] may be regarded not simply as one form of social organization but potentially ... as the dominant institution of the modern world.

We can see clearly from this that the fully blown idea of stakeholding dated from 1932 at the latest, *and that it originated in the context of a theory exalting the role of managers and proposing to replace the profit motive, the rights of shareholders, and the capitalist system itself.* There is no doubt that, in the 1930s, the idea was fresh and appealing. Even today, it exerts a certain charm, and its objectives – to democratize the economic system and run it for the benefit of all citizens – are totally consistent with those of this manifesto. But, sadly, the theory of stakeholding was flawed because it undermined normal capitalist market mechanisms without having a better resource-allocation system to propose. In practice therefore the idea of stakeholding had quite perverse effects. It wanted to make corporations act more in the interests of society as a whole, but in practice it gave positive power to managers and negative power to employees and took power away from customers and society as a whole. The result, wherever there was a serious attempt to allocate resources ignoring the market (or treating it only as an unwelcome constraint), was that resources were wasted and sectional groups within the firms were rewarded regardless of their contribution to society. Let's see what happened.

Towards the managerial state

The primitive stakeholder theory of the 1930s explicitly rejected contemporary capitalism and groped for a new idea of how the economy should be run. Berle and Means were in no doubt about this: [7]

There has resulted [from the development of the modern large corpora-
tion] the dissolution of the old atom of ownership into its component
parts, control [management] and beneficial ownership [shareholding].

The dissolution of the atom of property destroys the very foundations
on which the economic order of the past three centuries has rested. Private
enterprise, which has molded economic life since the close of the middle
ages, has been rooted in the institution of private property ... private
enterprise has rested upon the self-interest of the property-owner – a self-
interest held in check only by competition and the conditions of supply
and demand. It has been assumed that ... [the profit system of capital-
ism] can be relied upon as an effective incentive to his efficient use of any
industrial property he may possess.

In the quasi-public corporation [the modern large publicly quoted in-
dustrial corporation with fragmented ownership] such an assumption no
longer holds.

Berle and Means argue that society is moving from industry based on the entrepreneur, who is both owner and manager, to industry based on the manager
who is not a substantial owner; and in doing so the whole system and its objectives moves away from individual profit and capital. They also argue that large
corporations are oligopolies and have tremendous market power, and that therefore the rules of the capitalist market no longer operate. They are still fuzzy on
the type of new economic system that might emerge, but they conclude their
argument, immediately after outlining (what we now call) the theory of
stakeholding, by suggesting that the new economic state would be based on
new non-capitalist economic principles and corporate law:

The rise of the modern corporation has brought about a concentration of
economic power which can compete on equal terms with the modern state
– economic power versus political power, each strong in its own field ...
The future may see the economic organism, now typified by the corpora-
tion, not only on an equal plane with the state, but possibly even super-
seding it as the dominant form of social organization. The law of corpora-

tions, accordingly, might well be considered as a potential constitutional
law for the new economic state, while business practice is increasingly
assuming the aspect of economic statesmanship. [8]

Nine years later, in 1941, James Burnham asserts that managerialism was a total
replacement for capitalism. Burnham argued persuasively that both socialist
Russia and Nazified German were organized along the same anti-capitalist,
state-managerial economic lines, with the common theme being the social and
economic dominance of the managers. Burnham asserts that the replacement
of capitalism by managerialism was inevitable and that America would not be
far behind Russia and Germany in discarding capitalism [9]:

> *The theory of the managerial revolution predicts that capitalist society will*
> *be replaced by 'managerial society' ... that, in fact, the transition from*
> *capitalist society to managerial society is already well under way.*
>
> *The ideologies expressing the social role and interests and aspirations*
> *of the managers ... have not yet been fully worked out ... They are*
> *already approximated, however, from several different but similar direc-*
> *tions, by, for example, Leninism-Stalinism; fascism-Nazism; and, at a*
> *more primitive level, by New Dealism and ... 'technocracy'.*

Burnham comments that although most American managers believed that
their role depended on the capitalist structure, they were wrong about this.
The financiers depend for their position on capitalism, but not the managers:

> *The position, role and function of the managers are in no way dependent*
> *upon the maintenance of capitalist property and economic relations (even*
> *if many of the managers themselves think so); they depend upon the*
> *technical nature of the process of modern production.*

In fact, according to Burnham, the dominance of the managers and their
independence from the capitalists necessarily means that capitalism, with its
payments to owners, is redundant:

... disintegration of the social domination (that is, control over the instruments of production) of the capitalists is ... going on within the very womb of capitalism, and domination by new groups, above all the managers, is growing.

Burnham's managerialism (which he observed and predicted rather than advocated) is therefore not the managerial capitalism which has actually prevailed in the West's large private sector corporations, but a form of state socialism (or fascism) where the market is replaced by central direction as the main allocator of resources: [10]

There is nothing in the nature of factories, mines, railroads, airplanes, radio transmitters, that compels their operation to be dependent upon monetary profit. This dependence results merely from the specific economic relations of private enterprise, of capitalism. When these relations are gone, the need for profit is gone also. With the help of centralized state direction, managed currency, state foreign-trade monopoly, compulsory labor, and prices and wages controlled independently of any free market competition, branches of the economy or the whole economy can be directed toward aims other than profit. The managerial economy is no longer 'the profit system'.

In managerial economy, the regulation of production will not be left to the 'automatic' functioning of the market but will be carried out deliberately and consciously by groups of men, by the appropriate institutions of the unlimited managerial state ... the necessarily decentralized economy of private enterprise makes impossible such deliberate regulation of production as a whole. Under the centralized economic structure of managerial society, regulation (planning) is a matter of course.

For Burnham, the key economic reality is that managers manage. Like many or most of his contemporaries, Burnham sees little difference whether the managers were in the public or private sectors, or, conversely, whether government or 'private enterprise' were nominally in control:

> *The actual, day-to-day direction of the processes owned and operated ...*
> *or controlled ... by the government is in the hands of individuals strictly*
> *comparable to those whom we have called 'managers' in the case of private*
> *industry.*

And he observes:

> *already in the United States half or more of the population is dependent*
> *wholly, or in determining part, upon government for the means of living.*

The United States is therefore, during World War II, well on the way to the kind of centralist managerialism that had replaced capitalism in Russia and in Germany.

Why drag in the past to discredit stakeholder theory?

Today, of course, the statist managerialism of Red Russia is largely gone and that of Nazi Germany is hardly even a memory. Why, you may therefore ask, are we bothering to link early managerial and stakeholding theory with anti-capitalism and state socialism? Are we trying to establish stakeholding's guilt by association?

The point is that it is impossible seriously to pursue the stakeholding idea – either in theory or in practice – within the capitalist framework. The idea of managers balancing the rights of different groups of stakeholders and allocating resources to strike a fair balance between them – and this is *the* central idea of stakeholding, without which it is merely a set of exhortations for managers and corporations to behave responsibly – makes no sense at all unless there is to be a new decision-making apparatus which is different and better than the capitalist mechanisms. The managerialists and proto-stakeholder theorists of the 1930s were logical and acute thinkers. They realized that the whole point of freeing managers from the domination of the owners and financiers was to improve the allocation of resources, to create a more productive and fairer economy.

Stakeholder theory reduces shareholder claims

The stakeholder argument, then and now, revolves around replacing or limiting the claims of the people variously known as the owners, the shareholders or the capitalists. Industry can then be made to serve wider social purposes, or, put another way, serve, to a higher degree, the stakeholders (other than shareholders). The argument so carefully made by Berle and Means is that the returns to capitalists are no longer *necessary* economically (though Mr Berle, the lawyer, was clearly worried about upsetting traditional property rights, at least until the law had been redefined). Giving the shareholders high dividends could not affect economic performance, since the managers and not the shareholders are in charge. In theory, money could be used to motivate the managers, so what used to go to the shareholders (or some of it) could perhaps be diverted to the managers, to incentivize them to higher productivity. But Berle and Means speculate that managers aren't really that interested in money, and are responsive to social motivations anyway. The key point is that the profit motive is redundant, so why bother with capitalism and its costs?

Stakeholder theory rejects markets

The parallel point, made by Burnham and by Means later, is that markets are not needed to allocate resources. Large, oligopolistic or monopolistic corporations, acting at the behest of the state, or in concert with it, or independently but in pursuit of common social objectives, can allocate resources, these writers claim, at least as well as the decentralized market. This seems a strange argument to most of us today, but remember that in the 1930s it was widely believed that the world's two most effective, efficient and dynamic economies, and the only ones that could make full use of society's resources, were those of Russia and Nazi Germany.

Today it is not necessary to prove the virtues of decentralized markets. Experience of capitalist market economies or branches of the economy, compared to both state sectors within predominantly capitalist countries and to non-market economies in socialist countries, has vindicated the theories developed by Adam Smith and elaborated by the classical economists. But the very intelligent thinkers of the 1930s did not have this experience. What they *could* see was the emergence of large corporations, run by managers who were not the entrepreneurs pursuing individual profit maximization. This world *was* very different from that of Adam Smith. Moreover, the 1930s thinkers could observe the fundamental changes wrought by democracy. It was no longer ethical, or even feasible, to think of running the economy in the interests of a narrow elite, the former ruling monied classes, the capitalists. Hence the theory of managerialism and the gropings toward stakeholder economics.

The fundamental fallacy in the 1930s thinking is exactly the same as that of modern stakeholder thinking. *The common fallacy is to assume (what initially seems perfectly logical) that the main reason why capitalism gives returns to capitalists (owners or shareholders of large companies) is either to motivate them to maximize returns – the economic motive – or to uphold a certain social structure and provide high returns to the privileged – the social motive.* If this is so, it is entirely logical, in an era of large companies run by managers rather than owners, to 'save' the surplus value that would otherwise go to shareholders (which serves no economic purpose) and to allocate it to the benefit of broader and more deserving elements of society. To undermine capitalism in this way, if the assumption is correct, is economically sensible and socially justified.

Stakeholder theory misses the link between capital and customer markets

But the assumption is wrong. The reason for capitalism to allocate return to owners is that it is only through free capital markets that resources can be allocated efficiently. Economically, it doesn't matter much to whom (to which people or class of people) the returns to capital go. As long as the recipients or their agents want to maximize their returns, it matters little who they are.

The reason that free capital markets are so important is that they serve to allocate resources according to the wishes of consumers. It is impossible to have consumer sovereignty

*without also having capital markets seeking to maximize returns. Otherwise, the pro-
ducers will produce what they think best.* Both logic and experience tell us that
there is a huge difference in the efficiency and (more importantly) the dyna-
mism of economies where consumers, rather than producers, are dominant.

Thus, free capital markets and the desire to maximize returns on capital are
the incidental but absolutely necessary absolute accompaniment to market
economies and consumer sovereignty. Unless capital markets are seeking to
maximize returns, the market economy doesn't work, and there is tremendous
waste.

Now, the argument appears to get much more complicated when it comes
to large companies, which is where the 1930s thinkers went wrong. As these
thinkers correctly realized, there is no compelling reason why managers should
seek to maximize profits if they are not owners. And in fact we can observe that
managers *do* pursue many other goals than corporate profit maximization, not
least their own rewards, both individual and collective. Managers look after
other managers, and, almost as a tribal instinct, create far more managerial jobs
than are necessary. So why shouldn't the whole capitalist system break down,
foundering on this clear fact (which Berle and Means and most contemporaries
found uplifting, and I find depressing): that managers and not owners are in
charge, and might prefer to pursue different (higher or lower, depending on
your perspective) goals than profit maximization?

Managerialism could have prevailed – and sunk capitalism

The answer is interesting, and I don't think has been given quite in these terms
before.

*The answer is that it could. The capitalist system could have, and still could, founder
on this rock.*

In the 1930s this was expected, and objectively quite likely. Yet, it didn't
happen. And the reason it didn't, has little to do with managerial self-interest,
and a great deal to do with accepted ideas of how managers should behave,

with the surprising resilience of custom and practice in the capitalist economies, with what Marxists and some other academics call 'ideology'.

*The truth is, that managers went on behaving largely as if they were capitalists, even
though they weren't, and had no great economic vested interest in capitalism — arguably
quite the reverse, until in fairly recent days stock options and other paraphernalia simu-
lating capitalist interests for managers became widespread. The reason the managers did
not sink capitalism was lack of imagination, lack of developed alternatives to conventional accounting systems and capitalist allocation methods. In short, they had no well-
developed stakeholder theory.*

This was a very lucky accident. If managers in private industry had behaved
'managerially', as Berle and Means, and Burnham, had assumed they would,
capitalism would have ground to a halt. Managers in public enterprise did behave managerially: the number of managers and workers swelled well beyond
any economic need, the wages of managers and workers rose independently of
market requirements, and customers were systematically ignored. In striking
the 'equitable balance' between stakeholders, without any need to pay off shareholders, and without any need to make profits, managers followed the lines of
self-interest and least resistance. Those inside the organization were more voluble
and powerful than those outside. Though customers were thought of as stakeholders, they suffered along with shareholders.

By way of contrast, contrary to the 1930s expectations, large private sector
corporations run by managers *behaved more like small corporations, more as they
would have done if run by their owners,* than they did like public sector corporations. This was true except when labor unions usurped power within private
enterprise, or when managers entered into implicit alliances with labor to promote the interests of all workers at the expense of all consumers, and when
oligopoly blotted out consumer power — as in the case of the oil industry before 1973, and the steel industry until international competition spoilt the producers' game in the 1980s.

The 1930s expectations were entirely reasonable (and were to some extent
fulfilled in the 1970s, especially in the United Kingdom and the more socialis-
tic Continental European countries). It was just that American capitalism proved

more resilient as an ideology, and more successful in practice, than anyone could reasonably have expected.

In the late 1940s and the 1950s and 1960s, the golden age of post-war capitalism, American managers – who controlled the leading part of the West's production, and set the tone for most of the rest – continued to allocate resources in order to increase the profits and stock market value of their corporations. They listened to the market. They competed. They sought earnings per share increases. If they didn't, they were likely to be fired. It is true that managers feathered their own nests too; this tendency slowly accelerated (and in the 1980s and 1990s, as far as top management went, threatened to escalate out of control). It is also true that managers tended to be soft on labor, until Japanese competition forced them to do otherwise in the 1980s (a highly ironic result, since other parts of the Japanese economy were stuffed full of unnecessary management and labor). But, by and large, managers did not follow the siren voice of the stakeholderologists. They followed the market – the inseparable dictates of the capital market and the customer market. They followed conventional accounting conventions. If they themselves had owned the companies, the managers would have shed labor and management (as they eventually did in the 1980s and 1990s, respectively, because they had to), but otherwise they would have behaved in much the same way.

Quite why managers did this, when their class interests dictated otherwise, will always be a mystery to economic determinists. My best explanation is that the silent majority of conventional economists and business thinkers – the inbuilt majority of residual influence, stretching back to Adam Smith, solidly reinforced by the Manchester School of free traders and the classical economists of the late 19th century, and upheld most vigorously in the 1930s by the Austrian and German economists who fled Hitler's national socialism – proved able to resist the heresies of Marx and his followers, of the revolutionary capitalists after 1880s, and the developed heresies of the 1930s. We can be thankful that Hitler, unlike Stalin, was happy to exile rather than murder most intellectuals.

Stakeholder theory nudged managers to take more than their cut

Stakeholder theory never developed a viable alternative resource allocation mechanism to replace that of the capital and customer markets. Not having this at their disposal, managers used the existing capitalist method. But stakeholder theory, whenever it became known, was always popular with managers. Its natural tendency was to exalt the role of managers as the arbiters of different stakeholder interests, and to dignify and encourage the skimming off of the corporate surplus by managers, both individually (through higher compensation and, more importantly, unnecessary corporate expenditure) and collectively (through expanding the numbers of managers employed).

This was true right from the start of the stakeholder idea when Berle and Means, writing in 1932, strongly implied that the managers who were now running corporations had the right to arrogate to themselves at least part of the money that traditionally went to shareholders. Managers had this right because it was only they, and not the shareholders, who could now be motivated to improve the economic performance of the corporation [11]:

> *Those in control [the managers] of that wealth [of the corporation], and therefore in a position to secure industrial efficiency and produce profits, are no longer, as owners, entitled to the bulk of such profits ... the stockholders, on the other hand, to whom the profits of the corporation go, cannot be motivated by those profits to a more efficient use of the property.*

And here is Berle and Mean's charter for the fat cats (1932):

> *... we have already seen how the profit motive has become distorted in the modern corporation ... if ... all the profits reach or be held for the security owners, they prevent profits from reaching the very group of men whose action is most important to the efficient conduct of the enterprise. Only as profits are diverted into the pockets of control [management] do they ... perform their second function. [12]*

Berle and Means seek what is economically rational and fair. James Burnham, during World War II, chides Berle and Means for being naive. Burnham argues that Berle and Means catch-phrase, 'the separation of ownership from control', is pretty meaningless, since those who have the practical control will soon ensure that they have the ownership too [13]:

> *Where there is such a controlling group in society, a group which, as against the rest of society, has a greater measure of control over the access to the instruments of production, and a preferential treatment in the distribution of the products ..., we may speak of this group as the socially dominant or ruling class in that society ...*
>
> *... the two chief factors in control (control of access and preferential treatment in distribution) are closely related in practice. Over any period of time, those who control access not unnaturally grant themselves preferential treatment in distribution.*
>
> *Ownership means control; if there is no control, there is no ownership...*

The ruling class hits the beach – and loses control to managers

In an amusing section, Burnham argues that the capitalists only had themselves to blame for their loss of control, and (he foresaw) the loss of their property and civilization. If ownership cannot be defended without control, the rot began to set in when the capitalists sought the high life: [14]

> *We find that [the big capitalists] have more and more withdrawn, not merely from production proper, but from active and direct participation of any sort in the economic process. They spend their time, not in industry or even in finance, but on yachts and beaches, in casinos and traveling among their many estates; or, others of them, in charitable, educational, or even artistic activities ... To rule society, let it be remembered, is a full-time job ...*

> *One consequence of the withdrawal is necessarily the assumption of*
> *more and more power … by the managers.*
>   *It could not be otherwise. Someone is going to do the actual managing*
> *…*

It is not only the capitalists who will be, effectively, expropriated by the people they thought were just their paid lackeys:

> *Similarly, the managers will exploit the rest of society … They, too,*
> *through the possession of privilege, power and command of educational*
> *facilities, will be able to control, within limits, the personnel of the mana-*
> *gerial recruits; and the ruling class of managers will thus achieve a certain*
> *continuity from generation to generation.*

Burnham's prophecies should make us think: both why he was right and why he was wrong. Like most prophecies that prove correct, Burnham's were based on extrapolation of what he could see already, in the Third Reich and Stalin's vast empire. Hitler's world was reaching its monstrous zenith when Burnham's book came out; it lasted but another four years. Thanks, however, to Roosevelt and Churchill, and the war-weary popular democracy of the West, Stalin's equally monstrous and more efficient tyranny was allowed to expand and continue its evil unabated until he died, and, in more limited form, for decades thereafter. And what happened in the Soviet Union with the managerial class was exactly what Burnham had predicted. The managerial class in industry, in the armed forces, the police, and the bloated state bureaucracies, perhaps 15 per cent of the population, exploited the rest. This was stakeholder theory in practice, word for word as Burnham had said.

And in the West? Burnham's description should make us, too, pause. For what is the American dream, the middle-class lifestyle developed in the 1950s and exported as a model throughout the world, but a broader version of domination by the managerial classes? At the center of the dream sits the middle manager in a large multinational corporation, driving back in a large automobile, parking in the drive-way outside the two garages, to be greeted by his wife and two children, children who are being carefully educated to follow daddy's footsteps. Has there not been a certain continuity of managers from generation to generation? And do not executives in the media, the world of arts and entertainment, and even academia, increasingly resemble the business middle manager?

To be sure, this is not state-based managerialism, as Burnham expected. In the battle between the state and the stock exchange, the latter has finally got the upper hand. Stakeholder theory and practice have not replaced capitalist market theory and practice. And, in different countries, the demands of democracy have been to varying degrees effective in breaking the middle class monopoly of good education and hence of access to the managerial classes. Managerial capitalism has thus evolved as no-one predicted: a compromise between managerialism and capitalism, between two opposites, that everyone in the 1930s, of whatever political persuasion, would have thought unlikely and unsustainable. On the whole, the compromise has worked extremely well. But it has worked better economically than socially. Capitalism has been allowed to produce the goods, subject to surplus value being skimmed by the managerial middle classes. Those outside the magic circle, the bottom third of the population, have also benefitted economically. Markets have worked. But stakeholding, apparently a generous and democratic doctrine, has been perverted in practice into giving power and privilege to the elite class of managers at the expense of society generally. And, in recent years, the greatest benefit has gone increasingly to the very narrow elite at the top of the managerial zoo. This is not likely to prove sustainable. Democracy can, should, and will assert its claims.

Stakeholder theory led to socialism or managerialism

Stakeholding ideas must lead either to socialism – where the managers are the dominant class, the rest of society is exploited, and the country's wealth is held back – or to some other kind of managerialism. In practice, the only form of non-socialist managerialism the world has seen is that of managerial capitalism, which is neither managerialism nor capitalism but a compromise between them, where the capitalist system remains largely intact, but managers preserve their power and perquisites. Western managerial capitalism has generally been more strongly weighted toward capitalism than managerialism. But there have been some interesting exceptions.

Modern managerial capitalism: a personal reminiscence

When managerialism has become a stronger part of the managerial-capitalist mix – when capital and customer markets have been largely ignored, in order to favor producer interests – the tendency has been for managerial capitalism to become unstable, and to tip over heavily in the socialist direction. I have lived through this.

When I first became a (very junior) manager, in England in 1971, I worked in a very managerial industry (oil) and a very managerial company (Shell). No-one around me talked about customers, and very few about profits. Though I worked in an oil refinery, this simple production plant was blessed with hordes of highly paid managers, organized into all kinds of service departments (there was even one called Organization & Methods, whose sole job was to help other managerial departments organize their managers better), whose output was paper and yet more managers. Unnecessary managers like me were 'rotated' through the plant in order to 'gain experience' before being sent to another facility somewhere else in the world. Our main role and function was to become culturally integrated into the managerial elite. We served no useful business function at all; we were cost, pure and simple. Now the refinery runs with a quarter of its 1971 headcount. Few of the survivors are managers.

Rampant managerialism: the slippery slope to socialism

I then saw the UK economy teeter, in 1973–79, on the very point at which rampant managerialism, pushed by even more rampant trade unionism, nearly turned into socialism. Markets ceased to allocate resources; increasingly, this was done by the managers, the trade unions, and the government, operating in tripartite concert. Inflation approached 30 per cent in 1975. Stakeholder theories enjoyed unprecedented vogue. I espoused them. Only international money markets, operating through the International Monetary Fund in 1976, forced the government to slow and eventually reverse the process. Then democracy swept Margaret Thatcher into Downing Street in 1979 and amazing luck kept her there throughout the 1980s. She completed the task of restoring capitalism by crushing the public sector unions and then subjecting large parts of the public sector to privatization and, eventually, to competition. Managerialism retreated to its junior position in the managerial–capitalist coalition. Slowly, the waters of socialist managerialism abated.

Compare this experience with the fate predicted for capitalism in America and the other capitalist countries by Joseph Schumpeter in 1942: [15]

> In no country will war taxation of business and of the business class be reduced in the proportion in which it was reduced after 1919. This may in itself suffice to paralyze the motors of capitalism for good and thus provide another argument for government management. Inflation ... may well do the rest ... Moreover nowhere will war controls be liquidated to the extent ... after 1918 ... They will be put to other uses... Finally, there is no reason to believe that governments will ever relax the hold they have gained on the capital markets and the investment process. To be sure, this does not add up to socialism. But socialism may, under such conditions, impose itself as the only practicable alternative to deadlocks and incessant friction.

What Schumpeter expected after World War II in America, was almost exactly what nearly happened in Britain during the 1970s. Taxation reached penal levels, investment seized up, the stock exchange became a backwater, hyperinflation began to erode civilization, and the government became the focal point of all important economic decisions. All of this began with business managers ignoring the market and preferring producer to consumer interests.

One good point made by stakeholder theory

One unresolved issue – spotted by Berle and Means – remains. Is it not unfair that the same rewards now go to passive shareholders, that used to go to active entrepreneurs? The honest answer is yes.

The market system requires that shareholder rewards be preserved, in order to guarantee the integrity of the capital market, and hence of the customer market. If capital does not seek the highest returns, and obtain them, investment will not serve customers and resources will not be efficiently allocated.

Yet, as Berle and Means saw, investors who are not active in a business do not create the wealth that they appropriate. Modern shareholders are passive coupon clippers. It is left to the capital markets, and to the managers acting at the behest of the capital markets, to ensure that capital earns high returns. Since no skill is required by investors, it does not matter economically who these investors are. If an elite collars a disproportionate share of these investor returns, there is a social disbenefit and no economic benefit.

If we want to act in society's interest, we should seek to reallocate the investors' returns not to managers – they already have more than enough to induce them to perform their role well, as international comparisons show beyond doubt – but to citizens as a whole. We can do this without interfering with economic efficiency, since it does not matter who the investors are. The way to reduce the unfairness noted by Berle and Means is to redistribute capital, so that everyone gets a fair shot at enjoying the unfair rewards of capital. Chapter 8 shows how this can be done without tears. The big difference between my proposals and those of stakeholding theory – or any other form of social democracy or socialism – is that I want to increase rather than reduce the market's power.

Conclusion

The best idea that social democracy can muster, to reform our corporations, is the idea of stakeholding. This is an idea whose time has gone. It came from the 1930s and should be consigned back to the lumber-room of that decade, when capitalism was faltering and the hopes of mankind rested, cruelly, on managerialism and its socialist or Nazi incarnations. To be effective, for good or ill, stakeholding requires legal forms that are inconsistent with capitalism: the state corporation, state direction of industry, and/or other means for allocating resources that replace the allocations that would otherwise be made by capital and customer markets. The ideas of stakeholding and managerialism – twin cherries on a single stalk – negate capitalism and, if taken seriously, create non-market economies where there are no capitalists and not much wealth.

In practice, in the West, managerialism and stakeholding have had a limited, though still pernicious, effect. Under managerial capitalism, the basic capitalist system has been allowed to work its magic, though managers have skimmed off far too much of the surplus. Only the rules, conventions and accounting systems of capitalism have kept the managers tolerably honest and productive. Whenever the stakeholding ideas have become powerful, they have threatened to tip capitalism over into socialism.

Though managerialism and stakeholding are a much worse alternative to capitalism, capitalism today is far from perfect. Stakeholding and managerialism arose from noble and worthy ideals, ideals that were partly or wholly democratic. Like many ideals, they led to horrid results. But ideals, like persistent spirits, wander the world until they find a suitable home. That destination is not social democracy, stakeholding or managerialism, but something both noble and viable – democratic capitalism.

To see how radical democratic capitalism is, and how far it parts from capitalism today, we need a new critique of capitalism. Previous critics have missed the point. It is high time for a fresh democratic critique of capitalism, one freed from the discredited delusions of the past.

Endnotes

1. Tony Blair (1996) when leader of the British Opposition Labour party in a speech to the business community in Singapore, 8 January 1996.
2. James Burnham (1941) *The Managerial Revolution: What is Happening in the World*, New York, The John Day Company, p. 71.
3. John Plender (1997) *A Stake in the Future: The Stakeholding Solution*, London, Nicholas Brealey, pp. 16–17
4. Adolf A Berle Jr and Gardiner C Means (1932) *The Modern Corporation and Private Property*, New York, The MacMillan Company.
5. *Ibid*, pp. 355–6.
6. *Ibid*, pp. 356.
7. *Ibid*, pp. 7–9.
8. *Ibid*, p. 357.
9. James Burnham, *op. cit.* (see reference 2 above), pp. 29, 73, 91, and 110.
10. *Ibid*, pp. 129–30, 132, 109, and 107.
11. Adolf A Berle Jr and Gardiner C Means, *op. cit.* (see reference 4 above), pp. 8–9.
12. *Ibid*, p. 350.
13. James Burnham, *op. cit.* (see reference 2 above), pp. 59–60 and 92.
14. *Ibid*, pp. 101 and 126.
15. Joseph A Schumpeter (1942) *Capitalism, Socialism and Democracy*, New York, Harper & Row, pp. 374–5.

Chapter Four

A New Democratic Critique of Capitalism

Democracy believes in 'one man, one vote' (equality of political power), while capitalism believes in letting the market rule (in practice, great inequalities in economic power) ...

... capitalism is perfectly compatible with slavery. The American South had such a system for two centuries. Democracy is not compatible with slavery.

– Lester Thurow [1]

The answer is quite startling: 70 percent of the rise in average family income [between 1977 and 1989 in the United States] went to the top 1 percent

– Paul Krugman [2]

A society in which the top 1% earn more, collectively, than the bottom 40%, will not long be tolerated in a democratic state.

– Charles Handy [3]

Summary

- Capitalism has been greatly improved by changes in custom, practice and law in the past 160 years – changes driven largely by the forces of democracy.
- For the first time since the 1840s, capitalism is being subjected to fewer and less onerous democratic constraints. The revival of global *laissez-faire* capitalism, last seen to any great extent before 1914, has raised world economic growth but has rolled back the long term trend toward greater equality. *Fin de siècle* rampant capitalism is not compatible with democracy or with a good society.
- The problem is not purely that capitalism is unconstrained. It is more complex than that. One issue is the perversions inherent in the modern form of large corporations quoted on the stock exchange. Large, diversified, publicly quoted firms are the last redoubt today of undemocratic socialism.
- Big business should be subjected to much greater degrees of both market discipline and democracy. Big business should be largely dismantled. That which remains should behave increasingly like small business.
- The full answer is to reform capitalism using the power of the market to arrive at a wealthy and egalitarian society, one that liberates and facilitates the happiness of all its members. In a word, to make capitalism democratic.

Are capitalism and democracy friends or enemies? The intellectual consensus in the first half of our century was that they were deadly foes in a battle that, sooner or later, capitalism would lose. The consensus was nearly right. Democracy, the second revolution, was not a force that the first revolution, capitalism, could safely ignore. From 1945, capitalism made an unexpected recovery, but only by shifting its ground toward democracy.

Under democratic pressure, capitalism has reformed. 1945 was a watershed. Thereafter, in North America, in Western Europe, in Japan, and in other countries that have maintained or adopted capitalist systems, the state – enforcing the claims of democracy – intervened in a much stronger way than before to ensure that capitalism did not override basic human rights: to education, to employment, to reasonably safe and civilized working conditions, to workers' protection by trade unions, and, in most places, to a minimum standard of living and decent health care. These are the achievements, today perhaps frayed at the edges, but real nonetheless, of social democracy, the system that most of us, including Americans, have lived under since 1945. The democratic megastate and capitalism, yoked together, sometimes in harmony, sometimes in uneasy truce, often contend the boundaries of their influence, but never seek to destroy each other.

Capitalism has changed. At least in developed democracies, out have gone compulsory 12 hour days, life-threatening sweatshop conditions, environmental destruction, punitive supervision, blatant cartelization, and the arrangement of the economy for the specific benefit of a small elite. In have come civilized standards of behavior, decent wages, corporate pensions, employee development, the creation of mass markets, the commitment to ever-greater value for the customer, and an accommodation – perhaps too great an accommodation – with social democracy and the liberal state, including the willingness to fund without complaint large portions of state expenditure. In the process of society's democratization, ordinary people – those whom Marx called 'the masses' – have come to own, both directly and through their savings, insurance and pension funds, a majority of business assets. In a way unthinkable at the start of this century, capitalism and democracy, the two great revolutions of the modern world, have learned to live together.

Yet, capitalism is still far from democratic. And recent trends are making things worse.

The defects of capitalism today

Capitalism has grave flaws. Its democratization is half-hearted and incomplete. Capitalism in the 1990s, when left to its own devices, has returned to its old vice: that of reinforcing rather than reducing inequality. This inegalitarian, undemocratic capitalism is not good enough. In the end, democracy will not and should not tolerate too unequal a society, one in which there is a great gulf in the way of life, expectations and de facto rights of the rich and the poor, one where there is not a decent standard of life for everyone, and where the poorest citizen cannot feel the same dignity and pride as the richest. So what should we do?

The solution is not to restrict capitalism further, to hedge it about with social-democratic constraints. That has already been done. I do not complain at the results; they have not been bad. Social democracy has done far more good than harm. But social democracy is yesterday's solution. As the century draws to its close, it has become apparent that when we restrict or replace markets, we pay a high price in inefficiency; and that the state is a rather poor mechanism for delivering value to customers and citizens. The good state has to stand up for democracy, and for the least privileged citizen, but it cannot do this effectively by puffing itself up or extending its direct economic power. Democracy has learned that it has to find other means than the mega-state to do good. But, equally, the good state would be very naive to trust unreconstructed capitalism to solve all of society's problems. Those who have lived through the 1980s and 1990s know precisely what would happen. The rich would get richer and the poor get left behind.

Fortunately, there is a third way, that of the third revolution, the integration of capitalism and democracy. This requires the democratic reform of capitalism, not from outside, via social democracy and state restrictions, but from within. As we shall see, the state has an essential role in setting up democratic capitalism, but once set up, the new form of capitalism will run itself. Part Two gives a primitive blueprint for democratic capitalism. Before we get there, we must dispose, in this chapter and the next one, respectively, of today's great consensus illusions – that of the center-right, that capitalism has pretty much reached its ideal form, and all that it needs now is global roll-out; and that of the center-left, of social democracy, that markets are OK provided they are contained by judicious government intervention.

Capitalism's failure to progress far enough toward democracy falls into two arenas: that of the corporation and the capitalist economy, and that of capitalist society.

Defects of the capitalist economy

Big business or small business?

The critics of capitalism earlier this century got it exactly wrong. They held that the small business sector, the world described and glorified by Adam Smith, was anachronistic and inherently antagonistic to democracy; while the salvation lay with big business and its transition beyond capitalism.

Yet is it not clear that private businesses are inherently more democratic than big businesses? In most small enterprises, those who add most of the value are owners or part-owners. Those who are not owners are likely to be fairly rewarded for their contribution, and if they don't feel that they are, they can, and often do, go off and start their own small enterprise. The barriers to setting up a business are low, at least compared to larger and more complex corporations. To make the small business sector even more efficient and democratic, all we need to do is to make it easier for individuals to own capital themselves, and/or to gain access to capital. In further democratizing small business, we are leaning on an open door. The world has never before had so many small businesses or so many entrepreneurs, and their numbers are growing rapidly.

So small business tends to be both democratic and efficient. But the large business sector, the world of managed, publicly quoted corporations – the world that was meant to transform capitalism for the better – is neither very democratic nor very efficient. The closer we look at large corporations, and the large corporate capitalist system, the more imperfect they appear.

Is 20th century capitalism ahead of Adam Smith?

Adam Smith has often been patronized for living too early. The standard line is that Adam Smith's capitalism was fine in its day, the day of the entrepreneur and a handful of employees, but that the huge modern corporation requires a different economic framework.

Actually, Adam Smith *did* know about the modern large 20th century corporation, in all its essentials: because he knew its remarkably similar ancestor, the 18th century joint-stock corporation, typified by the East India Company. Adam Smith knew all about the separation of ownership and control in large corporations. He was familiar with managers who were not owners, and owners who were not managers. *Adam Smith knew all these things, and disliked them intensely!* To him they were a perversion of economic responsibility and harmful to society. How acute Smith is on the evils inherent in modern managerialist capitalism! [4]

> *The trade of a joint stock company is always managed by a court of directors [what we would call a board of directors]. This court, indeed, is frequently subject, in many respects, to the control of a general court of proprietors [shareholders]. But the greater part of those proprietors seldom pretend to understand anything about the business of the company; and when the spirit of factions happens not to prevail among them,* give themselves no trouble about it, *and receive contentedly such half yearly or yearly dividends, as the directors think proper to make to them. This total* exemption from trouble and from risk, *beyond a limited sum, encourages many people to become* adventurers *in joint stock companies,*

who would, upon no account, hazard their fortunes in any private copartnery [partnership with unlimited liability].

The directors of such companies ... being the manager rather of other people's money than of their own, it cannot well be expected that they should watch over it with the same anxious vigilance with which the partners in a private copartnery will watch over their own ... Negligence and profusion therefore must always prevail, more or less, in the management of the affairs of such a company. It is upon this account that joint stock companies for foreign trade have seldom been able to maintain the competition against private adventurers.

Adam Smith's logic is impeccable. His system is not to be judged against corporate forms. Rather, the corporate forms are to be judged against his system. The system of competition works for the benefit of all. No corporation, however modern, large and powerful, should escape this discipline.

The managerial heresy

Large modern corporations can and should operate within the rules of Adam Smith's capitalism. They can be made to work as if they were small corporations, owned by the people who run them and who add value to customers. As I show in Chapter 10, they can do this by becoming democratic corporations.

Why should we make large corporations resemble small ones? First, for economic efficiency. Big businesses run like small ones are the most successful of their ilk. This is no accident. It is because of the robustness of the competitive system that Adam Smith described. More creativity, better service to customers, less waste: the market rewards these traits.

But a second reason is democracy. Small corporations tend to be more nimble and democratic than large corporations: more easily influenced by employees below the top level, including the very lowest; faster to incorporate what works best in direct contact with customers. Large corporations can be made much more democratic than they are. This is likely to lead to raised profits and value, both to investors and consumers, of the companies concerned. But, even more importantly, it is also likely to raise the motivation and happiness of those who work in them. The latter effect, in large part, causes the former. But democracy, and the happiness of producers, are ends in themselves.

The great enemy is the theory and practice of managerialism. Championed by our friends Berle and Means, managerialism asserts that the managers in large corporations should be exempt from the iron laws of capitalism: free from competition, which forces attentiveness to customers; free from the supervision of owners and the profit motive, which stop the waste of society's resources; and free from any real system of accountability, which inculcates responsibility. Fortunately, managerialism has not subverted the basic laws of capitalism or put forward a viable alternative system. But what it has succeeded in doing, to the immense cost of owners, customers and society generally, is creating and rewarding a managerial class far larger and richer than is economically necessary.

Managerialism creates a self-perpetuating managerial oligarchy, sometimes very narrow and sometimes rather broader, but always a small minority of the total workforce. Whether this elite is correctly viewed as paving the way for democracy, by being, however narrow, nearly always broader than the group of original owners; or, alternatively, as a vested interest determined to hang on to power at the expense of the broader group of producers, is an interesting debating point, but one that need not detain us. There is a better model than managerialism: better for customers, better for investors, better for society, and better for all workers except the privileged elite of managers; and against this better model, the model of democratic capitalism, managerialism stands no chance. But first, the charge sheet against managerialism needs to be documented.

There are four charges: managerial socialism, managerial gigantism, managerial market manipulation, and managerial greed. Nearly all large corporations and their managers are guilty of at least one charge, usually of two or three, and some, all four (combining managerial socialism and managerial greed takes a particular brand of effrontery, but one not beyond the skill of our most talented top managers).

Managerial socialism

Managerial socialism is the insulation of business from competition and market pressures, with the result that resources are allocated without regard to customer preferences and with scant regard to internal democracy. Now that the USSR has imploded and China has become state-capitalistic, there are very few genuine socialist polities left (Cuba perhaps being the most conspicuous dinosaur). But socialism survives in some of the world's largest quoted corporations. These centrally planned economies subvert or mitigate market pressures, allocate resources according to their own dictates, sell wherever possible to captive customers (notably those inside the corporation), and smother or suppress fledgling attempts at internal democracy. Proclaiming themselves bastions of free enterprise, these large socialist multinationals practise double-think on an Orwellian scale; and, like the old USSR, they can survive only when there is little competition and they can liquidate the seedcorn of the past. The socialist corporation is running out of time.

Good service and good capitalism go together. One great virtue of capitalism is that markets and competition enforce attention to what customers want. If one firm can find a better or cheaper way of delivering a product or service to customers, it will be rewarded with more business – and competitors will either have to meet the new standard or see their sales fall. This system only works directly, however, if the producer is serving a customer. If the producer serves another producer within the same firm – and this process can be multiplied many times – the customer becomes much less relevant and powerful. Most of us have experienced the frustration of dealing with an unsatisfactory product or service, only to complain to the front-level employee, and be told that she would like to see the service improve, but is dependent on other, less responsive people in the organization. Whenever organizations become large and 'integrated' – meaning that the producer serves internal customers and not real customers – most stages of the value-added chain are not subject to markets and the valuable disciplines that they bring.

If the economy were composed exclusively of large, integrated corporations, with most exchanges being internal, this would be more a socialist than

a capitalist economy, because the market would only operate at the final stage
and at earlier stages. The market would be less powerful than the internal planning and co-ordination mechanisms of the large corporations. This would be a
largely socialist economy, even if there were no public sector and all the corporations were privately owned. The key concern for efficiency is not that corporations are owned by individuals, but that markets exist and call the shots.
Otherwise the customer is powerless, and the spur to superior performance is
lost.

Managerial socialism has been most blatant in corporations specifically set
up for the purpose of ignoring customer preferences: namely nationalized state
corporations. But since Britain's Margaret Thatcher ran out of money in the
mid-1980s and therefore started the then-daring practice of returning state
corporations to stock market pressures, later followed rather more slowly by
returning the newly privatized corporations to competitive pressures, and since
governments around the world have discovered that privatization can help
their state finances (and, of much less concern, their citizens as consumers), the
state corporation has become an endangered species.

Managerial socialism has survived and prospered, however, inside the so-
called private sector, within large publicly quoted – the 'public' is a warning
signal – corporations.

Make any business complex enough, and its executives can enjoy managerial socialism. Backward integration or forward integration can guarantee an
outlet for the firm's products, an outlet that is not immediately dependent on
market pressures. The real customer becomes an internal customer. We all
know that internal customers are a great deal less demanding, or can be more
easily ignored, than external customers.

But backward or forward integration are just a start. If a firm makes enough
different products, serving different markets, distributed through different channels of distribution, the whole shooting match can be made so complex and so
interwoven that customers lose an effective voice and can be safely ignored by
each individual manager.

In a complex corporation, nobody is clearly accountable for anything that is
clearly related to customer satisfaction. It is an index of seniority to be insulated
from the pressures of the outside world, starting with customers.

Have you ever had a complaint about a product or service, and tried to reach someone senior in the offending firm? In a small enterprise, it is easy. For one thing, the boss may actually answer the phone herself. In a large but simple company, selling just one main family of products, you stand an outside chance. Most likely you will reach the senior person's secretary or PA, and get no further. In a large and diversified company, it is virtually impossible to speak to anyone really senior. With size and complexity comes managerial impunity to customers. The manager may worry about her boss, but rarely or never about her customers. But even with her boss, the criteria by which her performance is judged are likely to bear little or no direct relationship to value delivered for customers. In a small and simple corporation, this is impossible. In a large and complex firm, it is routine.

Head offices are great redoubts of managerial socialism. Head offices are curious things. They have no customers, no competitors, no operations, no real business except finance and paper-shuffling. They are intermediaries between those who provide funds – bankers and investors – and those who run real businesses that do have customers, competitors and operations, those who do things and provide value to customers.

Head offices are parasitic. If they did not exist, it would not be necessary to invent them. The businesses that do add value could raise the money themselves, from venture capitalists and bankers, and if large enough from the stock market, without needing the head office. The head office is there, like some anachronistic family that is still in charge of an industrial empire though not active in the business, simply because it owns the business. It is true that most head offices, unlike our mythical family, add some value. But it is equally true that all head offices destroy value, usually large amounts of value. The net value added by head offices is normally negative, often heavily negative. (This, incidentally, is why breaking up multi-business corporations releases huge value. No new value is created, but value destruction by head office is removed.)

Even though their net economic value is normally negative, head offices exist. This would not happen in any effective market economy, where value delivered to customers is the only *raison d'etre*. The existence of head offices, and of unaccountable, senior executives, insulated from customers, is ample evidence that managerial socialism is alive and well. You would think that competitive pressures, and the ability to make money by dismantling managerial socialism, would cause it to disappear fairly quickly. And there are firms which engage in this sort of arbitrage – like Hanson plc, the Anglo-American conglomerate, that grew rich by dismantling managerial socialism [see box].

Yet competition is often a weaker force than social convention and class interests, particularly when these are disguised as normal economic reality. Our industrial fat cats, like true felines, don't cannibalize their own species. Large and complex corporations are conspiracies organized for managers and against the interests of non-managers. Market forces can only make headway if one significant large corporation in a competitive system starts to behave non-managerially, against the interests of its own managers, and for the interests of its investors and customers.

Armies can be inefficient because they compete only against other armies. Police forces can be even more inefficient because they compete only against criminals, who are also effectively their clients (if criminals did not exist, there would be no need for police).

Similarly, the inefficiency of large corporations has, until recently, been constrained only by competition from similarly inefficient large corporations. Managerial socialism is now in slow retreat, as smaller corporations begin to compete against their larger brethren, and as larger and more complex corporations simplify and make themselves smaller through breakup (spin-offs, demergers and unbundling).

Managerial socialism is also evident when historically successful large firms live off their past. Given the imperfections in financial markets, especially the stock market, where investors cannot accurately assess the future cash flows of any large, complex corporation, it is possible for a company with a good historical track record to continue growing well beyond the time that it has ceased to add surplus value. It is even possible for a less efficient corporation to take over a more efficient competitor. Anomalies like this arise because stock market analysts judge companies on their historical and near-future earnings per share records.

The hunter and the hunted: Hanson and Imperial Foods

Starting with a tiny business in Yorkshire, England, James Hanson and his partner Gordon White, had by the mid-1980s built up a huge empire of basic industrial businesses in Britain and America. Hanson and White were early devotees of shareholder wealth maximization. Their focus was never on the particulars of the businesses they owned. White, the man in charge of the group's operations, liked to boast that he had never visited any of his factories. They concentrated instead on the tricky business of making managers behave in the interests of shareholders.

Hanson was one of the very first people on either side of the Atlantic to realize that the Managerialist Corporation – all of the businesses he took over were run *by* managers *for* managers – contained huge amounts of waste, and that, for all their ritual obeisances to shareholders, most managers did not care very much about enriching shareholders.

Hanson may have been the first active business leader since Alfred Sloan to attempt to re-fashion the corporation in accordance with a clear theory. Whether he realized it or not, Hanson borrowed Sloan's emphasis on de-centralization allied to a rigid central reporting system, but whereas Sloan's system had focussed on industrial objectives like market share, Hanson's focussed narrowly on profits and on each managing director's personal responsibility to achieve them. Here is Hanson's explanation:

> The best results flow from three systems which we operate simulta-neously and continuously. The first is the identification of the man or woman on whose performance the business will succeed or fail – the Manager ...
>
> The second is financial discipline. We work hard to get our oper-ating companies to understand the concept that budgets are some-thing you intend to achieve, not something you hope to achieve.
>
> The third is motivation. I believe very firmly in the combination of carrot and stick. We make it crystal clear what the manager's task is, but don't just leave him to it or allow him to get on with it. We require him to do it. This has a dramatic effect on the individual. Possibly for the first time in his career he senses the meaning of personal responsibility.

Here is the basic formula, since greatly elaborated but never improved, whereby the modern large business corporation is to be run, not for the benefit of managers, but for the benefit of shareholders. This is primitive capitalism updated to take account of the fact that large organizations exist. In fact, it is something even more ambitious: the attempt to use organizational expansion via often-hostile takeovers to build a machine for perpetual shareholder enrichment.

Hanson and White had two insights that powered their money-making machine. One was that the Managerialist Corporation – the type of firms they took over – left a great deal of shareholder money on the table. When Hanson attacked the Imperial Group during the run up to Christmas in 1986, I was working as a consultant to Imperial Foods, one of the Group's three main divisions.

Imperial Foods was run by an intelligent, hard-working and hard-driven manager, who had come up the hard way out of the East End, London's traditional working class area. Yet Imperial Foods was a bureaucracy within a bureaucracy. It had its own large headquarters, based in Bedford, separate from the many operations it ran, all of which reported to Bedford. Bedford, in turn, counted the cash and drew up elaborate plans, assisted by an army of expensive consultants, to expand the Food Division. The main objective here was to put a better case for using the center's large cash flow than the Tobacco Division or Drinks and Leisure Division could. The recommendations from the divisions were all clothed in shareholder-friendly gobbledegook and projected the earnings per share impact into the 21st century, but the basic intention was to expand into a larger and more complex business. The lyrics were for the shareholders, and the managers needed help from consultants who were high priests of financial projections, but the basic tune to which we all danced was Managerial Expansion.

Here was value subtraction in action, run by energetic and talented people. The center of the Imperial Group, a large bureaucracy housed in a mammoth building overlooking Hyde Park Corner, subtracted value from its Divisions, by interrogating plans, semi-ignorant second-guessing, and taking away a sense of responsibility and ownership of their businesses. It turned managers into politicians. Then the Divisional Head Offices subtracted huge amounts of value from the individual businesses they managed, like the frozen food business or the snack business. It was a wonderful way of enriching consultants and managers, but it did much less than nothing for the customer or the shareholder.

Hanson won the Imperial Group after an epic struggle (my firm was engaged to defend Imperial, and produced, under another partner, a brilliant and appropriately one-sided critique of the Hanson money machine). Thanks to the defence, Lord Hanson ended up paying an 80 per cent premium to the share price before he got involved. Yet, as he knew, he still got a bargain. Imperial's businesses, run by Hanson, were worth well over double what they were under the old Imperial regime. Some businesses were sold; but most were kept. Out went the whole central bureaucracy. Out went all the divisional head offices. Instead, each managing director in charge of the real businesses (those with customers and competitors) was told to produce a budget showing significant profit improvement, and was then required to meet the budget. Suddenly, unnecessary costs, built up over generations of managers out-foxing the center, were axed by the managers themselves. They alone knew where the bodies were hidden, where the waste luxuriated. For the first time in their careers, as Hanson knew, they were serious about producing profits for shareholders. For the first time, they achieved what could be achieved. The release of energy and enterprise was truly staggering. When I talked three years later to the head of one of the most remote businesses, the man who had bitched and moaned about the Imperial Foods Head Office and the Group Head Office had nothing but praise for the Hanson system. Those who did not like the system had left within months. Those who stayed and produced the goods felt that they were living in a different world. Yet all that Hanson had done was to cancel out the center's value subtraction.

If Hanson's first insight added real value to the businesses by subtracting value subtraction (since two negatives make a positive), his second insight enriched shareholders but added no economic value at all. The Hanson strategy was to build up a record of ever-growing earnings per share, attain a stock market rating (expressed in the Price Earnings Ratio) above the market average, and then take over under-performing companies that were rated by the stock market at below the average Price Earnings Ratio. Since Hanson then improved their performance (by the means discussed above), there was economic value released and the profits rose. But for a long time there was also a second source of stock market value for Hanson, a 'double-whammy'. This came from the arbitrage between the Hanson Price Earnings Ratio (high) and the Victim Price Earnings Ratio (low). If Hanson stood on a PER of 17 and the Victim on an initial PER of 8, perhaps increased by the bid to 13, then Hanson plc could automatically increase its earnings per share even without improving profits. This game was played most merrily for a long time, vastly enriching the Hanson shareholders.

Eventually, as it always does, the music stopped. There was one fatal and increasingly apparent flaw in the Hanson strategy. Hanson was good at producing large profit increases in the first years after acquisition, through the elimination of waste and the full exploitation of price increases. Thereafter, however, growth was difficult. The businesses Hanson acquired were mainly in low growth markets. That was one reason why they were cheap to buy. Profit growth could be generated initially, but not sustained at the rate the stock market had grown to expect. To generate constant earnings per share growth, Hanson had to acquire more and more bigger and bigger companies. This would work for a while, but could not continue indefinitely, since at some stage Hanson would end up owning everything. And it could not continue at all once investors suspected that the game had a finite shelf life. Once investors realized that Hanson was a money machine whose profit growth was bound to slow, they marked down its shares from an above average rating (PER) to a below-average one. Now the financial synergy based on automatic earnings enhancement switched into reverse. Hanson had to pay more for each pound or dollar of profits it took over than its own shares were worth. Despite picking shrewd targets, Hanson turned from a stock market winner to a stock market loser. For years, Hanson had added real economic value but seen its stock market value increase way above this level. Now, Hanson continued to add economic value but subtracted shareholder value.

And, in the end, there was another fatal flaw, a highly ironic one. Hanson became a large company by stripping other large companies of their management bureaucracies. They eliminated waste and held managers accountable to shareholders. But as it grew, Hanson grew increasingly like its victims. At the end of *Animal Farm*, the oppressed animals turn from Man to Pig and from Pig to Man, and cannot tell which is which. Hanson was never as bad as this, but did become increasingly tainted by size and complexity. Perhaps the rot set in when Hanson decided to move into the old Imperial Group head office, rather than selling the lease at a premium. In 1996, Hanson announced plans to latch on to the very real value-creating phenomenon of breaking up its own business into four parts. The hunt was finally over.

A company with a good earnings per share record can lead analysts to expect continuing good increases over the next couple of years – few analysts look much further ahead – even after the base business has started to slow or even go into reverse. Use of accounting reserves and short-term cost cutting measures can keep earnings per share growing long enough to make a major acquisition of a better business with higher growth potential. The better business may be smaller, less well known and/or have a less impressive historical record in growing earnings per share – perhaps because it follows more conservative accounting principles – and therefore be on a lower price earnings ratio than its larger predator. If so, the acquirer can gobble the good business and automatically enhance its own earnings, even if the process of acquisition subtracts net value.

This type of managerial socialism is decreasing in the world's largest stock markets, partly because accounting standards are being tightened, partly because analysts and investors are now more astute, and partly because firms are becoming smaller and more focussed, and hence more transparent.

Opacity is the friend of socialism, transparency is that of the market. Most large multi-business corporations can still be glimpsed from the outside only through a mirror darkly.

Managerial gigantism

The pursuit of size for its own sake is biological. Organisms evolve slowly into larger and more complex beings. Corporations evolve the same way, but more quickly. Self-interested managers are the catalyst.

Increased size may add or subtract economic value. But managers prefer increased to decreased size, even when increased size decreases value, or when decreased size increases it. This is why there is a false market in acquisitions, where large companies routinely buy other firms at well beyond their true value, often offering an acquisition premium of 25–50 per cent (or even more) to the previously ruling market price. (The existence of a premium is not *ipso facto* conclusive evidence that the acquirer is over-paying, since the 'synergy' added may cover or more than cover the premium, but a large number of careful studies have demonstrated that, on average, virtually all the synergy benefits from combining two firms go to the shareholders of the firm taken over, to the people who sell out, take the money and run, and virtually none to the shareholders of the predator; and since this is the average, in about half the instances, increased size destroys value for the predator's owners.)

The reason is plain. Most senior managers would rather manage a larger company than a smaller one. With size comes prestige, perks, greater compensation, greater insulation from customers and other nuisances, and access to yet further size. Size establishes who's who in the zoo. To grow is exciting, interesting, challenging. To contract profitably may be even more challenging, but much less exciting and stimulating.

Irrefutable evidence of managerial gigantism and its cost for shareholders and society is provided by one of capitalism's greatest current beneficial trends: that of breakup. Under breakup (also known as 'spinoff', 'demerger', and 'unbundling') a large and complex company is broken up into two or more new companies. This creates greater value simply because it removes the managerial value subtraction inherent in having everything in one big company. In 1995, J P Morgan, the international investment bank, looked at the performance of 77 spinoffs since their independence. During the first 18 months after the breakup, the average spinoff performed 25 per cent better than the stock market, with the out-performance steadily increasing over time. But, even more tellingly, the spinoffs of smaller companies – those with an initial market value of under $200 million – beat the market by a staggering 45 per cent (again over 18 months). Small and simple is clearly better than large and complex ... for everyone except the managers wanting to run giant companies.

Having studied these spinoffs, David Sadtler, Andrew Campbell and I [5] found that in virtually every case, breakup happened because of external pressure. Though managers later came to like the results of breakup (because performance improved and they had a clearer purpose) nearly every senior management team within the parent corporation initially resisted the idea of breakup, principally on emotional grounds. Therefore, there are still fewer breakups than is economically rational. Investors have to apply pressure because there is an inbuilt management bias toward gigantism.

Managerial market manipulation

Managers can and do manipulate product/service markets and they can and do manipulate financial markets. In doing so they often add to their profits and the value of their firms on the stock market, but only at the expense of economic efficiency. Customers suffer. So does society generally, since resources are poorly allocated. (So too do some competitors and some investors, but these narrow effects tend to net out and be neutral overall. What matters is that markets are distorted and cannot do their job of allocating resources to the economic units that add the most value to customers.)

Product/service market manipulation is conceptually familiar. It happens whenever a firm establishes a monopoly not purely based on efficiency (some monopolies do arise as a result of efficiency, if as a result of scale and accumulated experience a firm has much lower costs and can deliver much higher value to customers than can any competitor: such cases are easy to spot because in these markets prices go down faster than in other markets).

All business people, whether they are entrepreneurs or managers, are tempted by market manipulation. Managers and non-managers alike can resist anything but temptation. It is not that managers are made of weaker moral fiber than their counterparts in smaller, entrepreneurial firms. It is just that the opportunities for abuse tend to be greater in large firms; the temptations are many and greater.

Larger firms have more privileged access to capital, new technology, established and new channels of distribution, and even to more refined market intelligence. (Do not believe that market research always helps firms serve customers better; often it helps firms exploit customers better, especially where they are price-insensitive.) If you doubt this, ask yourself this question: if Coca-Cola were not a natural monopoly, because of the strength of its brand and its ability to tie up the largest bottlers and distributors in most countries – if, in other words, there were a dozen competing suppliers of Coca-Cola in each country – don't you believe that Coke would be lower priced and that the profit margins on Coke would fall? The Coca-Cola corporation does nothing illegal or unethical; it serves customers and investors well, it is admirably focussed and well run. It is simply exploiting a monopoly and enjoying high returns as a result, something a smaller competitor could not do.

Managers manipulate financial markets. Some of this is illegal, and some legal; some blatant and some invisible. Every time there is a major financial scandal, like the Robert Maxwell/Maxwell Communications or the Asil Nadir/Polly Peck affairs in Britain, or the Recruit scandal in Japan, or the financial improprieties that sent Michael Milken and Ivan Boesky to US gaols, we are amazed that such successful manipulation could go on on such as scale for so long. Boards of directors, eminent non-executives, highly paid and intelligent accountants, tireless regulators, honest senior managers – all these mechanisms, checks and balances somehow prove absolutely ineffectual against powerful magnates. Yet, contrary to public perception, these blots on the face of contemporary capitalism are not typical; and even in these cases, the majority of those involved are not cynical or corrupt. Most market manipulation is altogether more tame and less harmful. But it is also prevalent and unremarked.

A whole new industry has burgeoned in the past 20 years: investor relations (corporate PR focussed on important buyers of shares, the large investment institutions). This industry enjoys high profits and returns on capital because it adds value to its clients. It sends their shares up.

The value added by investor relations is entirely derivative. All the investor relations professionals in the world add absolutely *nothing* to the value of products or services delivered to the customer. Yet investor relations professionals do add value to the managers who hire them. In the fields of real economic value, the investor relations experts spin not, neither do they reap. But in the world of the chief executive seeking to maximize his share price, these specialists deliver mightily.

The investor relations industry (like the stockbroking industry and the funds management industry – but we cannot afford to digress) consumes resources but adds zero to net economic value. Investor relations spin-doctors would not exist but for managers' desire and ability to influence financial markets via cosmetic attractions rather than transparent and eloquent bare economic performance. True, the harm done is minor. But it is another illustration that managerialism operates in a universe parallel to that of real value added. The opportunity cost of the talent – managerial and specialist – is not negligible: the executives and spin-doctors could be doing something useful. When markets become efficient and democratic, they will.

Managerial greed

We come last to the charge most often levelled against senior managers by the media: what is called in the UK the 'fat cat' issue. Though this is perhaps the least important charge economically, it is laden with social and symbolic significance.

The charge, at least in the United States, is wholly justified. The separation of ownership and control in big business, far from bringing to the fore disinterested managers who administer companies in the interests of society – astonishing as it is to recall, this was the consensus opinion in the first half of this century – has given us instead powerful and selfish self-perpetuating cliques of executive directors who have packed their boards with men (nearly always men) who award them huge personal pay and severance packages, so that regardless of success or failure they will get rich.

During their time in the executive suite, the top brass enjoy a life of luxury that only the most wealthy and extravagant private citizens would dream of paying for from their own pockets. On any intercontinental flight, it is almost certain that nearly all the first class seats are occupied, not by rich individuals paying their own way, but by corporate executives, virtually the only modern citizens who can enjoy luxury without even thinking about the cost. At their beck and call is an army of personal assistants and secretaries who attend to every whim, including frequently private business quite unrelated to that of the corporation. These corporate servants shield the top dogs from any unpleasant reality in the world outside, and often from the world *inside* the firm too.

The grasping selfishness of some top executives is rampant and rising almost beyond belief. Plato suggested that the top man in an organization should be paid no more than five times the amount paid to the most junior person [6]. In Japan, a typical multiple is less than twelve times.

Corporate America, from the 1930s onward, pushed this up to 40 times. Until the 1980s, the lowest paid worker might be on $10,000 and the boss on $400,000. Nice work, but perhaps justifiable.

Yet now pay levels for American fat cats have escalated beyond any such multiple, beyond precedent, beyond any international benchmarks, beyond reason, and beyond any sense of decency. In 1996 the total compensation of Roberto Goizueta, head of Coca-Cola, reached $1 billion for that one year! (this is not a misprint: it is *billion* and not *million*). This is an entrepreneurial return of extraordinary magnitude, that is justified in a capitalist system for someone who started a business that created enormous value. But Mr Goizueta, who died at the age of 65 in 1997, did not start Coca-Cola. He did not even take a small and modestly successful company and build it into a global giant. Born in Cuba, he joined Coca-Cola in 1954 and worked his way up the top by 1981.

The standard response to criticism of astronomical industrialist pay is that the market determines who is worth what. Don't the critics believe in the market?

There is a certain type of 'market logic' that can justify $1 billion annual pay. During Mr Goizueta's tenure at the Coca-Cola Company, its market value rose from around $4 billion to $150 billion, an annual increase of 25%. Certainly impressive, though far from unique. But was it necessary to pay Mr Goizueta $1 billion to secure his services or commitment? By all accounts he was wedded to Coke for other reasons.

Neither Mr Goizueta's rewards, nor his access to them (by getting the CEO position), were determined by a disinterested market. They were determined by a small group of people who should be, but no doubt are not, ashamed of themselves. This is oligopoly and social convention at work, not markets.

Take another example. When he was boss of Chrysler, Lee Iacocca 'earned' *36 times* more than the head of Honda [7]. Guess which company performed better! (Clue: it wasn't Chrysler.)

The thin elite is not guilty alone. Our corporate accounting and legal systems are also to blame. In most countries, including the United States and United Kingdom, the most gigantic elements in top executive compensation, stock options, do not even have to be reported as a corporate expense against the profit and loss statements. Any disinterested system would put an instant end to this abuse of managerial power.

Managerialism versus democracy

Most large quoted corporations are guilty as charged on one or more of the four managerial sins: socialism, gigantism, market manipulation, and tycoonery. These sins are correlated with size and complexity. They happen much more in large, publicly quoted companies than in smaller and unquoted ones.

They are transgressions of managerial elites, not, in general, of individual entrepreneurs. They are sins against democracy. They would be much less likely to happen if information was transparent, readily available to everyone, if customers' interests were paramount, if competition was free and active, or if decisions were made by employees collectively rather than by a narrow elite.

It is not necessary to argue that the managerial sins would be totally absent if all the workforce were shareholders, or if every large firm were replaced by a large number of small firms. There is a natural tendency for producers to sin against consumers, whenever they can do so with impunity. But the opportunity for successful sinning is greater in larger, more complex, more internally focussed corporations. The sins are market imperfections. They thrive in less democratic and open corporations and markets.

Managerialism sins are sins against efficiency and the sovereign market. The market is the most democratic and efficient mechanism known to mankind. Making the democratic market work well, through democratic corporations, while not losing the terrific benefits of size is one challenge for third-revolutionaries. One way is to reform the way corporations work: making corporations smaller, simpler, less managerial, and less fixated on short-term stock market manipulations; making them more like Adam Smith's world and less like that of Adolf Berle, Gardiner Means, James Burnham, Joseph Stalin or Adolf Hitler; making them, in short, more democratic, more subject to the control of all the individuals in society, both as producers and consumers.

Beyond the corporation, too, much needs to change.

Defects of capitalist society

Conspicuous consumption and conspicuous destitution – the two faces of inequality – are as characteristic of capitalism today as they ever were. They sit ill with democracy.

It is tempting to equate modern individualistic capitalism – the world of 'greed is good', bombastic bond dealers, buccaneering billionaires, and resurgent yuppies – juxtaposed against the helpless and the homeless of society, the exploited young, the prostitutes, drug–abusers, drop-outs and the new urban underclass – with Victorian capitalism, the world passionately described and denounced by Dickens and Marx. What has changed, when extremes of wealth and poverty co-mingle within an indifferent capitalist system? Nature has no compassion. Is capitalism the same? Is the inevitable consequence of capitalism an uncaring individualism, where there is no such thing as society, where wealth is a badge of virtue, and where the poor are told that they deserve their poverty?

We are witnessing a rejection, intellectual and practical, of the systems that have threatened capitalism – socialism, the state, even, to a degree, social democracy. Individualistic capitalism may never have been as powerful or as unrestrained as it is today. Global capitalism is forcing competition into hitherto protected national nooks and crannies. Everything appears to be at the mercy of undesigned, unrestricted, individualistic capitalism. Market forces determine employment levels, the value of currencies, corporate profits or losses, interest rates, wage levels, and many other things that national (and sometimes democratic) governments used to control. Where market forces rule supreme, the rich get richer and the poor poorer.

In the United States social inequality has been rising for the past 20 years. *Average* real living standards have risen slowly and fairly steadily. But the bottom 10 per cent of households have actually seen their real incomes fall, while the top 10 per cent have seen big gains. And it is at the very top that the gains have been most spectacular. Between 1977 and 1989, of *all* the increase in real incomes, a staggering *70 per cent of the total increase* went to the *top 1 per cent* of income earners. This reflects both market forces and the increasing disinclination to do anything to modify or mitigate them.

Something else is happening, this time throughout the world: it's called the *winner-take-all* phenomenon. The very top players in all professions, from sport to entertainment to business, are making 'super-star' earnings: tens or even hundreds of millions of dollars a year. The next level down, those not quite at the very top, make nowhere near as much. This is a new and accelerating phenomenon. There are good economic reasons for *winner-take-all* – intriguing reasons, but we cannot afford to digress here [8] – further demonstrating that giving free rein to market forces is bound to increase inequality.

Is it good to release market forces? Economically, *yes*, without question. But is increasing inequality, and what seems to go with it, all this rampant individualism, this uncaring capitalism, is *this* all good? No. At some point, the social costs outweigh the economic benefits, and the economic benefits will not be sustainable if there is a social backlash. Is increasing inequality and social division inevitable under capitalism? No. Is it the only form of capitalism that is, or could be, on offer? No. Is there a way of getting all the economic benefits without the social costs? Yes. Are capitalism and democracy enemies? No. Have they been allies? Yes. Can they be friends? Yes, absolutely, they can. Can you have the benefits of a full-blooded capitalist system without the defects of rampant individualism, without extremes of wealth and poverty? Of course you can. Why haven't democracy and capitalism come together? Because both democrats and capitalists have lacked imagination.

Capitalism is evolving, not fixed

Capitalism is *not* a static, defined, immutable, inflexible economic system bequeathed to us by God, Adam Smith, Frederick A Hayek, Milton Friedman, nature, or any other relatively stable and predictable cosmic force. Capitalism is not a set of given rules, not a consistent economic system, nor a definable phase of civilization. To be sure, capitalism *is* something definable. It is possible to know when an economic system, or a society, is capitalist, and when it is not (see the box in the Preface for my definition of capitalism). But there is not *one* form of capitalism. There are many. Capitalism today, even in the United States, probably the most unrestricted capitalist society in the world, is light years away from the capitalism of Victorian England. It is better and more democratic. So: what makes us think that we have to tolerate the abuses of current day capitalism, that inequality is intrinsic to capitalism?

Capitalism requires a relatively unrestricted market system, at least in the core of economic life. I want vibrant and unconstrained market systems in all parts of economic life. But capitalism, like any economic and political system, sits within a social context, partially delineated by laws, but mainly ruled by a thousand unspoken social conventions and internalized standards of behavior.

Most of us don't go around stealing our neighbor's cars, cattle or concubines, even if we could with impunity do so. Most of us don't lie and cheat. Most of us don't shoot people, even if they are rich or our competitors. All of these activities are compatible with a form of capitalism. It would not be a very pleasant form. By the same logic, what is to prevent us having a more acceptable and ethical form of capitalism than we currently tolerate?

The answer is: no economic principles – simply social and behavioral *mores* – custom, practice and laws. There is nothing that stops us constructing a better form of capitalism, one that leads to the greatest happiness of the greatest number, and that eliminates misery, one that is, in shorthand, democratic.

How can we deal with the problem of swaggering yuppiedom and the socially irresponsible deployment of wealth, without in any way impeding the wonderful motor of capitalist wealth creation? I really don't think this is very difficult. At one level this is a question of cultural norms and values. We need to educate people – via sitcoms, novels, mundane conversation – in the enjoyment of wealth. Wealth should be enjoyed as it often used to be – unostentatiously, unobtrusively, invisibly, privately; or generously, socially, for the benefit of friends and the wider community. Not everyone will see the point at first. Polite society should shun such low-lifes.

Already there are some hopeful signs. Jim Taylor and Watts Wacker, in a fascinating recent survey of trends for the next 500 years (!), note:

> *the movement away from conspicuous consumptions to stealth wealth and 'downward mobility', with its demand not for many things but for a few good things.* [9]

Yet changing conventions and values is a slow process. We should accelerate it, using some market mechanisms of our own. For instance, we might remove or reduce most taxes on income (whether 'earned' or investment income) but slap very heavy taxes on luxuries, on goods bought by the high rollers at the point of purchase; not so heavily on the everyday luxuries enjoyed by the many, but more on the unusual luxuries enjoyed by the few. Income and investment taxes are easy for the rich to avoid. But consumption taxes are not. The major civilized countries of the world, including the United States, Britain, France, Italy, and wherever the current reader is situated – anywhere the rich want to visit – could tax luxuries and conspicuous consumption at roughly consistent, high levels. The amount of tax raised may not be very much, because the rich are still statistically insignificant. But it would take the edge off social discord.

The problem of the irresponsible rich is, however, much less important than that of the poor, whether responsible or irresponsible. Modern capitalism is good at delivering for ordinary working people. The problem is the underclass. In some capitalist societies this is a small group, well under one person in twenty, sometimes fewer than one in fifty. In others, it is a larger group: in South Africa, 40 per cent of blacks, the great majority of the population, are unemployed. In yet other societies, like the United States, the problem is limited but heavily concentrated within certain minority groups, like young non-white people in inner cities. These minorities, large or small, are people for whom the capitalist system isn't working. And no capitalist system is working well when it isn't working well for everyone.

It doesn't have to be like this. We don't have to accept minority unemployment and misery. It's not intrinsic to capitalism. In the 1930s, when unemployment in the capitalist world affected most people, the conventional wisdom was that capitalism could not cope with unemployment. If you wanted jobs for most people, you had a choice between fascism and socialism. Even in 1944, F.A. Hayek, writing *The Road to Serfdom* [10], his passionate apologia for capitalism and against socialism and Nazism, did not claim that capitalism could deliver full employment, or even that capitalism would lead to better economic results than socialism. He justified capitalism on grounds of freedom rather than economic performance. Yet, after 1945, the West was able to engineer not just individual freedom from the state, but also a transformation of living standards and the abolition of poverty and, largely, of unemployment, all within a capitalist system. Why, then, do we in the 1990s think that we cannot engineer a solution to rising inequality, and the reintegration of the underclass into affluent society, within capitalism?

Three responses to the underclass

One, the social-democratic response, is to dispense welfare. This alleviates the problem and removes immediate misery (not, incidentally, unworthy achievements) at some cost to economic efficiency. But it provides no long term solution. Over time, the underclass becomes larger and more dependent.

The second and increasingly prevalent response is to ignore the problem, or claim that any action will make it worse. This is the favored response of most who would today call themselves capitalists. This is the way the world is going, with a reversion to *laissez-faire* capitalism. It is wrong. It is also short-sighted. It will not work for long in democratic societies. Democracy has tolerated capitalism only because, along with greater overall wealth, capitalism has been manipulated to produce greater equality too.

There is no automatic mechanism by which capitalism produces greater equality or inequality. There is no satisfactory theoretical reason why capitalism should lead inevitably or tend toward greater equality or greater inequality. Marx argued that surplus value was always appropriated by the capitalist, leading as wealth increased to greater inequality. The case was not well argued from first principles, and Marx appealed to experience – to the evidence of the immiseration of the masses – to buttress his case. Experience in the later 19th century in fact went the other way, and it is now generally accepted that living standards of workers made huge strides forward. Joseph Schumpeter, in 1942, stood Marx on his head by arguing that most of the benefits of capitalism go to ordinary people, and disproportionately to the poor [11]:

> Broadly speaking, relative shares in national income have remained substantially the same over the last hundred years. This, however, is true only if we measure them in money. Measured in real terms, relative shares have substantially changed in favor of the lower income groups. This follows from the fact that the capitalist engine is first and last an engine of mass production which unavoidably means production for the masses, whereas, climbing upward in the scale of individual incomes, we find an increasing proportion is being spent on personal services, and on handmade commodities, the prices of which are largely a function of wage rates.
>
> Verification is easy. There are no doubt some things available to the modern workman that Louis XIV himself would have been delighted to have ... – modern dentistry for instance. On the whole, however, a budget on that level had little that really mattered to gain from capitalist

achievement ... It is the cheap cloth, the cheap cotton and rayon fabric, boots, motorcars and so on that are the typical achievements of capitalist production ... Queen Elizabeth (I) owned silk stockings. The capitalist achievement does not typically consist in providing more silk stockings for queens but in bringing them within the reach of factory girls in return for steadily decreasing amounts of effort.

But this is too loose an argument. Inequality is difficult to measure, but historians are agreed that inequality in pre–1914 Britain was extremely high. It is clear also that inequality throughout the capitalist world declined markedly from 1918 to about 1980. It strains credulity to believe that this was unconnected with social democratic reforms that deliberately redistributed incomes and provided increasing amounts of welfare to the bottom half of society. Since 1980, as social democracy has retreated, and *laissez-faire* capitalism advanced, inequality has surged back towards the previous levels. This is a global trend, but has been most pronounced in the United Kingdom, which has seen the greatest *proportionate* movement towards *laissez-faire*, and in the United States, which has the freest markets in the world. The evidence is absolutely clear: untrammeled capitalism leads to unacceptable inequality.

Capitalism and inequality:
The United States, the United Kingdom and Europe

Capitalism can remove poverty. For a time it can reduce inequality. But then inequality seems to sprout up again, and the more unrestricted the capitalism, the greater the apparent inequality.

We have a perfect object lesson in the experience of the United States and Western Europe (excluding the UK) over the past two decades. In general, the US has started with a freer and less restricted form of capitalism, and has increasingly allowed markets to operate with progressively less interference. Taxes have been lowered and government expenditure as a proportion of national wealth has also been reduced, to around 30 per cent. By contrast, continental European countries have raised the level of government expenditure, from around 45 per cent in 1980 to about 50 per cent today. Employers in Europe have also been

required to contribute large payroll taxes to support social security programs. What have been the results of these two quite contrasting policies, the American one favoring individualistic capitalism, and the European one of social democracy, allowing capitalism to operate but with
restrictive labor markets and superimposing heavy taxation on business
and income earners to support a large parallel social security system?

The American experiment scores heavily in terms of aggregate wealth
creation and jobs. Taking inflation out of the picture, the real US gross
domestic product (GDP) per head between 1973 and 1995 rose by 36 per
cent, and aggregate employment rose. By contrast, there was no increase
in the total number of jobs in Europe and the unemployment rate went
from half that of the US to double that level: a four times relative increase in European unemployment. A greater degree of capitalism generated greater productive wealth and more jobs.

But whereas in Europe inequality by most measures is substantially
lower than in the US and inequality did not increase substantially in the
past two decades, in the US a higher degree of unrestricted capitalism
has led to a galloping gap between the fortunes of the rich and the rest.
Total real wealth per head in the US rose by 36 per cent (1995 versus
1973) but the real hourly wages of non-supervisory workers – the majority – actually fell by 14 per cent. In the 1980s, all of the income gains
went to the top 20 per cent and at least 64 per cent of the gains went to
the top 1 per cent of earners! The pay of the average Fortune 500 chief
executive started the 1980s at 35 times the pay of the average production worker – and ended the decade at 157 times that level!

Social democracy invented the progressive income tax in the first third
of this century, not just to raise revenue but also to reduce inequality.
This experiment has failed. In the US the failure is most apparent. The
richest 1 per cent of the population now controls more than 40 per cent
of total wealth, which is double the proportion held by the top 1 per
cent in the mid-1970s and in fact back to the percentage prevailing in
the late 1920s, before the introduction of progressive taxation!
(See Lester C Thurow (1996) The Future of Capitalism, New York, William
Morrow & Co/London, Nicholas Brealey, Chapter 2)

So we need a third way – a form of capitalism that is rigged to do what capitalism will not naturally do: to promote an acceptable degree of equality – without losing the power of markets to increase total wealth.

The only long-term solution is to bring all members of the underclass into
capitalist society, to make them part of it, to make them participants within it.

If we tried to do this, we might at first fail. But when we try long enough, hard enough, and imaginatively enough, we will succeed. This will be the result of the third revolution, the integration of capitalism and democracy.

The main reason that capitalists have not solved the problem of the underclass is that they have not tried. Those who might have tried have not been capitalists. They have wasted their efforts on a washed-up creed, socialism, or, more recently, social democracy. It is time to convince those men and women of goodwill, the social democrats, to try a different route, one that uses rather than restricts the power of markets. Markets can be manipulated to produce democratic results, without losing any of their awesome ability to create ever increasing wealth.

Endnotes

1   Lester C. Thurow (1996) *The Future of Capitalism*, New York, William Morrow & Company/London, Nicholas Brealey, pages 17–18 and 242.

2   Paul Krugman (1994) *Pedling Prosperity*, New York, W W Norton & Company, p. 138.

3   Charles Handy (1997) *The Hungry Spirit*, Hutchinson, London, p. 40.

4   Adam Smith (1776) *An Inquiry into The Nature and Causes of the Wealth of Nations*, Book V, p. 800.

5   David Sadtler, Andrew Campbell and Richard Koch (1997) *Breakup!*, Oxford, Capstone.

6   I am indebted for the reference to Plato and for much else in this paragraph to Robert A. G. Monks (1997) *The Emperor's Nightingale*, Oxford, Capstone, Chapter 3.

7   Charles Hampden-Turner and Fons Trompenaars (1997) *Mastering the Infinite Game*, Oxford, Capstone.

8   See Richard Koch (1997) *The 80/20 Principle*, London/Sonoma, Nicholas Brealey, especially pages 206–212. See also Robert Frank and Philip Cook (1995) *The Winner-Take-All Society*, New York, Free Press.

9   Jim Taylor and Watts Wacker (1997) *The 500 Year Delta: What Happens After What Comes Next*, New York, HarperCollins / Oxford, Capstone, page xv. 'Downward nobility' is an attractive concept, defined as 'The decline in the value of formerly status-laden items and the simultaneous growth in the status value of just being satisfied. Self-affirmation will come by underspending incomes and exercising independence as consumers and workers, not by depending upon objects to establish worth.' (p. 286).

10 F.A. Hayek (1944) *The Road to Serfdom*, London, Routledge & Kegan Paul. Hayek even appears to imply that socialism may perform better economically than capitalism: 'It is essential that we should re-learn frankly to face the fact that freedom can only be had at a price and that as individuals we must be prepared to make severe material sacrifices to preserve our liberty.' (p. 99 of 1986 edition).

11 Joseph A. Schumpeter (1942) *Capitalism, Socialism and Democracy*, New York, Harper & Row, p. 67 (1962 Harper Torchbook edition).

Chapter Five

Markets Unbound

We may therefore acquiesce in the pleasing conclusion that every age of the world has increased, and still increases, the real wealth, the happiness, the knowledge, and perhaps the virtue, of the human race.
— Edward Gibbon [1]

We have arrived at a period of truncated equilibrium where the long plateau of history is poised for a huge leap forward .... enormous possibility — true democracy, true equality of opportunity, true individualism, true freedom — lies just on the other side ...
— Jim Taylor and Watts Wacker [2]

The rapid economic development of East Asian 'tiger economies' is unprecedented in economic history ... [these economies] have moved beyond the scarcity of specific things, like profits and property, to the abundance of diffuse processes, like knowledge generation ...
— Charles Hampden-Turner and Fons Trompenaars [3]

Summary

- In the past 250 years capitalism has achieved economic miracles that dwarf anything achieved before in the whole history of mankind. A world composed of hundreds of poor subsistence economies is becoming one very rich global economy. This is a fantastic and grotesquely under-celebrated achievement.
- Though it is correct to ascribe this achievement to capitalism, the real driver of progress is free markets. Until recently, capitalism had a monopoly of the free market system. But it is not capitalist social relations, or Western individualism, that drives progress: just the willingness to let markets work their magic. Free markets can work successfully in very different types of society, including ones that are neither democratic nor capitalist in any meaningful sense.
- Markets work so well because they use technology and knowledge to drive improvement; because resources are redeployed to more productive uses; because they give information about what people value; because they provide control and motivation in an extremely light, efficient and decentralized way. None of these processes require a materialistic, individualistic, divided or seriously unequal society. There is some evidence that markets work best within the context of a rich and variegated civil society with high degrees of trust, collaboration and common social purpose.
- Markets are a wonderful means to an end, but they are neither perfect nor an end in themselves. Markets are useful where they conduce toward a happier society, and not when they don't. Though markets are still under-used, a society using markets for everything would be intolerable.
- For democrats, setting limits on markets, and rigging those that exist to produce the best results for society as a whole, are as important as extending markets into arenas where they are still taboo.

In 1798, Thomas Malthus, a mathematically inclined English parson, worked out that the population was increasing at an alarming rate. He saw clearly that the growth in population would far outstrip the food available. He predicted mass starvation and famine.

Malthus got the population explosion right; in fact, he greatly under-estimated it. But the reason that the English peasant did not starve in the 19th century was that by then agriculture and capitalism had created unprecedented wealth. From 1780 to 1880, a wealth increase of 3 per cent per annum was enough to take England from a subsistence, rural economy, where ordinary people – peasants – were continuously vulnerable to malnutrition or semi-starvation, to a mixed rural and industrial economy where living standards for ordinary people – now more industrial workers and domestic servants than peasants – were in a different league: and all this despite a massive increase in population.

The modern market miracle

This was the pattern for the modern world: first in Britain, then in America and Germany, later throughout the rest of the civilized world.

The same things happened everywhere. Industry grew stupendously. Land, always the center of society, became of marginal importance. Wealth exploded. For the first time, countries became single economic systems. Distances were defeated. In the first half of the 19th century, it took three weeks to travel from Chicago to New York. By 1857, the new railroads had reduced this to three days. The railroads made fast, all-weather transportation possible for the first time in history. This created a mass market in manufactured foodstuffs. New miracles followed: the telegraph, the water-closet, the telephone, national postal services, gas, electricity, oil, urban mass transit, the department store, refrigeration, cheap steel, the automobile, the aeroplane … These 19th century inventions transformed society, turning it inside-out, upside-down, and making the modern world utterly different from anything seen before. The world shrank. Free trade offered the hope, and eventually the reality, that economic common interest would render war between civilized nations an atavistic anachronism. And the 20th century has seen further massive breakthroughs: mass production on a previously unimaginable scale; cheap drugs to combat disease; the extension of mass production to services; the invention of economic space, that requires almost no physical space; miniaturization; the computer; the micro-processor; bio-technology ...

All this capitalism has done. And it is in the nature of capitalism to continue, ceaselessly, the process of invention, innovation, improvement, extension and quality enhancement. It is difficult to grasp the enormity of what has happened, the qualitative and quantitative change, the implications for society and for individuals. But let us try. Let's look at three aspects of the change: wealth creation; the effect on ordinary people and the poor; and the effect on the political process.

The pattern has been repeated in every single country that has embraced the market. Poverty and the threat of malnutrition have been banished. Agricultural work used to require nearly 100 per cent of the workforce; now it is 2–3 per cent, and yet agricultural production has multiplied. Living standards for ordinary people have also multiplied; in most cases, the standard of living has increased beyond recognition. Can anyone name a poor country that has a free market system?

The free market is the only social and economic system known to man that reliably and consistently ends poverty. Where capitalism has held sway for any extended period of time, starvation, the threat of starvation, malnutrition, and hunger – the most dangerous and evil conditions of the poor – have been permanently banished.

Massive and unprecedented wealth creation

Consistent and sustained economic growth is a modern phenomenon. Before the 18th century it did not exist. Since 1750, economic growth under capitalism has averaged at least 2 per cent per annum compound, and probably closer to 3–4 per cent if we use hourly productivity as our measure (and therefore include the benefit of increased leisure). Over each century, this means a *50 times increase* in equivalent wealth; over two centuries, a *2500 times increase*, over 250 years, since capitalism started motoring, a *50,000 times increase*.

The mind struggles with these astronomical abstractions. Let us try again. From Roman times until the end of the Middle Ages, the stock of wealth in the world scarcely rose at all; it may even have fallen. From the Renaissance until about 1750, the stock of wealth in the world increased modestly, but almost certainly never doubled during the course of a century, during the life of a very old man. During the last two and a half centuries, a tiny fraction of history's span, wealth has increased at a rate that is not only many times greater than ever before – at the very least 25 times greater – but also to a level that simply would have been unimaginable to anyone. This is discontinuous change of a quality, quantity and intensity that has never been seen before in the whole course of human history.

What really caused the world's wealth explosion: capitalism or the steam engine?

I have made some large claims about what capitalism 'did'. But how can we be sure that it was capitalism, and not something else, that created our modern, unprecedentedly wealthy, society? What actually explains the wealth creation – the link between capitalism and wealth creation? And how can we be sure that there weren't other causes of modern wealth, not necessarily linked to capitalism? Maybe it was the invention of the steam engine that did it all!

I think not. For one thing, there have been many dramatic periods of invention that could theoretically have led to escalation of society's wealth levels long before the 18th century, but which did not; and they did not, because there was not a sufficiently pervasive capitalist system in place to commercialize and spread the inventions and extend them to other spheres. As Peter Drucker has pointed out, Roger Bacon (died 1294 or earlier) invented eyeglasses and they were quickly and widely used by the rich elderly; but because there was no profit-based system and no Eyeglasses Inc. to spread the invention, it remains narrowly used. Drucker [4]:

> It took another 200 years – until the early 1500s – before Bacon's invention had its second application: eyeglasses to correct near-sightedness. The potter's wheel was in full use in the Mediterranean by 1500 BC ... Yet the principle underlying the potter's wheel was not applied until AD 1000 to women's work – spinning.
>
> Similarly, the redesign of the windmill around the year AD 800 ... was not applied to ships for more than 300 years [in designing sailing ships to replace oared ships] ...
>
> The inventions of the Industrial Revolution, however, were immediately applied across the board, and across all conceivable crafts and industries. They were immediately seen as technology.

Of course, this does not prove that capitalism wrought the change that used every new technology for all possible uses – the steam engine for powering factories of all types, for new steamships, for railroad locomotives, and so on. Perhaps people suddenly got good at extending new technology. Perhaps. What makes this implausible is that capitalism empowered the inventor and the entrepreneur in a totally new way – with ready access to whatever funds were required, and with the prospect of becoming rich and rising rapidly in the social scale.

Roger Bacon, the inventor of eyeglasses, lived and died a Franciscan friar. No-one told him that he could become a capitalist. James Watt (1736–1819), the redesigner of the steam engine, became an entrepreneur. So did his partner, Matthew Bolton (1728–1809), who took the steam engine out of mining and into textiles and all other industrial applications; and so too did Robert Fulton (1765–1815), the steamship inventor. It is too simple to say that these gentlemen were actuated by the profit motive. What is clear is that the new capitalist system allowed them the freedom to make their obsession their profession, and gave them the means to maximize useful output.

Since then, capitalism has given virtually everyone and anyone who has an idea about making something better or cheaper, and the passion to pursue it, the opportunity to prove themselves right or wrong. Only under capitalism has there been a ready market for capital to be used by entrepreneurs, enabling anyone with skill, knowledge and a tiny initial capital base to play in the market. Then the good ideas – the ones that prove commercially successful – spread like wildfire. There is a constant incentive and opportunity to refine successful methods, since even a small improvement can make a fortune for at least one individual. This is surely the reason for the more rapid deployment and extension of inventions and innovations since the mid-18th century. Capitalism puts a price tag on knowledge and multiplies it accordingly.

Capitalism and the internationalization of wealth

Capitalism is the first economic system that has deliberately aimed to create wealth, not just in one nation or region, but throughout the world. Britain under Queen Victoria was the first country to become a thoroughly capitalist society. Victorian Britain pursued a policy of free trade whose explicit goal was to create other industrial economies that could share in, and further multiply, Britain's industrial cornucopia.

The policy worked. First Germany and the United States, and later all Western European countries, became industrial-capitalist economies with wealth levels, by 1914, rapidly converging toward British standards.

After the 1917 to 1945 hiatus, the policy was resumed. The United States aimed to make Western Europe and if possible other parts of the 'free world' (meaning countries that were capitalist, even if not all of them were free) as rich as the US itself. Again, the policy worked, first in Europe, then in Japan, then across other Asian countries. Competition from the expanded free market world actually continued to enhance – as the classical theory of free trade predicted – the wealth of the United States.

Now, with the fall of communism, there is the opportunity to make virtually all nations of the world substantially as rich as the leading capitalist nations. If the policy is energetically pursued, it will work again.

Capitalism and prosperity: evidence from history and geography

One striking illustration of market power is a comparison of Russia and Japan [5]. Both were backward feudal societies until the middle of the 19th century. Russia was, however, less backward and more powerful than Japan: Russia was always counted one of the Great Powers. Russia defeated Napoleon in 1812 and secured a standoff against France and Britain in the Crimean War of 1854–56.

From the 1860s, the ruling elites in both Russia and Japan pursued vigorous modernization programs, abolishing feudalism and promoting capitalist enterprise. Both economies grew fast up to World War I.

From 1917 until 1991, Russia rejected capitalism and espoused socialism, while Japan continued under capitalism. Both countries were devastated by World War II. But Russia in 1991 was clearly a relative economic failure, leading the world in no product category at all, while Japan had decimated international competition in a host of consumer electronics categories and become one of the world's most successful economies. Living standards in Japan were at least three times greater than those of Russia, and probably a much higher multiple.

Another illustration is how much more successful the West German economy was under capitalism from 1946 to 1989 when compared either to the German economy under Nazism from 1933 to 1945 or to the East German economy under communism from 1946 to 1989. Similarly, the Soviet economy in Russia and Eastern Europe under communism greatly and progressively under-performed Western Europe and North America under capitalism. The migration of five million people from East to West Germany prior to the building of the Berlin Wall, and the migrations that preceded and followed its destruction in 1989, says it all.

Further, we have available many comparisons between the economic performance of state *sectors* and capitalist sectors in the same countries at the same time. In every single case, the capitalist sectors performed much better. Whenever state businesses have been privatized, their value has soared; losses have turned into profits and services to consumers, whenever subject to competition (the true test of free markets), have improved dramatically.

We also have evidence from Japan and the Asian 'tigers' of the huge growth and wealth creation that flows from converting feudal or socialist to capitalist economies. There is not one single case where conversion of a country to capitalism has not led, within a generation, to a wealth explosion. Given the large number of examples, the link between free markets and prosperity is crystal clear.

Capitalism and marketism

Though it is correct to describe the modern economic miracle as the fruit of capitalism, the real driver of progress is free markets. This may seem an unnecessary distinction, since historically 'capitalism' and 'free market economy' have been synonymous. Capitalism has been the only system that uses the device of the market to allocate resources. This may not be true in the future: China is a fascinating and very important case in point. Since 1975 China has increasingly used free markets to enormous effect, but China is neither democratic nor 'capitalist' in the usual sense of the word (see box). China is – for an important part of its economy – marketist, but it is not capitalist.

China: marketism without capitalism

Does China represent a new, effective and sinister model of economic development, neither capitalist nor democratic, but state-dominated, managerial and marketist? Or is it simply in transition to capitalism, or, more optimistically, to capitalism and democracy?

Even the facts about China appear highly disputable. Is it amongst the most successful economic miracles of all time and on track to become the largest economy in the world within the next ten years? Or is it merely a fast-growing, very poor developing country that will remain a developing country well into the 22nd century?

Actually, both contentions are true, and not so incompatible as first appears. The statistics show that China has been growing by at least 10 per cent per annum over the past 15 years. Between 1989 and 1996, China's GDP per head grew by 136 per cent, an annual growth rate of 13 per cent, putting it at the top of the world's growth league [6]. The International Monetary Fund (IMF) projects that China will overtake both the United States and the entire European Union as the world's single largest economic unit by the year 2005 [7].

If this sounds threatening, relax. The statistics come from the communist authorities in Beijing, who in turn derive them from local officials, whose bonuses are tied to their region's growth. Also, inflation is understated, so the real rates need to be corrected for this. The best estimate is that annual growth in China has been running recently at around 5–10 per cent rather than at 10–15 per cent, and it is probably unrealistic to project future long term growth at more than 6 per cent per annum [8].

Moreover, even taking the official statistics at face value, the estimate that China will become the world's largest economy depends on calculating incomes on the basis of what they buy locally (what economists such as the IMF, who use this method, call the 'Purchasing Power Parity' or PPP value). If instead we use the dollar value, which is often dramatically lower for developing countries, we find that even by 2015 China's economy would be only about 27 per cent as large as that of the US.

It is even more important to realize that the absolute size of China's economy will not impinge greatly on the rest of the world, at least not for many decades. China's economy is so big because it has so many people. But they are still very poor people. Measured by PPP, the average person in China has an annual income of $1,600; measured in international currencies, this shrinks to $370. The economist Lester Thurow [9] has estimated that over a hundred years from now, in 2100, China's average income will only be 70 per cent of that of Japan (using the PPP method) or less than 20 per cent of Japan's (measured in international currency).

Nevertheless, China's economic success over the past 20 years is stunning. It matters greatly whether it is simply a case of a transition to capitalism, or whether it marks a genuinely new and unique system of economic management, different from both communism and capitalism. If China is and can remain simultaneously state-dominated, managerial and marketist, this would be a new cocktail. The Nazis and communists combined the state and managerialism, but never deployed markets properly.

What sort of economy is China's? Various commentators call it 'capitalist', 'Marxist-capitalist', 'state-capitalist', and 'market-Leninist'. These terms are all partly true, but the key is to realize that China has three economies in one. There is a peasant, agricultural economy; a socialist economy; and an advancing market economy. These three economies co-exist and are not rapidly converging. Each economy is held in place by the absolute political and economic power of the state.

First, there is the agricultural economy, which is partly feudal, partly socialist, and partly capitalist. About 20 years ago, China began to give peasants leases, which effectively gave them ownership of their land. To a large extent this marks the transition from socialism to capitalism, and the market liberalization raised output, between 1978 and 1984, by two thirds [10]. Agriculture is now largely 'marketist', but it retains tinges of socialism – because the state still owns the land – and even feudalism, because some agriculture is still subsistence-based, with limited exchange of crops for cash.

Then there is state-run industry. Most of China's traditional industrial base remains state-run and socialist. China's Premier, Li Peng, interviewed in 1997, noted that most of industry is state-owned and would remained so [11]:

> ... the problems facing state-owned enterprises are exaggerated.... They still take up a large portion of the national economy ... Such important economic lifelines as iron and steel, chemical, oil, coal, and electric-power industries are state-owned enterprises ...
>
> Some of our state-owned enterprises have set up joint ventures or cooperative schemes with foreign firms and domestic private enterprises. We have also allowed some enterprises to raise funds from capital markets by issuing stock, including stock overseas. Such enterprises will increase in number, although the majority will still be controlled by the state.
>
> Generally speaking, large state-owned enterprises perform better ... Those in difficulty are mostly small and medium-sized [state] enterprises. We have adopted some flexible policies toward them, allowing them to issue stock, become cooperatives, or be sold to individuals. But for the great majority, the nature of their ownership will remain unchanged.

Alongside the socialist economy, there is a large and growing market economy, growing not so much because it is invading the traditional industrial economy but because it is being allowed, within well drawn boundaries, to create its own new world. The degree to which market forces have been unleashed varies greatly from area to area. The greatest marketist moves have been made in special economic zones, generally on the coast. The export sector is now largely marketist, the import sector and goods that are not traded internationally are still largely socialist.

This is not a capitalist economy, or even a simple case of transition from communism to capitalism. To some extent it is a patchwork quilt of socialism and marketism. Agriculture, small retailing, personal services, housing, export industry, and a limited amount of other industry – these are largely subject to market forces. Much of the rest of industry is socialist, run in the traditional centralized communist way. In between there are decentralized experiments, partial privatizations, public-private sector partnerships. This may look to Western eyes like a controlled transition to capitalism, but it is not. The state remains firmly in charge, with regional economic warlords making decisions on political as well as economic grounds. The whole mentality of China's leaders is statist and authoritarian. Li Peng, the Premier, concluded his interview with ringing words that underline this:

> The 1.2 billion Chinese people are determined ... to continue his [the late Comrade Deng Xiaoping's] great cause of building socialism with Chinese characteristics. Our people will rally round the CCP Central Committee with Comrade Jiang Zemin at its core, working hard as one to fulfil all our tasks for this year and the Ninth Five-year Plan period, and to realize the grand blueprint drawn up by Comrade Deng Xiaoping for the next century.

No-one can know what will happen in China.

The experiment with marketism may be terminated if it leads to unacceptable demands for political reform. Given a choice between economic growth and the retention of its iron grip, which way do you think the communist central committee would jump?

Or, China may implode like the USSR, riven into different areas, each controlled by its own economic and political warlord, some perhaps converting to a market economy and some reverting to traditional socialism.

Or perhaps a reformer will seize power, or the contradictions between markets and state control become untenable, resulting in the triumph of capitalism and democracy. Many countries, including Spain, Portugal, Greece, Chile, Brazil, Argentina, South Africa, and Russia and virtually all the countries of Eastern Europe, have become democratic shortly after economic 'takeoff', when per capita incomes reached around $2–3,000, which will happen to China in the next ten years [12].

A fourth possibility is that the current course is taken to its logical conclusion, with the privatization of nearly all state industries but the retention of absolute political power by the communist party. This would represent a new phenomenon, breaking the historical correlation between marketism and democracy. How long such a phenomenon could be sustained must be an open question.

Or something totally unexpected may occur, like war between China and Japan, resulting in yet another permutation.

If China remains communist, with no concessions to democracy, yet largely marketist, and very successful at growing its economy, it is possible that this will be used as a model for other developing countries, particularly those ruled by an elite, regardless of political ideology. A proliferation of such states represents the dark scenario for the next century.

There is further evidence, from other parts of East Asia, that it is not capitalist social relations, or Western individualism, that drives progress; rather, it is simply the willingness to let markets perform their magic. Charles Hampden-Turner and Fons Trompenaars [13] have pointed out that between 1990 and 1996, the East Asian 'tiger economies' grew faster than other capitalist economies have ever done – for example, Singapore doubled its GDP per head. Hampden-Turner and Trompenaars convincingly argue that the exceptional growth has been driven by the ability to integrate Western individualistic values with Eastern co-operative values. I would add that the market economy is much larger in most East Asian countries, with the state economy only comprising about 20 per cent of the total, compared to 30 per cent in the United States, 40 per cent in the United Kingdom and 50 per cent in continental Europe. Despite the Asian economic crisis of 1997–8, caused by imprudent over-expansion, Asian countries continue to demonstrate the force and the heterogeneity of marketism.

Perhaps, then, if we wish to define the source of progress, we should get used to talking about 'marketism' rather than 'capitalism'. In many ways, 'marketism' is a more accurate as well as more comprehensive descriptor. There is a market for capital, a market for labor, a market for entrepreneurs, and a market for goods and services. Although the name might suggest it, capitalism is not, in fact, controlled by capital or the owners of capital. This would be no more effective or sensible than a system controlled by the army or the aristocracy. Capital does not control capitalism. Neither do entrepreneurs. Neither (though they often think otherwise) do managers. Neither do the providers of labor. Neither does the government. In fact, no-one and no force – except anonymous and ever-shifting market forces – controls capitalism. This is its great virtue, both for productivity and for freedom. Capitalism is market anarchism.

In future it might be possible to use the word 'marketism' to mean the free market system, and 'capitalism' to describe the co-existence of free markets with undemocratic social conditions, where the fruits of free markets are enjoyed disproportionately by elites. 'Capitalism' would then become a subset of 'marketism', alongside 'communist marketism' (as in China) and 'democratic marketism', the system proposed in this book. In order to avoid confusion, however, outside this section I consistently use 'capitalism' in its currently accepted sense of a free market economy (regardless of social relations or political trappings) and 'democratic capitalism' to describe the fusion of democracy and capitalism in the third revolution.

Why do markets work so well?

The market system is decentralized. Any business, however large or small, is allowed to use society's resources if and only if it can generate a profit or promise credibly to do so in the future. Profits are derived from satisfying customers' needs better or cheaper than other suppliers can. The market system is based on the entrepreneur shifting resources from low value to high value applications. Money rather than rank or perceived merit or worthiness is the basis for allocating resources; anything that uses money well will therefore tend to be done, and anything that does not, will not. This is a wonderfully decentralized system where improvements can be made by anyone on an experimental basis without the need (except in large business corporations) for bureaucratic approval. What works well tends to be done more. What works poorly tends to be done less. The market for goods and services is a brilliantly efficient way of deciding what should be produced to satisfy the aggregate demand of consumers and intermediate customers. If purchasing power is reasonably equally distributed, the market for goods and services is also a very democratic instrument.

Market systems tend to produce improvements in aggregate value created of around 3–4 per cent per annum, not every year, but reliably over long periods. Over a 20 year period, this leads roughly to a doubling of value, which can be taken in any way: products and services become more plentiful, better quality, have more features, are safer, or become cheaper; or those who produce them have better working conditions and/or shorter working hours. This is an amazing attribute of markets, and explains how poverty can be abolished quite quickly. And though the result is amazing, the process can be understood in two words: technology and improvement.

Technology

Technology derives from the Greek word *teche*, meaning skill. But the modern sense of technology, meaning the application of knowledge to improve tools, processes, products and services, dates from the 18th century, the period when marketism began to explode. Systematic analysis and the application of all forms of knowledge to improve products and services is both the cause and the result of marketism. Big breakthroughs in living standards result not from extra effort but from new ways of doing things, which are often not new in any fundamental scientific sense, but new in their extension and application to useful processes.

Technology and markets have a symbiotic relationship. They nurture and reinforce each other in a unique way. Technology can, of course, be used by non-market economies. Feudal lords and cardinals were allowed to have eyeglasses. Socialists were allowed to use the steam engine and the internal combustion engine. But all the evidence and all the logic shows that technology is created, multiplied and used far more and far better when the economic system is based on markets. Universities have always been hotbeds of knowledge. What is different since marketism took hold is that individual entrepreneurs and large corporations have a vested interest in using and extending whatever useful knowledge is available. State institutes and state corporations can do this under direction, but without the market for capital dictating where the funds are used, they will be wasted, or at least not applied efficiently. Without the market for goods and services, technology will do what the state wants – pyramids and arms and space programs, for example – rather than what the people want. Without the market for entrepreneurs, talent will not be directed to invent, innovate and spread technology for what ordinary people want.

Improvement

Improvement – continuous improvement – is the other reason why markets produce continuous productivity gains. Be it ever so small, a tiny improvement in producing goods or services – a better mousetrap, a lower cost material, using less labor, doing things slightly faster or more intelligently – can make an individual entrepreneur, and sometimes a whole corporation, rich. The constant quest for those few extra points of return would not happen – did not happen – without the market system. And the more open and free markets are, between corporations and between countries, the more improvement there is.

We have had classical liberal theory about markets and capitalism for well over a century, and yet only now are we beginning to grasp how markets make progress happen. Classical theory was basically static and one dimensional, dealing in optima and equilibria. It was elegant and internally consistent, but rarely observable. All of the truly great economists, from Vilfredo Pareto (1848–1923) to John Maynard Keynes (1883–1946) to Joseph Schumpeter (1883–1950) to scholars like Paul Krugman today, have paid attention to the dynamic movement of the economy over time: mysterious, chaotic, yet curiously predictable. Schumpeter said that capitalism proceeded via 'creative destruction', with better methods replacing inferior ones. He argued that even if capitalism at any time exhibited oligopolistic behavior, with large firms colluding to deny free competition, ultimately the best methods would triumph through the application of technology.

Death: a useful market ploy

There is a clear link here with pain and death. Business progress requires change. Better methods, better firms, must replace inferior ones. Markets makes this happen. What is odd about this list of America's 12 largest corporations as the 20th century began: the American Cotton Oil Company, American Steel, American Sugar Refining Company, Continental Tobacco, Federal Steel, General Electric, National Lead, Pacific Mail, People's Gas, Tennessee Coal and Iron, US Leather, and US Rubber? Answer: only one of them, GE, has survived intact today. Capitalism, not revolution, devours its own children most conspicuously.

Free markets allow change in the economy. Companies are taken over or die. People become unemployed. People change their jobs even when they do not lose them. Resources are diverted. In non-market economies, these changes

– often very painful and visible – do not happen or happen more slowly. The victims of change are evident. The beneficiaries – society at large, through productivity improvements – each benefit far less than the victims, and do not notice any individual benefit. And yet, without the change, living standards could not rise relentlessly. The pain of markets is less than the progress they foster. All societies before capitalism – and all socialist economies – became set in their ways, ossified, stagnated. Pre-capitalist societies plateaued and produced no increase in wealth for centuries. Market economies cannot and will not do this.

Decentralization: free markets' other secret weapon

The ultimate virtue of capitalism is that it combines a comprehensible and universal measure of performance – profit – with the most extreme decentralization. It thus provides order and rules, easily and unanimously followed, without any external authority taking decisions for people. This fits well with everything we know about how to make human beings productive and happy. What we do of our own volition, we do well. But unless we are also accountable to each other, we grow lazy, complacent and self-centered. The greatest virtue of markets is that they allow us to make all our own decisions, but ensure that these decisions are made in the full knowledge of what other people want, with economic rewards for following those wishes, and penalties for not doing so.

As Adam Smith understood, markets impose discipline relatively painlessly; they align self-interest with social interest; and they do so without external compulsion and hierarchy. Markets give us information about what others want. Markets allow us to fulfil others' needs in original and idiosyncratic ways, so that we can be selfish, original and fulfilled, yet also useful. Markets allow full deployment of individual skill, and provide high rewards for entrepreneurs. Yet the absolute size of the rewards seems to matter less than the freedom of an individual or family to plough an independent furrow and make a good living. Entrepreneurial activity seems to thrive whenever markets are free, regardless of the potential to become a millionaire or billionaire. There is only a weak and tenuous connection between entrepreneurship and tax rates. Japan achieved 8–10% annual growth when top tax rates were 80% [14].

Market processes do not require society to be materialistic, excessively individualistic, divided, or grossly unequal. There are examples of very successful market economies, including many of the East Asian tigers, which are none of the above. There are other examples of 'market' economies, such as post-communist Russia, which just do not work well, because the non-market context is not benign. There is no living memory of honest entrepreneurship, no impartial civil law, no depth of intermediate social institutions which are necessary to create trust between strangers, no sense of common purpose, and no perception that the system is basically fair. Markets appear to work best in countries which have a rich legacy of non-market values, that have a rich and variegated civil society, many well-supported voluntary organizations, and a high degree of trust, common values and social consensus [15]. Thus, paradoxically, the extension of market values to all corners of life may actually undermine the effectiveness of markets. The best combination – even from a narrowly economic perspective, that is, the maximum economic growth – is probably a very large market economic sector, a tiny state economic sector, a well respected state, a vibrant set of voluntary and social institutions, a strong sense of community identity, and a milieu where integrity has not been undermined by cynicism.

Implications for democrats

The important point for democrats is that rampant inequality is not necessary for markets to work, and may even be economically harmful. A market-based system is compatible with a wide range of values and many ways of organizing society.

The awesome power of markets should be fully recognized. Even capitalist apologists rarely state the case for the free market strongly enough. There is no other way to multiply wealth and human dignity. I will argue in Chapters 7 through 11 that democrats should leave virtually the whole economy to market forces, including 'social' areas such as education, health care and all forms of welfare provision that have previously been taboo, no-go zones.

Markets are wonderful wealth-creating machines, but neither markets nor wealth are perfect passports to happiness. The test for any market extension is not: will this create more wealth? This is too easy a test for markets to pass. The test should be: will market extension enlarge happiness? I will argue later that in large and important areas of life, including education and health care, the answer is: almost certainly. But I would like to close this chapter with one small but telling case, where market sovereignty would reduce the quality of life for almost all city dwellers.

Parks. There is very little to be said for feudalism, but parks are a relic of feudalism, and a heartily welcome relic. No market system would institute parks on anything like the scale we now enjoy. From a market perspective parks are wasteful and unnecessary. If people wanted parks, they would pay for them: this would be the market argument. And I doubt very much, that, for example, if Central Park in New York did not exist, citizens would club together to buy up prime Manhattan real estate in order to raze it to the ground, plant trees and listen to birds. Yet, whatever the economic cost, who can doubt that it is better to have Manhattan with rather than without Central Park? Or that it would be a sad day if New York City decided to auction off the park, even if it distributed the proceeds to its citizens?

The existence and virtues of parks do not undermine the case for markets. Parks are simply a useful example to remind democrats that the extension or curbing of markets must be a pragmatic decision based on what is best for ordinary people. Though a huge extension of free markets may be the result, democrats should remember that increasingly free markets are only useful if they lead to increasingly free people.

Conclusion

Any previous age could have used the power of markets by making them central to society. But until the past 300 years, markets were restricted to limited parts of society, to seaports and coastal regions, or to limited roles within society. Merchants were tolerated but subordinated to feudal society. Political power was more important than economic power, and in general resources were not allocated by markets but by hierarchies.

Today the genie is out of the bottle. Markets have become dominant. Barring a catastrophe like nuclear or climatic apocalypse, there is no way back to pre-market society.

The liberation of markets has exploded wealth. As history would predict, those at the top of society have appropriated more of the wealth explosion than those below. But the arrival of modern democracy, partly caused by the market revolution, and partly by new ideas, has created a new possibility, and in the most advanced societies a new reality, quite outside the experience of previous history. This is the liberation of ordinary people, achieved through the liberation of markets and the liberation of democracy. Democracy appropriates a large slice of the wealth explosion for the benefit of the people at large.

The history of the 20th century is the history of the tension between democracy and capitalism, on the one hand, and all the old recidivist tendencies of mankind, history's legacy of war, oppression from above, and dysfunctional cruelty, on the other. Between them, capitalism and democracy render this legacy of history obsolete. The agony of the 20th century, the worst wars and mass murder in history, should be seen as the last throw of atavistic evil, technology deployed by hierarchies to do things that technology renders unnecessary and senseless, democracy perverted by demagogues for ends that a civilized, educated, well-informed and well-fed populace would never sanction.

We are well over the worst, and not too far from the best. What stops further qualitative progress is that the tension between markets and democracy has not yet been resolved. Markets have been unbound: the first revolution. Democracy has been unbound: the second revolution. Both have liberated more human beings than ever before. But true liberation for all individuals in society requires that markets and democracy fuse together their values and systems: the third revolution.

Endnotes

1   Edward Gibbon (1776) *The Decline and Fall of the Roman Empire.*

2   Jim Taylor and Watts Wacker (1997) *The 500 Year Delta: What Happens After What Comes Next*, New York, HarperCollins/Oxford, Capstone, p. 7.

3   Charles Hampden-Turner and Fons Trompenaars (1997) *Mastering the Infinite Game: How East Asian Values are Transforming Business Practices*, Oxford, Capstone.

4   Peter F. Drucker (1993) *Post-capitalist Society*, Oxford, Butterworth-Heinemann, p. 19.

5   I am indebted to Michael Conway O'Dowd for this comparison. See M.C. O'Dowd (1996) *The O'Dowd Thesis and The Triumph of Democratic Capitalism*, Johannesburg, FMF Books.

6   The World in 1997 quoted in Charles Hampden-Turner and Fons Trompenaars (1997), reference 3 above, pp. 1–3.

7   IMF Economic Outlook, quoted in Report Back on the 1997 Annual Meetings of the IMF and The World Bank, 23–25 September 1997, Johannesburg, Society Generale Frankel Pollak.

8   For an illuminating discussion of China see Lester C Thurow (1997) *The Future of Capitalism*, London, Nicholas Brealey, pp. 47–58.

9   *Ibid*, pp. 51–52.

10 *Ibid*, p. 53.

11 Leaders magazine (1997), July September 1997, volume 20, number 3, p. 53.

12 Is this just an extraordinary coincidence? Not according to Michael O'Dowd (see reference 5 above) whose 'O'Dowd Thesis' first stated in 1996 was that industrialization led to capitalism and democracy. Before dismissing this as naive economic determinism, note that Mr O'Dowd's record of successful predictions is second to none. There is clearly something in the thesis, though I am not sure why. It may be partly because economic growth is inseparable from an educated workforce, which

demands influence and eventually democracy; and partly because it is very difficult to run a modern developed economy without decentralizing power.

13 See reference 3 above.

14 World Economic Forum (1989) World Competitiveness Report, Geneva, p. 261, quoted in Hampden-Turner and Fons Trompenaars (1997), see reference 3 above.

15 See Francis Fukuyama (1995) *Trust*, New York, The Free Press. This explains why post-communist Russia has found it difficult to move to a proper market system.

Chapter Six

The Answer

All animals are equal but some animals are more equal than others
— George Orwell, *Animal Farm*

In a capitalist society, some people are exploited by other people — in a communist society it is just the other way round
— Peter Ustinov

Summary

- An economic system based on markets is the only way to create continually more wealth. Using markets to allocate resources in society as a whole is an experiment mankind has only tried in the past 250 years. It has been spectacularly successful.
- The market system has been incarnated within capitalism. The key paradox of capitalism is how it has managed to combine extraordinary economic achievement, benefitting everyone, with consistent unpopularity. The answer is not that capitalism has favored the few at the expense of the many. The answer is that capitalism's values have been and remain incompatible with those of democracy.
- Democracy is the best human invention of all. It has raised mankind above nature. During the past 250 years, democracy has been a surprising and stunning success.
- None of the attempts to square the values of democracy and capitalism have been successful. Nor have non-capitalist systems, ostensibly more democratic, proved to be compatible with democracy. At the moment both democracy and capitalism appear to be triumphant, and important exceptions, such as China, are brushed aside. But capitalism and democracy are still set on a collision course and there are dangers from outside to both of them.
- The market system has burst out of the shell of capitalism. Markets can be used by the communist state, as in China. Markets can also be used by democrats to create a society that expands fairness and fraternity as well as wealth.
- Capitalism is the first revolution and democracy the second. The third revolution subordinates capitalism to democracy's values, but also extends market principles into the heart of democracy. Part Two describes how democratic capitalism can work.

The market system – organizing the economy by consumer-led markets – is by far the best economic system that has been, or could ever be, devised. Until very recently, the market system was synonymous with capitalism, since capitalism was the only working embodiment of the market system. Capitalism has proved an unprecedented economic success.

Since markets became central to society, in the last 250 years, living standards in capitalist countries, in the world's leading economies, have escalated quite off the scale previously experienced by humanity. Capitalist countries have experienced a population explosion that would in all other ages of the world have led to famine and destitution, and yet have managed to create average levels of wealth that previously only tiny elites could enjoy through exploiting the masses. Free markets, linked to the unprecedented creation and dissemination of useful knowledge, have achieved this prosperity. Free markets can continue to deliver ever greater wealth to each succeeding generation.

The market system does better than any other economic system because it is the most decentralized; because it centers around the individual, as both producer and consumer; because the consumer calls the shots; because it rewards improvements in efficiency and imposes economic discipline, in the interests of all, in the most painless and least obtrusive manner; because it is the most meritocratic system, giving resources to the productive, and taking them away from the unproductive, multiplying more effective solutions and retiring less effective ones; and because it is the most prolific generator and user of new technology. Marketism controls and socializes human behavior, for the benefit of all, while reinforcing rather than detracting from the autonomy and creativity of the individual producer.

The market is the best way to organize and multiply resources. Because capitalism gave free rein to markets, it was the first really important revolution in history.

Despite its incredible creation of wealth, capitalism has been hated and despised. Why? The stock answer – that capitalism benefits capitalists, the rich, at the expense of the poor – has been discredited. Everywhere it has operated, capitalism has created tremendous increases in wealth for every group within society. Nor is it at all easy to demonstrate that capitalism typically creates more *objective* inequality than any non-capitalist system. Sometimes capitalism increases inequality, and sometimes it lowers it. But what is true is that capitalism consistently offends our modern sense of what is fair and proper. It does not conduce toward a society that is fairer, that exalts human dignity and the personal liberation of each individual in society. The successes of capitalism, and of democracy, have continually and appropriately raised the standards against which the economic system is judged. Against this standard, capitalism is found wanting. In short, capitalism's values do not fit with those of democracy.

★ ★ ★

Shortly after modern capitalism, the first revolution, extended its sway, it ran into a second revolution, one only apparently operating in a different sphere.

Democracy is the best way to organize politics and society. Democracy is the best human invention of all. The greatest happiness of the greatest number, and liberty for each individual, are the right objectives and can only be achieved through a system where each individual has an equal right to set up and set aside the government. Modern democracy is even younger than modern capitalism, yet is already irrevocably built into modern civilized life. All decent people are liberal democrats, and there is no intellectual or practical case for any other system. In the modern enlightened world, democracy is unique in combining right and might.

★ ★ ★

Capitalism and democracy have had a checkered relationship. They have not been natural bedfellows. The economic system, at least up to 1945, benefitted society's most privileged elements, who often reaped more than they sowed. Capitalism was a system for capitalists. Increasingly, in the first half of this century, capitalism gave manifestly unfair rewards to capitalists. Capitalists became absentee industry-lords. Economically, managers became more important than capitalists. The capitalists retreated to the beach, the casino, the art-gallery, the charitable institute. In Russia and Germany, the managers, acting in concert with the state and in the name of democracy, seized power. Elsewhere, they flexed their muscles, creeping toward ascendancy.

Democracy, an egalitarian system run for the masses, could not tolerate capitalism, an inegalitarian system run for the few. A better system shimmered. Whether called communism, socialism, fascism, Nazism, or – the best generic description – managerialism, a new economic system was on offer that promised to organize economics for the benefit of society as a whole rather than for the upper classes. That is why nearly all democrats took, or wanted to take, this road.

The road to hell was paved with democratic intentions. Between 1917 and 1941, capitalism's share of world economic systems, measured by value, fell from around 95 per cent to well below 40 per cent. By 31 December 1941, when the United States joined the European War, the United States and the British Empire were the only important states on earth that were still willing hosts of capitalism. A free press guaranteed that the intellectual consensus against capitalism gathered force even in the US and Britain. By 1941, few informed and intelligent observers expected, or wanted, to see capitalism survive.

★ ★ ★

Since 1945, non-capitalist economics, non-market economics, have become discredited and, increasingly, unwound. The apparently better economic systems, centered around the state and the manager, have proved in practice to be worse systems. They have impoverished, and often enslaved, both the rich and the poor. The power of markets, though far from complete, has increased and is increasing. Capitalism and democracy, both in their ways tolerant systems, have finally come to tolerate each other.

★ ★ ★

Yet we have not reached the end of history. Contemporary capitalism is dynamic and creates wealth with devastating force. But capitalism is not democratic: not in its intentions, nor in its institutions, nor in its results. Capitalism serves those who have money: not just capitalists, it is true, but the possessors of purchasing power. Somehow, today's free market economy often produces greater and greater inequality of wealth. So the system appears to serve, inherently, disproportionately, and increasingly disproportionately, those at the top of society. This is what Marx claimed capitalism did. This was plausible then and it is just as plausible now. Whatever the truth about capitalism and inequality – and it is difficult or even impossible to establish the objective truth – it is clear that *laissez-faire* capitalism will not lead to an increasingly equal and fair society. Democracy is rightly programmed to demand something that contemporary capitalism cannot deliver.

The conflict between democracy and capitalism goes beyond results. It is a conflict of values, of inputs as well as outputs, of objectives and process even more than outcomes. The problem is not markets, but the institutions through which our capitalist society lets markets work. The problem is most acute with regard to the large business organization.

Big business is not democratic. It is elitist. Whichever animal metaphor you prefer, it is run for the top dogs, for the fat cats. The ordinary employee is not enfranchised.

So what is democracy to do? Accept free markets as the price of freedom and wealth, whatever the consequences for social cohesion and fairness? This is, in practice, the American way. Allow markets to operate, but restrict them somewhat and tax society to redress the worst inequalities? This is the social democratic way, still being followed by Japan and most European countries, as well as many developing countries. Neither solution works well.

The American solution, a reversion to unrestrained capitalism, contains the seeds of its own destruction. A widening gap between rich and poor is not sustainable in a democracy. The social democratic solution leads to reduced international competitiveness, higher unemployment, greater waste and poorer service to customers. And, ultimately, the logic of global markets makes it impossible for the American solution and the social democratic solution to co-exist. Social democratic economies will be forced to loosen the restraints on capitalism or else opt out of the global free market economy. It will seem a cruel choice.

Sooner or later, the siren voices of managerialism and socialism will re-awaken, probably – because it has not been widely tried recently – in an updated fascist incarnation. Democracy will again be seduced by anti-capitalist programs. Social protest will revive, because there is much to protest.

Alternatively, if it is impossible to have free markets, social fairness and a liberal democracy, the latter may be chopped. It is possible for an authoritarian regime, claiming to act in the interests of the people, to use markets on its own terms. There is no automatic link between the extension of markets on the one hand, and the extension of capitalism or democracy on the other. For example, if the Chinese government tells many of its citizens (as it has done) to buy their own houses – at an effective cost greater than the previous heavily subsidized rents – it is extending market power but in a way that is completely foreign to both democratic and capitalist principles. China is but the most extreme example of a system that benefits from using markets without importing the capitalist or democratic institutions that we have wrongly thought inseparable from markets. To a much lesser degree, a country like Singapore combines social control with market forces. The Singaporean system is accepted because it is egalitarian and wealth-creating (a very desirable combination) even though it is not very democratic.

China should be both a warning and an example. A warning because liberal democracy no longer has a monopoly of the market system, so that the rulers of third world countries do not need to accept democracy as the price of economic development. An example because it shows us that market forces are quite compatible with non-capitalist institutions. It gives us this challenge: to design new market-based institutions that reflect society's quest for fairness and purpose without compromising the personal freedoms of liberal democracy. Democrats should use markets to expand fairness and fraternity as well as wealth, to create a society of fully liberated individuals.

★ ★ ★

The hope, and the probability, is that in most places the third revolution will forestall the resurgence of socialism and managerialism, and frustrate the propagation of Chinese-style market-communism. The third revolution is a union and synthesis of the first two revolutions, capitalism and democracy. The world since 1945 has been tolerable – and by most standards, extremely successful – because capitalism and democracy have learned to live together. The hope for the next century is that capitalism and democracy fuse together to produce an extremely prosperous, socially cohesive, and politically stable free world.

Economically this world will be driven by free markets. Politically and socially – and in all our important institutions, including business corporations – this world will be driven by democracy. Though markets will operate freely, the way that they operate will be rigged toward equality. The state, though it will do nothing else in the economic sphere, will see to that. The values of capitalism will be subordinated to those of democracy at the same time that market principles will be extended into the heart of government.

Markets do not have to be inegalitarian or undemocratic, either in the way they operate or in their results. Indeed, the market, serving the sovereign consumer, is the most democratic mechanism imaginable, provided only that purchasing power is fairly equally distributed. Conversely, democracy is the nearest political expression of market forces that could be contrived.

Markets are neutral. They process the data they are given. The political market is democratic because it has been set up that way. The economic market is not because it hasn't. But it could be.

A market system can serve the ruling classes or the state. But the simplest and best markets are inherently decentralized, even anarchic. Capitalism is potentially a very democratic system, provided there is reasonably equal purchasing power, provided the suppliers of labor and entrepreneurship compete on fair terms, provided large organizations are forced to respond to markets and democracy, and provided everyone has some capital to join the game.

The third revolution will make capitalism irrevocably democratic, and democracy irrevocably capitalist. The third revolution will provide capital and knowledge for all, will redistribute surplus capital to those who have little or none, will create a broad spread of purchasing power throughout society, will make big business accountable both to democracy and the market, and will increasingly dismantle big business altogether.

It is time to glimpse how the third revolution will merge capitalism and democracy for the benefit of all.

Policy

Chapter Seven

The Four Principles of Progress

It is now often said that democracy will not tolerate 'capitalism'. If 'capitalism' means here a competitive system based on free disposal over private property, it is far more important to realize that only within this system is democracy possible.

— Friedrich August von Hayek (1)

If men were actuated by self-interest, which they are not — except in the case of a few saints — the whole human race would co-operate. There would be no more wars, no more armies, no more bombs.

— Bertrand Russell (2)

How selfish soever man may be supposed, there are evidently some principles in his nature, which interest him in the fortunes of others, and render their happiness necessary to him, though he derives nothing from it except the pleasure of seeing it.

— Adam Smith (3)

Summary

- We should organize society to maximize human happiness.
- How is this to be done? I propose four Principles of Progress against which to judge specific policy proposals.
- Principle one is the Market Principle. Every economic activity should be market-based. This is the way to maximize wealth. Until material misery is banished from the earth, wealth creation should be a high priority.
- Principle two is the Democratic Principle. Each person's happiness is as important as that of the next person. Individuals are equally entitled to respect and autonomy. Power should always be given to individuals unless the Market Principle absolutely and necessarily requires aggregation of power. The Democratic Principle also demands attention to the common good, to community and fraternity, without infringing the dispersion of power in society.
- Principle three, the Principle of Inclusion, insists that all citizens must feel included in society and have a reasonable share of society's resources. What is reasonable is defined according to what society can afford. The way to achieve a tolerably equal society is to ensure that each individual is educated and free.
- The fourth and final principle is the Knowledge Principle. The key to progress is to acquire and use knowledge. A society that values and multiplies knowledge, and insists that it is universally distributed, will progress much faster than one that places a lower value on knowledge.

The two great revolutions of the past quarter millennium are, slowly but surely, fusing together in a third revolution, that will create unprecedented wealth for everyone in the new millennium. The third revolution puts democracy at the heart of capitalism, and capitalism at the heart of democracy.

Democracy is man's invention, and superb evidence that we can improve on nature (4). Modern democracy, the second revolution, is a noble experiment that, against all the odds, against all historical precedent, has succeeded and surpassed all expectations. Democracy is society with the people, for the people, by the people; where the ideal is the active and free individual, improving her lot and that of those around her, where society works in the interests of the people, all the people, ordinary people, and where the citizen is the protagonist, not the passive recipient of what is good for her. Democracy is opposed to elites running society for their own benefit, but also opposed to elites running society for everyone's benefit. Democracy is the unchaining of individuals' creativity and energy, so that they are free to pursue their self-interest unconstrained by the privileges of any class or clique, constrained only by rules that serve to protect the equal rights of other individuals. Wherever it has been tried, where the power of elites has been set aside to a sufficient degree to allow democracy to work, it been brilliantly effective. Contrary to 19th century expectations, democracy has led to stable, peaceful and prosperous societies, with degrees of personal freedom for all citizens that in earlier ages were available only to a tiny fraction of the population.

Capitalism is pregnant with democratic ideals

Capitalism, the first revolution, is still rather more controversial. It is accepted as necessary, because only capitalism can use the power of markets, and only markets can give us the wealth to which we have become accustomed. But capitalism remains unloved, an ideal, it seems to most people, only for the rich, the greedy, or the insane. Can capitalism be an ideal, when there is plainly so much wrong with it?

Yes – though it will require much change. Capitalism is not a fixed system. It is not, primarily, a means of allocating resources, or even an economic system. Capitalism is, as Hayek told us, a discovery mechanism; and, as Schumpeter said, an evolving and dynamic system. Capitalism is always deeply integrated into non-economic parts of society, into power groups, culture, science, ways of thinking, a whole nexus of relationships and behaviors that started by describing a small segment of society and has, in the past 150 years, become characteristic of society as a whole in most of the world.

Joseph Schumpeter was not wholly wrong, therefore, when he described capitalism as a scheme of values, a form of civilization that, in 1942, he lamented, was slipping away. One form of civilization, capitalism based on the power structures and ideology of the upper classes of the 19th century, was indeed fast abating. But other, more democratic forms of civilization were evolving. One of these was state-driven socialism and Nazism, the civilization of the Third Reich and Stalin's empire, which turned out to be a great deal less democratic than advertised. Another form of civilization arose in the West: more democratic, predominantly capitalist but with social-democratic constraints on capitalism, run largely for the benefit of the middle classes, a broad group comprising, in most countries, a majority of the population.

The embryonic third revolution democratizes capitalism, creating a new society which, although capitalist, is unlike any capitalist society the world has yet seen. And yet capitalism, though more often used to repel or limit than to advance democracy, embodies ideals that are totally compatible with democracy, and, indeed, absolutely necessary for democracy – emphasis on the self-starting individual, the liberation of the individual's talents, the satisfaction of the individual's needs and wants, independence of the individual from central authority, the advancement of science and technology as central components of society's advance, the belief in progress itself, and the desire to make individuals financially independent. These ideals are at the heart of successful capitalism – the market as a discovery mechanism, driven by the consumer and the active, unconstrained entrepreneur, in fruitful alliance with all branches of knowledge – and though certain forms of capitalism, tainted by elites or governments, do not fully live up to these ideals, they are less successful as a result.

The Third Revolution uses capitalism for democracy

The third revolution will be fully and primarily democratic. It will create a society run for the benefit of all individuals, run honestly and idealistically, to create the best possible society for all, and the greatest happiness of the greatest number, while respecting the freedoms of everyone, and removing, as far as possible, the misery of any member of society. The society must also be, to the maximum possible extent, a society where all members are active participants and reach their maximum personal fulfillment. It must be **actively** democratic, advancing the interests of all the people, not just defending liberal democratic rights and procedures.

There have been many attempts at creating democratic societies, but most of the attempts have wanted to replace, or at least moderate, capitalism. But the third revolution does something different. It uses the good ideals – it is possible to have bad ideals, those more likely to make the mass of people miserable rather than happy – of capitalism to create a way of running the whole of society in the interests of all. The third revolution exploits capitalism to the full, for democracy. To borrow from Franklin D Roosevelt, 'a program whose basic thesis is, not that the system of free enterprise for profit has failed this generation, but that it has not yet been tried', at least not to serve explicitly democratic purposes.

Capitalism can work for any set of interests. It can work, as it did in the 19th century, for the upper classes and the new class of capitalists, who rapidly integrated themselves into the upper classes. It can work, as it has broadly in the 20th century, for the middle classes and skilled workers of all classes. And it can work, as it must in the 21st century, for the benefit of everyone, and particularly for those who have been disadvantaged. Capitalism will not do this automatically. We have to set it up the right way.

So far, democracy has not tried this experiment. Democracy has set about taming capitalism, mitigating capitalism, and using the wealth created by capitalism to set up alternative systems – mainly welfare – to take care of those who were never successful at breaking into the benefits of the system or who were casualties of it. This has been the approach of social democracy, and, though it hasn't been a total failure, it has not worked as well as expected. Somehow the poor remain poor, and their numbers refuse to diminish. Indeed they increase. Some countries, especially in continental Europe, impose greater restrictions on capitalism and have larger non-capitalist (state) economies operating in parallel with the private sector. The result is less inequality, but also less employment and wealth generation. Other countries, like the United States, allow current forms of capitalism much greater latitude; they enjoy rising prosperity but rising inequality too. Neither approach is the way forward.

The third revolution uses capitalism – 100 per cent, pure, blue-blooded capitalism, though not the current variety – to serve democratic ends. And, as Hayek would add, only capitalism can serve democratic ends really well, because only capitalism places the emphasis where it should be: on the active, liberated, educated individual. But in order to marry capitalism to democracy – as opposed to the rather loose flings that each side has enjoyed to date – we need to reform capitalism. We need to make major changes to the way we run both society and business.

What are the principles of progress?

What changes, what reforms, will make capitalism work for the people? And how can we judge policy? What principles should it be based upon? If we cannot answer these questions satisfactorily we will end up with an ad hoc program, a lucky dip of good and bad ideas, not properly grounded in defensible principles.

In the next four chapters I outline some policy suggestions: a radical manifesto to democratize capitalism. But the policy ideas are illustrations of possible applications of democratic capitalist *principles*. The policy ideas often have the defect of originality; they are simply ideas, no doubt many half-baked, and some that may prove totally impractical. They are not the result of thousands of hours of investigation by public servants or think tanks. But the policy ideas *are* illustrations of the sea change in thinking that can derive from the application of what I call 'the principles of progress'. These principles are more important than the policy illustrations. If the principles are right, they can be used to generate, and to judge, any specific policy proposal. If the proposal fits the principles, it is worth experimenting with; if not, not.

If the principles are not logically coherent and attractive, they cannot help us. If the principles cannot clearly lead us to new policies that work, they are useless. If the four principles conflict with each other to the extent that it is not possible to derive policies compatible with all four principles, they will not supply many helpful answers. The discussion of the principles of progress in the rest of this chapter is therefore pivotal. If the principles are sound and compatible, they can soon generate successful policies. These policies may or may not bear a close resemblance to those tentatively put forward in the four following chapters. The policies are mere illustrations, early attempts to begin the brainstorming process. What matters most are the underlying principles.

Shortly, I will propose four Principles of Progress: (1) The Market Principle; (2) The Democratic Principle; (3) The Principle of Inclusion; and (4) the Knowledge Principle.

Even principles, however, require an overall objective. The overall objective I propose is *not* original; political scientists will recognize it as a modified form of utilitarianism, deriving mainly from Jeremy Bentham, the radical-liberal British political philosopher of the late 18th century. There are endless disagreements and refinements of political philosophy, and I am sure that the professionals will not be fully satisfied with the objective for society that I propose. Nevertheless, I think the objective should be able to command a consensus among most intelligent and benevolent readers.

The objective: the pursuit of happiness

Aristotle said happiness should be the goal of all human activity. The second revolution, democracy, points *society* in the direction of individual happiness. The Declaration of Independence proposes life, liberty and the pursuit of happiness. Soon after, Jeremy Bentham invented the concepts of 'utility' and 'the greatest happiness of the greatest number' (5):

> *By the principle of utility is meant that principle which approves or disapproves of every action whatsoever, according to the tendency which it appears to have to augment or diminish the happiness of that party whose interest is in question ... if that party be the community in general, then the happiness of the community; if a particular individual, then the happiness of that individual ...*
>
> *The interest of the community then is, what? – the sum of the interest of the several members who compose it.*

On the whole democracy, after some false starts, has delivered happiness. It *has* allowed and encouraged individuals to pursue happiness. It has organized society, not perfectly, but reasonably closely, so that we pursue the greatest happiness of the greatest number.

Modern political philosophers, in search of something new or of a system that supplies a total answer, quibble with Bentham's system. The quibbles are important. 'The greatest happiness of the greatest number' does not provide a calculus for deciding how to arrange this. Should we redistribute income from the rich person to the poor on the grounds that a dollar taken from the former will give more satisfaction to the latter? If so, when do we stop the redistribution process? What happens if an individual's happiness requires the misery of others, if utility is derived from sadism, envy, resentment or malice? And, most important of all, if we organize society for the greatest happiness of the greatest number, what does this say about protecting the rights of minorities or preventing the oppression of individuals?

These points can be accommodated within a liberal, democratic framework based on 'the greatest happiness of the greatest number'. The most attractive society is that which maximizes aggregate individual happiness, subject to two extra requirements: that individual liberty is maintained and no-one is oppressed; and that there is the opportunity for happiness for everyone – that nobody has an unacceptably low quality of life relative to what society can afford. Expressed more snappily, we could say that society should aim to maximize the aggregate happiness of its members, consistent with liberty and the opportunity for happiness for all. This is very close to the even more succinct Declaration of Independence phrase: life, liberty and the pursuit of happiness.

Within these principles, the important quibbles can be answered. Yes, we should redistribute wealth, because a rich woman's dollar can give more satisfaction to the poor woman, but we should not do this beyond the point at which it oppresses the rich woman or where it creates unfortunate by-products which detract from aggregate happiness – if, for example, redistribution stops wealth creation and creates dependency. There is plenty of room for argument here, but at least the starting principle is fair and clear, and at least we judge by results. In practice, we will find, democratic capitalism favors quite sharp redistribution of wealth, relatively shallow redistribution of income, and the removal of all dependency. We will see a society with a higher minimum quality of life, higher average individual wealth, and also many more rich and very rich people than today – but that is to get ahead of ourselves.

As for antisocial urges like envy and malice, these will be excluded from our utility function: anything that causes unhappiness to others, or is a perverted type of happiness, has no right to be maximized! And protection of individual liberty should be strengthened.

I therefore propose – carrying, I hope, most of you with me – that the best sort of society is one that maximizes the aggregate happiness of each individual within society, and that seeks at least a reasonable level of happiness for each individual, so that no-one's happiness is bought at the expense of another person's misery.

Even if we can agree on this objective, however, how far does it take us? Not far enough. It is very difficult to derive policy from this overall objective. In between the objective and the policy we need a small number of principles to guide us. The principles must be consistent with the overall objective of happiness, must be compatible with each other, and must be useful in deriving policy. Most thinkers who have tried to set policies for society have gone wrong by searching for just one principle. They end up with a panacea. Neither the market, nor democracy, nor any other single guiding principle, can comprise a satisfactory, universal guide to policy. But I believe there are four principles that, taken together, can. Here are my four principles of progress:

Principle one: the market principle

We start with the Market Principle because it is by far the best, and perhaps the only, way of constantly increasing the wealth of society, and because progress and happiness rest upon increasing the wealth of humanity. This view may seem controversial. After all, whole communities, many cultures, and most religions reject the basic premise that progress requires wealth creation. This is all very well for those who are happy with poverty or who have long since escaped it. But however much poverty may appeal to intellectuals, it has little attraction for the vast majority of the poor. Poverty blights lives, and the only way to remove poverty is to create wealth.

The pursuit of wealth

The pursuit of wealth should be an ideal, for society and for many or most of the individuals in it. With wealth comes freedom – freedom from starvation, freedom from the elements, freedom from want, freedom from drudgery, freedom from fear and dependence, freedom from the need to seek the favor of powerful people or institutions, freedom of thought, freedom of movement, and freedom to develop the body, mind and spirit. All of these are elements of life and liberty, and all are necessary preconditions for the pursuit of happiness.

There is a great deal of sanctimonious hand-wringing about the pursuit of wealth. In an age where material plenty has become possible for all, materialism has become a term of abuse. It is a shame that those who undervalue the wealth of society today cannot be transported back to the past. Ideally, the time machine would take them back first 50 years. Many familiar conveniences of life would be absent; many more would be primitive; general standards and freedoms would be lower. Then 100 years ago. Relative poverty would be the rule for most of the time travelers and work for them would be hard and long. Then 200 years ago. Most of our world's active and liberated individuals, save only those in the young United States, would be transported back to the land, to work as peasants in back-breaking labor for a bare subsistence in a fixed society that allowed little prospect of self-improvement and imposed the severest physical penalties for insubordination or minor infractions of the law. In the United States, many would be independent settlers, but many also slaves. Everywhere, as time rolled back, life would become increasingly Hobbesian: nasty, brutish and short.

Until we have a time machine, we will have to make do with an aeroplane to illustrate the point. Go to developing countries. See the places like Rwanda that cannot feed their people. Then hop to a wealthier African country, like Uganda, where there is still a great deal of deprivation and awful living conditions. Then go to a vibrant Asian country, Thailand perhaps, where there is still much poverty but a palpable sense that wealth is being pursued and things are getting better. Then visit Taiwan or Chile and see how much has been achieved over the past generation. Then tell us that wealth and the ability to pursue wealth are not valuable and correlated, to a degree, with people's happiness.

The idea that society should create wealth does not imply that individuals should mainly be concerned with making money. Society should facilitate wealth creation, firstly to remove poverty, and secondly to allow and encourage each individual to be creative and liberated. A wealthy society is not necessarily a materialistic society. Indeed, Abraham Maslow's famous 'hierarchy of needs' argues convincingly that only by satisfying physiological needs such as warmth, shelter and food, and later safety and security, will it be possible for higher social or love needs, and later 'self-actualization', to come to the fore (6). It is only a tiny fraction of humanity that has enough wealth and leisure to pursue self-actualization seriously. Therefore, until everyone has reached this happy state, or until a majority of the world's people rejects the modern world, society had better place a high priority on wealth creation.

The market principle as the way to create wealth

Now, if you accept that increasing wealth is a good thing, it should by now be abundantly clear that only market-based systems maximize progress, that only the market can motivate people to take under-utilized resources —

whether natural resources, labor, capital or human skills – and make better use of them on behalf of society, or, more precisely, on behalf of those who have purchasing power. The rewards of the market induce, in the most painless and unoppressive way possible, all workers to deploy their labor in the most productive way, and induce entrepreneurs to make great efforts to move resources from low-value to higher-value applications, the source of all economic growth.

I do not argue that markets are fair or that they automatically lead to the greatest happiness of the greatest number; markets, like nature, are pitiless, remorseless; and in the short term serve only those who have the money to dictate what should be produced. Nor do I argue that unchecked markets will necessarily and always even produce the greatest aggregate wealth in society, regardless of the distribution of that wealth. I think it is clear that intervention in markets can sometimes actually raise aggregate wealth as well as produce a fairer society: the post-1945 economic miracles have largely been based on conscious intervention, at national and international levels (especially the Marshall Plan – see box), to create mass purchasing power where the unassisted market would have done so much more slowly or not at all. But what is absolutely clear is that a *market-based* system creates a continuous increase in society's wealth, and that no other system can do this as well.

The Marshall Plan, 1947–1951: how intervention can reinforce the Market Principle

The Marshall Plan is one of the best illustrations of the compatibility of intervention, and concern with the common good, with the Market Principle. The story also demonstrates the naturally supportive linkages between the Democratic Principle and the Market Principle. Despite being one of the most successful American initiatives of this century, the story has conveniently been forgotten by today's radical right.

After the Second World War, all European countries – victors and vanquished alike – were devastated. A generous and imaginative European

Recovery Program was put together by the Truman Administration. General George Marshall, the Secretary of State, announcing the Plan on 5 June 1947, explicitly linked political and economic objectives:

> It is logical that the United States should do whatever it is able to do to assist in the return of normal economic health in the world, without which there can be no political stability and no assured peace.

From 1948 to the end of 1951, the Marshall Plan disbursed $12.5 billion via the Organization for Economic Co-operation and Development (OECD), which insisted that recipient countries expanded free trade and made matching contributions of their own. There were no other conditions. The funds were available to former enemies and neutrals as well as allies. Stalin forbade his bloc to accept aid, dubbing it a capitalist ruse.

Stalin was right. Marshall Aid secured democracy and capitalism, peace and prosperity, for the recipient nations of Western Europe for the rest of the century, and led, indirectly, to the eventual fall of the Russian empire in 1989–92. Conversely, it is possible that without Marshall Aid, capitalism might not have survived in Western Europe, possibly not even in America. If so, we can taste the delicious irony that massive state intervention, reaching across political boundaries, may have saved the only non-state economic system from extinction.

The historian, Norman Davies, wisely comments:

> In contrast to the 1920s, the USA was offering to finance Europe's recovery in the interests of the common good ... The 16 countries of Western Europe who benefited from Marshall Aid were able to forge ahead; the USSR and its dependents were cast into self-imposed isolation.

The broader lessons today are that appropriate government intervention to kick-start market activity may be beneficial, and that the Market Principle and the Democratic Principle can reinforce each other in surprising ways. Apparently altruistic pursuit of the common good may lead to greater wealth and a stronger market system.

Source: Norman Davies (1996) *Europe: A History*, Oxford, Oxford University Press, pp. 1063–5.

The Market Principle should, then, be stated as follows: every economic activity, including those designed to produce 'social' goods such as health care and education, should be market-based, unless basing the activity on a market or markets violates one of the other three Principles of Progress (in practice, we will find that this constraint is rarely if ever binding: the other Principles do not prevent market organization). Note, however, what the Market Principle as stated above does *not* say. It does *not* say that every economic or social activity should be run as a for-profit enterprise. It is quite possible, and I think highly desirable, to have many market-based activities, including education and health care, run by competing institutions, some of which aim to maximize profits, and others of which are co-operatives or charitable institutions. Nor does the Market Principle rule out intervention by governments to rig or improve markets, as long as markets remain at the core of the activity after the intervention.

Yet, despite these caveats, the Market Principle is not bland, nor does it describe current practice, even in America. Today, the Market Principle is only rarely applied to the parts of the economy controlled by governments, that is, to between a quarter and a half of all economic activity. Let's give an illustration of how things would change if we consistently applied the Market Principle. The illustration in education is that progress depends upon our knowledge of how to educate people efficiently and in the most socially useful ways, and that this knowledge will only be fully created and deployed if we create a market in education. It may still be desirable for the state to continue to fund education, or even to dramatically increase its funding of education, but purchasing power must be taken from the national and local state and given to the 'customers', to parents and students, via a voucher system or something similar. A thorough-going application of the voucher process would take the 25–50 per cent of the economy controlled by government and give it to individual citizens in the form of purchasing power. Markets would then ensure that the purchasing power produced dramatically better results. (How this might work is explored in Chapter 9.)

Why the market principle is better

The Market Principle may be contrasted to more traditional, centralized and hierarchical ways of attempting to induce progress. If we are trying to promote happiness broadly in society, we could – as early democracy did – decide to give power to those whose function it is to represent and promote happiness. This experiment resulted in the whole paraphernalia of the Welfare State: huge organizations, devoted to noble causes, attempting to dispense welfare and other desirable goods to the people. But this attempt at benevolent dictatorship or benevolent bureaucracy did not work, because markets did not operate and because those who were the beneficiaries were not allowed to be the decision-makers. Welfare ended up benefitting the welfare-providers, the professionals employed by the state, as well as, and sometimes much more than, the under-privileged. The right answer is to use markets to decentralize the power so that the individual herself decides how to use the purchasing power, and so that all providers have to follow best practice established by competition.

It is *much more* urgent for desiderata that are more social than economic – for things like education and health care and the alleviation of poverty, that affect life and the quality of life more profoundly than anything else – to be provided via markets, than it is for normal economic life to work this way. Yet this is contrary to all historical practice by democracies and, even today, to the prevailing intellectual assumptions. Margaret Thatcher denationalized moribund state economic corporations but did not dare to marketize the provision of social services. It would have been far better for Britain – and the rest of the world in imitating privatization – if Mrs Thatcher had left the provision of telephones, gas and electricity and water within the public sector, but had marketized education, health care and social security.

One of the great virtues of a market system is that it harnesses individual self-interest, and pursuit of wealth, in ways that are likely to be socially beneficial. We do not need to recite Adam Smith's words to demonstrate the point, because it is now widely accepted that the market mechanism is the best method available to reward individual effort in proportion to the extent to which consumers are satisfied and improvements in productivity are made. If consumers are, broadly, people at large, rather than a narrow clique or class, this means that society's resources are harnessed increasingly well to give most people in society what they want, relative to their purchasing power. Waste in society occurs most profusely in the non-capitalist sectors, where the interests of producers are put ahead of those of consumers, and there are only weak incentives for improvement in products and services. The more democratic and market-based a society, the more individual self-interest can be harnessed to the benefit of all. This is one reason why the Market Principle, though perhaps the most important basis of progress, is not a sufficient panacea. We need three more principles, starting with democracy.

Principle two: the democratic principle

The Democratic Principle is an essential complement to the Market Principle. The Democratic Principle states that society must be run for the benefit of everyone and by everyone, that individuals are equally entitled to respect and that one person's happiness is as important as the next person's, regardless of wealth, title, background, intelligence, character, merit or any other criterion, and that individuals should control their lives themselves without having to defer to external authority, subject only to respecting their impact on other people. The Democratic Principle further recognizes that in a modern society we are each tied to others, and that, as equals, we must recognize and promote the common good.

The Democratic Principle decentralizes power. It states that power should always be given to the people, to individuals, unless power is necessarily concentrated in a more aggregate form purely as a result of market forces, where the power of customers will tend to ensure that individuals call the shots. No power should be aggregated, rather than dispersed, unless there is a market justification (that the aggregation is necessary to maximize society's wealth) for the aggregation. Any powers not allocated by market forces should be given to the people. For instance, in education, power should go to parents and students as individuals, and not to the educational hierarchy. In organizations, power should go to individuals unless market forces *necessarily* decree otherwise. If market forces *can* be combined with giving power to individuals, without any loss of aggregate production and productivity, then the power *must* be devolved to the lowest possible level of aggregation, preferably to individuals.

In many ways, more than is realized, democracy is the political analog to marketism, the nearest we can come to marketizing politics, to distributing power in society. In this sense, marketism may teach us something about the real nature of democracy. Representative democracy of the type overwhelmingly practised today can be seen as a transitional step toward more genuine, decentralized democracy. Political parties are an increasingly blunt, irrelevant, and even obstructive, means of organizing individuals' political wishes. Moreover, the control exercised through public corporations and all the state and quasi-state institutions that infest modern democracies can be seen as profoundly obsolete and undemocratic. Power is taken from one elite in the name of the people and passed to another elite. Elites will always exist, but the elites that matter should be the elites of influence, where the ultimate decisions always rest with the people as individuals. Direct democracy, via electronic exchange of views and voting, is now possible and the market for votes need no longer be distorted by intermediate power blocs (parties and coalitions) with their own agendas.

Yet, though the Democratic Principle nicely parallels the individualistic Market Principle at many points, there is an ethical and communitarian aspect to the Democratic Principle which is totally lacking in the Market Principle, but which is an essential supplement to it if we are to create the greatest happiness of the greatest number. Republican traditions, derived from the American and French Revolutions, have clung tenaciously to the ideals of community and co-operation; politics should not be about the balancing of interests, or even the direct expression of individual interests, but about something that transcends purely economic interests. Whether expressed in terms of fraternity, community spirit, respect, loyalty, solidarity or altruism, these democratic concerns can be encapsulated in three words: the common good.

It is essential to recognize the moral force of the common good if we are to maximize human happiness. Though happiness depends on material security, happiness also requires non-material values – both those that consume economic resources, like leisure, and those that need not, like relationships. Moreover, the selfish gene is supplemented in humans – and this is the great and unique achievement of humanity, since in other animals co-operation is always used as a tool of competition or to achieve selfish or genetic goals (7) – by altruistic impulses. Now, democracy need not be any more altruistic than dictatorship, but democracy is given its moral force by recognizing and advancing the common good. In practice, democracy has tended to be more benevolent than even benevolent dictatorship, and there are good reasons for this. Concentrated (non-democratic) power corrupts, and even where it does not corrupt, it is inherently inefficient. The ruler cannot know how to pursue the common good as well as the common people themselves. And genuine altruism, expressed through public opinion, is nobler and tends to be more generous than imposed altruism.

Capitalism's great flaw: indifference to the common good

Capitalism has often been hostile, or indifferent, toward the idea of the common good. If the emphasis is placed on the individual, looking after his own interests and interacting with other citizens in the market nexus, what role is there for the state, the common good, or society? Margaret Thatcher, when Prime Minister of Britain, famously remarked: 'there's no such thing as Society. There are individual men and women, and there are families.'

She was providing a distorted echo of W.H. Auden's verse, *September 1, 1939,* on the eve of World War II:

> *There is no such thing as the State*
> *And no one exists alone;*
> *Hunger allows no choice*
> *To the citizen or the police;*
> *We must love one another or die.*

As Auden knew, there was indeed such a thing as the State: the Nazi state, the Fascist state, the Soviet state, all large, menacing, nasty conglomerations of police, military, para-military, politicians; instruments to repress certain individuals and mobilize others into the pursuit of the common evil. Also, there were Western states: governments, more or less honest, trying to get individuals and society to rub along peacefully toward greater prosperity and equality.

Auden was objecting to the *idea* of the State, the Hegelian–Stalinist–Hitlerian abstraction, a glorious entity meant to transcend individuals and have its own authority and legitimacy. He was not denying that there was such a thing as the common good, and he explicitly recognized interdependence.

Auden got it right. The practical reason for taking account of the common good is that a society of self-interested individuals, trying to maximize their well-being without regard to the common good, will very rapidly create a society that is unattractive, and cannot lead to the greatest aggregate happiness and liberty of individuals. There are powerful forces at work in the world, and particularly in free markets, that rapidly lead to unequal outcomes (8). Excessive inequality, devoid of a sense that there is a community that must take care of all its members, detracts from maximum aggregate individual happiness and liberty.

There is also Auden's emotional rationale for the common good. No-one exists alone; we must love one another or die. We need fraternity; we value it even if it serves no economic goal. Altruism, as both Adam Smith and Bertrand Russell realized, serves selfish goals. Without a degree of altruism, we cannot be happy. Without the sense of living in a society that is united and at peace with itself, that is organized for the benefit of all, we cannot attain full happiness. In this sense the common good is a 'free' addition to individuals' utility, not a restriction on or diminution of it.

Is the Democratic Principle incompatible with the Market Principle?

Does the Democratic Principle require a reversion to social-democratic constraints on capitalism? Are our first two Principles incompatible?

No! The answer is to use market mechanisms to produce the common good. This will not happen without intervention; left to their own devices, market mechanisms will *not* serve the common good, and in the process, will not maximize the good of all individuals.

It has long been recognized that intervention to set up the capitalist system correctly can enhance its force and value. In 1944, F.A. Hayek, scarcely a collectivist, carefully distanced capitalism from *laissez-faire* (11):

> *The liberal argument is in favour of making the best possible use of the forces of competition as a means of co-ordinating human efforts, not an argument for leaving things just as they are. It is based on the conviction that where effective competition can be created, it is a better way of guiding individual efforts than any other. It does not deny, but even emphasizes, that, in order that competition should work beneficially, a carefully thought-out legal framework is required, and that neither the existing nor the past legal rules are free from grave defects.*

But no-one has stopped to ask the crucial question: if we were aiming to set up the market system so that it served the interests of democracy and society – by maximizing the aggregate happiness and liberty of individuals – just how would we set up the system?

This is *the* question for democratic capitalism, founded on the concept of the public good, the good of individuals comprising the public. The concept is not just that each member of society should maximize her own well-being, but should also be part of a society that maximizes everyone else's too, if necessary by legitimately restricting or reducing the individual's freedom to maximize her own well-being when this is bought by greater reduction of the well-being of others. Only society can set up the rules to ensure this result. This thinking is well accepted, at least among collectivists. The originality of thinking that is now required, however, is to use markets to satisfy this criterion. Free markets will not do this automatically. But free markets, correctly set up, *can* attain this goal, and in fact can attain it to a much higher degree than any non-market mechanisms.

Principle three: the principle of inclusion

The Principle of Inclusion explicitly extends the Democratic Principle to cover all citizens. It also addresses a key question that the Principle of Democracy, as we have defined it, does not answer: whether, and how far, democracy requires redistribution in order to achieve greater equality.

The Principle of Inclusion states that ways must be found, consistent with the other Principles, to include all citizens within the same perceived polity. All citizens must believe that they are fundamentally equal members of society, and no citizen must be isolated, either by great wealth or great poverty, from feeling included in the society of which he is a member.

What does this mean for equality? We have adopted a subjective definition, because fraternity is much more important than equality. All empirical evidence (9) shows that what most people want is an absolute increase in their standard of living, and that inequality is not offensive as long as (a) there is the possibility of anyone becoming rich (b) the rich do not have unequal civil rights, and (c) there is no underclass, clearly cut off by poverty from the rest of society.

It might be argued that the greatest happiness of the greatest number inherently requires a high degree of egalitarianism, since, as mentioned before, a dollar means more to a poor person than it does to a rich one. But this is to ignore the second order effects. Taken too far, equality removes the incentive to produce, both for the rich and for the poor. This is especially dangerous if it removes the incentive for the entrepreneur to shift resources from low value to high value uses. Whereas at any one time there is only a fixed amount of wealth to go round, over time wealth is multiplied by allowing the possibility that some people can become very rich, and by channeling ambitious and able people into commercial (as opposed to military or political) pursuits. The inequality that arises from having a small proportion of very rich people – as long as these people do not lord it over others – is much less of a problem than having a proportion (large or small) of people who are very much poorer than the typical citizen. It is almost certainly true that the existence of rich people –

and what at least some of them have done to become rich – and the possibility of getting rich add to rather than subtract from aggregate social happiness, while the existence of people who are conspicuously poor relative to the rest of society detracts from aggregate social happiness.

The Principle of Inclusion therefore states that there is nothing wrong with some people having access to a lot more of society's resources – money, skill, knowledge, housing, food, etc. – than other people, provided that everyone has access to a reasonable amount of the key resources. In practical terms, we might decide that there should be no cap on individual wealth, but that no-one should have an income that is less than one half or one third of the median level of income. (There is no magic number. Popular perceptions and experience will show what is the right level for any society – determined of course through popular voting.) This 'income' can be distributed in ways that do not violate the other Principles, especially the Market Principle. We shall see in later chapters some ways in which redistributed wealth can actually enlarge, rather than diminish, the aggregate wealth in society.

The Principle of Inclusion is important not just for humanitarian purposes, and for the cohesion of society, but also to make the best use of human talent. All experience shows that excluded individuals make a negative contribution to society. They may be miserable and poor, but in aggregate (there are of course honorable exceptions) they suck up resources, create crime and disease, despoil the environment, and give little back to compensate. The existence of the poor is bad news for everyone, for the average citizen and the rich as well as the poor themselves.

By contrast, there is ample evidence that the poor can become valuable contributors to society, and that everyone born is capable of creative expression. There is thus a positive link between all three Principles discussed thus far: the Market Principle, the Principle of Democracy, and the Principle of Inclusion. The link is the active and liberated individual.

The active and liberated individual

All that is most worthwhile in Western civilization has come from releasing the creative energy of individuals. Chained up within feudalism, traditional society, poverty, or the bounded horizons that arise from ignorance, temerity, weak character, inherited religion or oppression, only individual geniuses transcend the prevailing morass of mediocrity. Released by tolerance, liberty, science and freedom from serious material want, and encouraged by the whole apparatus of civilized social engineering – schools, universities, apprenticeships, clubs, voluntary societies, newspapers, exhibitions, theater, visual arts, music, travel, and all the other stimulations that expand our capacity to think, feel and create – the active individual over the past few centuries has performed miracles that earlier societies could not imagine, let alone make real.

Not everyone in society is yet an active and liberated individual, and the definition anyway is subjective and fuzzy. But make no mistake. A society predominantly composed of active and liberated individuals – such as now exists in most developed countries – is an historically unprecedented phenomenon. There was no country in the world in the 19th century – save arguably some Swiss cantons or (even more arguably) the tiny Vatican State – where active and liberated individuals comprised, even on a very permissive definition, more than half the population. Of large countries, the United States probably came closest, and was the first to attain, some time in this century, that distinction. If, however, we roll back history to before the 18th century, the proportion of active and liberated individuals in society recedes towards vanishing point, re-appearing as a noticeable minority only in Roman and Greek times (supported by a large majority of slaves). The 20th century pioneered the society of liberated and active individuals. A world overwhelmingly comprising such actors will be the most significant achievement of the next century. For this we need democratic capitalism.

The link between democracy and the active, liberated individual may be evident. But what is the link with capitalism? Karl Marx knew the answer. He realized that the capitalism he saw reduced the number of active, liberated individuals (and this in large measure was why he condemned capitalism). He argued, very precisely, that it was the separation of ownership and management that was the root evil. The laborer lost control of his labor. It was alienated to the factory owner, beyond the control of the worker. The capitalist accrued the worker's surplus value; the worker wore out his life in the service of a machine beyond his control, a machine incapable of normal human decency. Marx's analysis was correct, but the trend he projected went into reverse. The worker, increasingly, got control of the machine. Capitalism, not through philanthropy, but through its relentless vested interest in effectiveness, discovered that it should make workers smarter and less alienated. It paid better to put the man in charge of the machine than the machine in charge of the man. The logic of capitalism's evolution was not the immiseration of the masses, but their activation and education.

And today? It is absolutely clear. And it goes back to Marx's insight. Capitalism has, to a degree, liberated the individual, but there is still a fatal flaw. This is the separation of ownership from control. *Pace* the thinkers of the 1930s, this was and necessarily would always be a retrograde step for humanity. The active and liberated individual must be in control of her time, her work, her ownership of her means of production. Reintegrating ownership and control – at work and in society more generally – is the only route to a society exclusively, or overwhelmingly, composed of active and creative individuals. People who can control their own future will make that future good. Those who can't, won't. Those who don't do it for themselves won't do it for others. Society will always sub-optimize its wealth and civilization exactly to the extent that individuals do not control their own value added.

Capitalism feeds on and feeds smart, motivated people: knowledge workers, entrepreneurs, scientists, and the huge army of self-employed people, from cleaners to prostitutes to concert pianists to professors, who meet the test of the market, do something for which others are willing to pay, and control, to a substantial extent, their own destiny. There is a problem with large business organizations – which as we shall see in Chapter 10 contain intractable islands of socialism, where results are not measurable or linked to rewards, resources are wasted and individuals alienated – but this is a problem that democratic capitalism can resolve. People who are smart and motivated at work do not stop having these characteristics in the rest of their lives, and vice versa. Whereas in Marx's time capitalism was not compatible with a society of active and liberated individuals, today capitalism requires such people and has done more than any other mechanism to encourage human development and responsibility.

Today, where people are not liberated and active individuals, the chances are that they are either working in large organizations (inside or outside the capitalist system), or beyond the reach of the system itself. People who are passive and under-developed are not, in general, active in useful work; they are unemployed, dependent, on welfare, or otherwise outside the normal economic system. Far from being what Marx called the reserve army of the unemployed, and a necessary part of the capitalist system, these people tend to be unskilled, unmotivated, demoralized, and increasingly disengaged from the market economy or any other role that gives dignity, satisfaction and personal development. Someone in an American inner city ghetto who has been unemployed for more than a year, or perhaps never even held a proper job since leaving school, has more in common with a person without hope in a developing country than with the investment banker whom she will see passing in the enclosed glass of a cab. At the extreme, the bag lady is not part of capitalism or even of normal society. If society were exclusively composed of bag ladies and bag gentlemen, capitalism (and much else besides) would collapse. Conversely, if everyone were engaged within the capitalist system, there would be no bag people. Before long, everyone would be a liberated and active individual; the discipline of the market requires that individuals produce results, and the self-interest of the producing system requires that individuals have the knowledge, training and other resources necessary to produce results most cost-effectively.

The appropriate response to unemployment, we shall see in Chapter 9, is not for the capitalist producers to shrug their shoulders and say it's not their problem, or even for them to subsidize the state to subsidize the unemployed, but to create market mechanisms whereby unemployment can be eliminated. If the market's so wonderful – which it is – why not use it to solve the unemployment problem?

If we want a society of liberated and active individuals – as dictated by the Principle of Inclusion – we should want a market economy; and if we want a society exclusively peopled with active and liberated individuals, they must all be roped into the market economy, directly or indirectly, so that they are able to deliver something of value to others and receive back the material means that are preconditions for activity and creativity.

There is a fourth and final Principle of Progress that will help us set policy and achieve a society of liberated and active individuals.

Principle four: the knowledge principle

The Knowledge Principle states that the best way for any individual, organization or society to progress is by acquiring and using knowledge. The Knowledge Principle also reinforces the Principle of Inclusion by stating that a key objective of the good state is to raise the skill level of all citizens and to ensure that everyone attains a certain minimum level of useful skill.

The progress of the world is, very clearly, based on the accumulation of scientific knowledge and the technologies for exploiting it for material benefit. As Francis Fukuyama has pointed out (10), modern natural science is the only field that everyone agrees is moving in a positive direction and where progress is cumulative; the same cannot be said for art or architecture.

Humanism is a very important and under-rated value in our society. Humanism means not only learning, but the noble independence of man (11) and a culture that values learning and the development of the individual through expansion of the mind. Today most people would regard humanitarianism – caring for the deprived – as a greater virtue than humanism. But humanism is a higher goal and also a means of reaching humanitarian ones. It is significant that the most successful and innovative pharmaceutical companies, like Astra of Sweden, have their research and development very closely tied into universities where the principal motivation is *not* commercial; and that countries with the ancient and flourishing intellectual cultures, like Britain, have been the source of so many inventions and technological breakthroughs. (And, incidentally, it does not matter that Britain has failed to commercialize most of its knowledge – the United States and Japan have done so much more effectively.

If the world had relied upon Britain to do so, we would all now be much poorer. One of the great things about knowledge, propelled by markets, is that diffusion and exploitation of knowledge proceeds at the pace of the fastest and most effective innovator at each stage in the chain from knowledge generation to commercialization to implementation and delivery to consumers.) Knowledge begets knowledge and wealth.

Knowledge enables us to generate new resources (skyscrapers substitute for land, the micro-chip substitutes for expensive and clunky machinery, bio-tech substitutes for nature) and to make more economic use of both new and existing resources. Knowledge finds a way to do things better or cheaper, provided there is an economic incentive. The market system gives individuals a clearer and more necessary incentive to acquire and deploy knowledge. The whole basis of enterprise is the entrepreneur, a term coined about 1800 by Jean-Baptiste Say: 'the entrepreneur shifts economic resources out of an area of lower productivity and yield into an area of higher productivity and yield.' Knowledge and technology are the necessary means of leverage for the entrepreneur and the condition for enhancing society's wealth.

Francis Fukuyama comments (12):

> ... the logic of modern natural science would seem to dictate a universal evolution in the direction of capitalism. The experiences of the Soviet Union, China and other socialist countries indicate that while highly centralized economies are sufficient to reach the level of industrialization represented by Europe in the 1950s, they are woefully inadequate in creating what have been termed complex 'post-industrial' economies in which information and technological innovation play a much larger role.

The Knowledge Principle requires a society where the pursuit of knowledge is universal. Every individual will be educated and will value knowledge. This will conduce toward the creation of more wealth, both because the individual at work will find ways of working smarter, and because there will be more inventions and innovations (even if, or perhaps because, *all* branches of knowledge are pursued, not just narrowly scientific or technological ones). But the main reason for the Knowledge Principle is the pursuit of happiness, which depends most critically (beyond a certain point of material wealth) on the expansion of the mind and spirit, on the active and liberated individual with broad horizons and an appetite for learning.

The virtuous circle

The Principles of Progress can comprise a virtuous circle, as shown in Fig. 1. All the Principles, but especially the Market Principle and the Knowledge Prin-

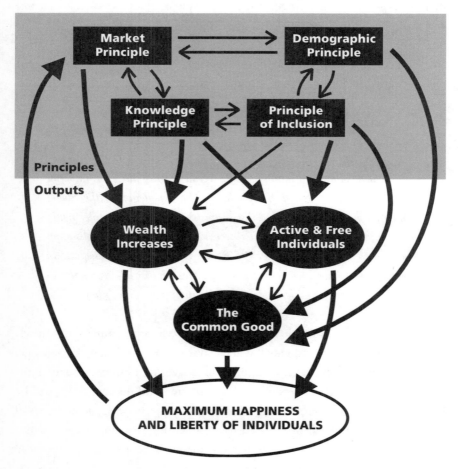

Fig. 1 The four principles of progress lead to a virtuous circle.

ciple, conduce toward progressively greater wealth creation. All four Principles create a society of active and liberated individuals, who in turn enhance wealth creation. The Democratic Principle and the Principle of Inclusion induce fraternity and take the common good to ever higher levels. Wealth creation, the common good, and a society composed of active and liberated individuals all lead to maximum individual happiness and liberty. In theory at least, the four Principles can support each other and lead to a continually improving society of the sort envisaged over 200 years ago by Edward Gibbon.

But will the Principles work in practice? Can we derive useful and better policy from our four Principles of Progress? Or will the Principles be vague and unhelpful, or, even worse, lead to contradiction? Let us see. In the next four chapters we attempt to use the Principles of Progress to construct some new and better policies. This foray is far from comprehensive, but five of the most important public policy issues are considered: redistribution (Chapter 8), education (Chapter 9), employment (also Chapter 9), the way our organizations are run (Chapter 10), and the role of the state (Chapter 11). The policies are only illustrations of the Principles; readers and others may be able to suggest better policies that are in line with the Principles. But let's make a start.

Endnotes

1   F.A. Hayek (1944) *The Road to Serfdom*, London, Routledge, p. 52 (Routledge paperback version).
2   Quoted in Samuel Brittan (1995) *Capitalism with a Human Face*, Aldershot, Edward Elgar, p. 31.
3   Adam Smith (1759) *The Theory of Moral Sentiments*, Indianapolis, Liberty Classics, 1976. Opening words.
4   Ivan Alexander (1997) *The Civilized Market*, Oxford, Capstone.
5   Quoted in Samuel Brittan, *op. cit.* (reference 3 above), p. 66. These are the opening sentences from Bentham's *Introduction to the Principles of Morals and Legislation*.
6   Abraham Maslow (1954) *Motivation and Personality*, New York, Harper & Row.

7   See Matt Ridley (1997) *Origins of Virtue*, London, Viking. According to Ridley, most co-operation between animals is competitive in intent. In dolphin society, co-operation is used mainly for achieving sexual goals: co-operation of two or three adult males to kidnap female dolphins. Chimpanzees co-operate in order to attain power.

8   See Richard Koch (1997) *The 80/20 Principle*, London, Nicholas Brealey.

9   See M.C. O'Dowd (1996) *The O'Dowd Thesis and The Triumph of Democratic Capitalism*, Johannesburg, FMF Books, pp. 42–4 for a convincing demolition of the case that most people value equality more than an increase in their living standards.

10 Francis Fukuyama (1992) *The End of History and the Last Man*, New York, The Free Press. Quote is taken from p. 72 of the 1992 Penguin edition.

11 See Ivan Alexander, *op. cit.* (reference 4 above), p. 174.

12 Francis Fukuyama, *op. cit.* (reference 10 above), p. xv.

Chapter Eight

Capital for Everyone

The top 1 percent of the population have 40 percent of total net worth, but they do not have anything like 40 percent of total IQ. There simply aren't individuals with IQs thousands of times higher.

— Lester Thurow [1]

Realized capital ... meets the worker as the property of the capitalist, as an autonomous power, although it has been created by labor.

— Karl Marx [2]

Summary

- The market system is the best way to create wealth, but it necessarily enshrines an injustice: the owners of capital can compound their wealth unfairly. The only way round this dilemma is to ensure that everyone has some capital and benefits from the capital multiplication game.
- A new type of Popular Privatization is proposed, whereby nearly all state assets are sold and distributed to individual citizens.
- Capital Start ensures that every person starting economic life has an asset base that can be used to acquire skills or start a business. Though the cost will be very high, the benefit to individuals and society will be astronomical. This scheme can be supplemented by Capital Renewal at later stages in life.
- Direct capital investment by individuals will be encouraged. Tax changes will make it easier for people to attain financial independence. Pensions will become capital accumulation funds run wherever possible by the interested individuals.

Introduction

I start with a proposal that both developed and developing societies should ensure that all their citizens have some capital, that they become active capitalists, and that (at least in developed societies) financial independence is an attainable goal for everyone.

Why? Which of the principles of progress does this reflect?

The Market Principle states that every economic activity, including those serving social goals, should be market-based, unless having the activity organized this way violates one of the other principles. Now, there is a problem about having everything market-based, and we had better be up-front about it. The market organizes resources better than any other system and is more decentralized than any other system — so far so good — but it gives unfair rewards to the possessors of capital. Capital is no longer necessarily or even largely provided by entrepreneurs themselves: capital comes to the meal separately, like a side salad. The market for capital serves a useful function, because capital is relatively scarce and it seeks the best return. But the *owners* of capital themselves may serve no useful function. In general, the owners do not direct the use of the capital; they do not act as venture capitalists; they are simply providers of funds. The owners of capital are there just because they happen to have the capital. The owners of capital derive a fat reward — returns to capital show absolutely no long term tendency to decline, despite specious arguments that talent is more important than capital (which it is) and that talent is gaining rewards at the expense of capital (which it is not) — just from being there. It might be argued that the owners of capital have scrimped and saved to build up their capital, but this argument is unconvincing too. Most large capital accumulation today is the result of inheritance and/or luck.

So: the market system has at its heart an injustice — that there is a free ride for the owners of capital. This is already causing social problems, as inequality widens in the most market-oriented societies like the US. Yet, the Market Principle asserts that we should go much further, in the interests of wealth creation, and make all economic activity market-based. This could tear apart the social fabric – *unless* we make capitalism, and the free ride that comes with capital ownership, available, at least on a modest scale, to everyone.

The Democratic Principle decentralizes power and supports the Market Principle in taking out the intermediate aggregations of power between the citizen and the market. But the Democratic Principle also insists that we should take care of and enhance the common good. Rampant marketism without a wider distribution of capital would increase the inequity and inequality in society and would not be consistent with nurturing the common good.

Above all, the Principle of Inclusion states explicitly that citizens should belong to the same perceived polity and that no citizen should be isolated, by great wealth or great poverty, from the society of which he is a member. The Principle of Inclusion states that there is nothing wrong with some people having a great deal of wealth or capital, provided that everyone has access to a reasonable amount of the same resources. Clearly, the Principle of Inclusion is incompatible with the burgeoning gulf between the super-rich and the underclass, evident in the most free market countries like the United States. If we take the Principle of Inclusion seriously, we must ensure that everyone has access to some capital, so that they can join the free ride.

Can this be done? I believe that it can. In this century we have already taken giant strides towards the wider distribution of capital, through the investment of savings of ordinary people in capital instruments. It is only in recent years that this process has stalled. I argue that we need to reignite the process, this time ensuring that *everyone* has some capital. And I argue that we can serve the Democratic Principle in the process, by taking resources – economic power – away from the government, and giving it to ordinary people.

The capital revolution stopped half-way

As democracy advanced in the 19th century, capitalism seemed increasingly indefensible, because it concentrated ownership of society's wealth – the means of ownership, distribution and exchange – in the hands of very few. During this century, the ownership of industry has passed from the few to the many, largely through what has been called alternatively 'pension-fund socialism' and 'post-capitalism'. Neither is a very accurate or helpful label for a very simple fact. Now, in developed countries, a majority of business wealth is owned by pension funds, mutual funds and insurance companies whose assets, in turn, are owned mainly by ordinary people. Some of these assets have been acquired through savings of various sorts; most by the accumulation of pensions paid by companies to their employees over a lifetime of service. The astonishing increases in the value of shares quoted on the stock exchange in this century has driven the process.

Though capitalism has continued to benefit those with most capital most, it has actually worked for the benefit of the mass of employees and self-employed people, and given a modest degree of independence to hundreds of millions of people around the world, albeit one mainly enjoyed in the sunset years.

This is real progress towards democratic capitalism, but it is not democratic capitalism. There are three important ways in which the status quo falls short of real democracy:

1   *Not everyone is a capitalist*, owner of part of society's productive wealth.
2   *Few people are active capitalists*, directly participating in the capital accumulation game.
3   *Few people can realistically use capital to establish their own independence during their working lifetime.*

We can remove these limitations, both in developed and developing countries.

Making everyone a capitalist

The capitalist game is a fantastic one. It is a perpetual motion machine that generates wealth that most societies in the history of the world could not have imagined, and that, to the limited extent imaginable, could only be generated by the slow, uncertain and ever vulnerable process of conquest and colonization. But the source of wealth is not generally well understood. It derives only to a limited extent from property, precious metals and other fixed assets. It derives mainly from the apparently infinite multiplication of industrial and commercial wealth, from the creativity of individuals and the beautifully yoked advance of business and science. In a word, it comes from business. So whether you are going to get wealthy, or share in the extra wealth being created in the world, year in and year out, does not depend in the first instance on your skills, or even whether you own property, but on whether you own a piece of business or its tradable equivalent. If you do, you're in the game, riding the surf of increased wealth. If you don't, you're not.

The business capital game – money for old rope

Over the past 70 years, business assets, as measured by US stock markets, have earned a real rate of return, over inflation, of 7 per cent per annum – and an increase over the period of a hundred times [3]. If the money had been put in long term Treasury bonds – loans to the government – the real increase would have been 2 per cent per annum and the value would have tripled over 70 years (three times versus one hundred times if put into industry!). If the money had been put into the bank or another savings institution, the real value would actually have gone down! The American experience is paralleled in all other business asset markets.

Multiplying your money 100 times over 70 years is one hell of a game. The problem for democracy is that not everyone has been in this game, so that those who were have benefitted hugely, at the relative expense of others.

One reason why the rich get richer, and the poor never catch up, is that the poor, even when they save, tend to do so outside the business asset (equities or shares) system. With the important exception of pension fund investments, when the decisions are largely taken for them, the poorer elements in society, and even most of the middling earners, put most or all of their money into banks, thrifts, savings and loans or their equivalent (building and friendly societies). Their savings get turned into loans. The rich, on the other hand, invest most of their savings in private businesses or the stock market. Small starting differences in wealth become massively exaggerated because of the difference in compound returns between business and non-business investments.

The myth of post-capitalist society – all power to talent?

The returns to capital – which, if anything, show signs of increasing rather than decreasing on trend over recent years – give the lie to those who assert that we are moving or have moved into a 'post-capitalist society'. In an astonishing lapse of normally sound judgment, the admirable Peter Drucker gave a recent book this title [4], and argued that capitalism today was fundamentally different because talent, rather than capital, was calling the shots.

This alleged recent 'change' in the nature of capitalism bears an uncanny resemblance to the predictions of the 1940s. Then managers and knowledge workers were the heroes of the hour; they were going to replace capitalists altogether.

In 1942 the young Peter Drucker argued in *The Future of Industrial Man* that the large business enterprise would become the community through which the individual would find status and function, with the plant community becoming the place in and through which social tasks would be organized – a view clearly influenced by fascist thinking and by James Burnham. Drucker also coined the term 'knowledge worker'.

Yet the 'change' in the terms of trade, the shift from capital to talent, whether in the 1940s or the 1990s, is much more apparent than real. Talent, especially entrepreneurial talent, was always at least as important as capital in driving capitalism forward. And when talent meets capital today, the latter is still remarkably powerful.

Yes, talent and knowledge are important. Yes, top managers in large organizations, especially in America, are raiding the till and paying themselves excess and unnecessary rewards that belong to the shareholders. But this hardly means that we are 'post-capitalist'.

There have never been more real capitalists around in the world, small business people (and a few large ones too) who own equity in their own companies valued, for each capitalist, in the millions, tens and hundreds of millions, or even billions of dollars. Small business is gaining share from large business at an unprecedented rate – hardly any indication that the entrepreneur or capitalist-entrepreneur is dead.

The astonishing thing is how *little* the capitalist system has changed in its essence, even though the beneficiaries of capitalism are now much more broadly spread in society and even though we have lived through the (now slowly abating) separation of ownership from control, an event that could truly have kaiboshed capitalism once and for all. We still have a capitalist accounting system, basically the same as that of the 1930s or even 1830s. We still have very high returns to shareholders. The system is the same even though roles have shifted.

If you doubt this, think about how difficult it is, even today, for budding entrepreneurs to take their ideas to market, and how high the returns are for the capitalists – the venture or development capitalists – who back them. Sit in on the negotiations. As someone who has been on both sides of the venture capital fence, I tell you that the people with the money hold the best cards. I have obtained an internal rate of return of around 100 per cent – money doubling on average ever year, for several years – out of two venture capital investments, one in hotels and the other in restaurants, where the entrepreneurs had great talent but no money. I was the only person they could find to invest and I drove a hard bargain. All I contributed was capital. Do not tell me that we are in a post-capitalist world where talent is scooping the pool and the capitalist can barely make ends meet.

It is the same with large organizations. To be sure, exceptional talent (and some that is far from exceptional) at the top is gathering entrepreneurial rewards, while taking little or no risk, which is a new phenomenon in capitalism (and one that we hope will come to an end when the bubble of unaccountability is burst). But for the great mass of so-called knowledge workers, the message of the organization is the same as before (and it is Peter Drucker who formulated this reality): *you need us more than we need you.* I hope this will change, as more and more talent shifts into small business and especially as wage slaves become entrepreneurs. But this will hardly mark a transition from capitalism.

These are important points, not made purely for fun. Capital is still reaping very high returns, if you like, surplus value. It has to, if we are to have an effective capitalist system. It is unfair. If you look at the people who benefit from the process, most of the capitalists, on any fair assessment, do not deserve the returns they get. But if we took the returns away from them, they would

have to go, equally unfairly, to someone else, if we wanted the system to continue its magic. In a democratic society, the only way to make the system less
unfair is to ensure that everyone has a chance – and perhaps even more than a
chance, a certainty – of joining the capitalist gravy train.

How can everyone join the capital game?

If we desire a cohesive and democratic society, we cannot have one class of
citizens who have latched onto the capital wheeze, and another set who
haven't. Particularly as there is no inherent justice or positive motivational
effect in being an owner versus a non-owner.

As our old friends Adolf Berle and Gardiner Means spotted back in 1932
[5], when the capitalist and the manager ceased to be one and the same animal,
returns to shareholders cease to motivate. The shareholders do not contribute
to the business as the former owner-entrepreneurs did. The stockholders became passive coupon clippers, giving nothing to the business except their initial capital.

This raises a tricky issue. For the market to work well, we need capital to
seek the highest return, we need the high returns to capital in order to drive
forward the process whereby each small bit of capital is used efficiently to generate a large amount of extra wealth. Capital must still seek the highest available
return, and to restrict returns to capital would lower economic efficiency. If
we artificially lowered the returns to capital, much of it would be diverted to
consumption or to projects that do not deserve to go ahead, projects that would
use society's resources – not just capital, but talent and labor too – to bad effect.
Only because capital is scarce is there the drive for continuous improvement.
But do passive capitalists *deserve* this high return?

The answer is no. And the high returns to existing capitalists are exacer-
bating inequality and threatening social cohesion. Yet we need the high returns to capital. Is there no way out of this impasse?

There is. Who owns the capital is, in the first instance, entirely irrelevant
to the process of wealth creation in society. Whether top-hatted capitalists
corner the market in capital, or bureaucrats working for pension funds manage the capital on behalf of skilled workers, or the capital is owned equally by

every man, woman or child in the land – in one sense, the narrowly micro-economic one, this matters not at all, because the owner makes no active and valuable contribution to companies quoted on the stock exchange. In another sense, following the social and economic consequences of capital ownership, it matters greatly. If capital is relatively equally distributed, there is no loss of economic efficiency at the level of the individual firm, yet there are social and economic benefits to society. Flatter capital distribution tends over time to raise aggregate purchasing power, to reduce economic activity that destroys happiness (such as crime) or that adds nothing to society's useful stock of wealth (such as police and security forces), and to reduce personal alienation and the divisions within society. More equal capital distribution leads to greater *real* economic growth (though the GDP statistics do not measure this, a new index could easily be constructed to exclude economic activity that is negative or neutral to wealth and happiness) and also to increase aggregate happiness.

This is not an argument for the confiscation of shares and their equal redistribution to the populace. There are obviously decisive arguments against such action. It cannot be done without invading personal liberties, causing widespread disruption and distress, and requiring the intervention of the oppressive state. In today's global market, it is impractical to confiscate wealth without exchange control, and this would probably be ineffective, cause capital flight and talent flight, discourage all inward investment, and permanently reduce the value of the national currency – all leading to the downward spiral that has destroyed wealth and happiness in places like Zimbabwe or Cuba. Such socialist policies would therefore violate both the Market Principle and the Democratic Principle. But the positive, fair and socially useful policy is to ensure that every family unit can benefit from the game of capitalist ownership, without removing existing market and personal liberties. I can see how to do this. Some will continue to have more capital than others, but all will have some. The rising tide will lift big boats more than small boats, but the idea that all boats will be lifted would no longer be a lie or a delusion.

How do we do this? How do we make each family, or even each citizen, a participant in the capitalist automatic-wealth-creation process? Here are four ideas which are all in accordance with the Principle of Progress: popular privatization, capital start, capital renewal, and the capitalist employee collective (CEC).

Popular privatization

A terrific immediate start everywhere around the world could be made by what I call Popular (or Democratic) Privatization. The basic idea is to take most or all the assets that are owned by the state, centrally or locally, anything that can be sold and turned into cash or tradable bits of paper, and give the proceeds directly to the people, to be kept and used as permanent business capital. Popular privatization is both more democratic, and more capitalist, than the privatizations with which most of us are familiar.

The first wave of privatizations, such as those practised by the British Conservative governments of 1979–97, did a very curious thing. They sold off state assets to the private sector, but then used the proceeds within the state sector. The proceeds went to the Treasury, which then promptly spent the money on providing much higher levels of welfare (in Britain, the real value of social security expenditure went up *80 per cent* between 1980 and 1995!). What the state gave up with one hand, it took back with the other.

The fact that Margaret Thatcher – long thought of as a passionate and innovative capitalist – was in practice a brilliantly successful social democrat, is a delicious irony. But the significant point is that for privatization to change the nature of capitalism, it has to avoid giving the proceeds back to the state. And it need not do so. *Popular privatization gives state assets back to the people as individuals.* It can give every citizen a lump-sum deposit that can initiate or reinforce the habit of successful saving and investment.

State businesses or other assets, especially property, are transferred to the private sector, as with conventional privatization, but the proceeds, instead of disappearing into the state coffers (where they will inevitably provide very poor value) are distributed as free shares to the population, either directly or via privatization funds owned by the public. Since nearly all states – including the United States – have massive public assets, this offers a way of giving all citizens a capital lump sum that, over time, can become important personal assets. Poland, the Czech Republic and Chile have already started to go down this road, with results that are already impressive. The long run vision is to remove all individuals from dependency on the state. Instead of 'pension-fund socialism', or 'capitalism without capitalists', we would have a world full of capitalists.

How might popular privatization work?

Every time a government asset is sold, the proceeds, either in cash or shares, are transferred to accounts earmarked for individual citizens. The most convenient way for this to work, at least initially, would be for the citizen to select a fund manager for the citizen's privatization account [6]. The fund manager would keep some or all of the privatization shares and invest the cash in other equities, so that the fund would generally be 100 per cent invested in shares. All dividends would be reinvested too. The individual would be the beneficial owner of the account, and the value of each individual's fund at any time could be checked by telephone or with an ATM card. But the individual would only be able to access the funds under certain conditions.

The conditions would vary from country to country according to the exact rules set up by the privatizing government, but most countries would probably restrict the use of funds to certain purposes like education, training, the purchase of shares in one's employer, and seed capital for starting a business: uses that would help the individual's future, rather than be dissipated in short-term consumer expenditure, and that would reinforce democratic capitalist habits. Some countries might allow certain funds to be withdrawn immediately to fund qualifying expenditure (the fund managers would only be allowed to credit qualifying recipient accounts); other countries might require the funds to be held for a minimum period. Some countries might allow funds above a certain level to be withdrawn for any purpose provided the minimum level was maintained. The fund would normally be supplemented over the first few years as new privatizations or sales of other government assets took place, so the fund, supplemented also by capital gains and reinvested dividends, could grow quite fast in the early years.

Who would the beneficiaries be? Again, this could vary from country to country. Some parties might propose to open privatization accounts for all citizens, or all those of a certain age. Other ideas would be to open privatization accounts for young people only, perhaps once they reached a certain age like

16 or 18. There could be many variations, and some governments might hold a referendum on different qualifying proposals. As long as the benefits were widely spread, any such scheme would qualify as popular privatization.

What sort of sums might be involved? A country with a state sector that has had limited privatization might be able to generate, over a few years, very high capital sums for its citizens. Another country, that has already had widespread privatization of a conventional type, like the United Kingdom, might be able to generate less via popular privatization. Nevertheless, the sums involved can be larger than one might at first think. In 1996–97, prior to the UK's election, I calculated that there were at least £25–50 billon ($40–85 billion) worth of UK state assets, including land and buildings, that could be sold off over a five year period, generating a fund of several thousand dollars apiece, perhaps appreciating within the period to $10,000 per individual, if distributed to all young people in Britain. The key to generating large returns is to sell off all state assets, including non-operational military land, airports, waterways, and the rights to everything controlled by government such as lotteries, radio frequency spectrums, and everything the government does that could be turned into a profitable business. Even the United States, which has always had a much smaller state sector than any comparable country, has a surprising number of public and quasi-public enterprises that could be sold off for very substantial sums.

Democratic capitalists should want to privatize almost everything. We could take services that are heavily subsidized by the state, such as public transport and all other social services, and privatize the service with a guarantee of a diminishing state subsidy over the next few years (say five to ten years) as a dowry on sale (minimum standards of service can also be imposed, with punitive fines for failure to reach them). This kills three birds with one stone: decreasing the public sector expenditure progressively over time; allowing 'unsalable' assets to be sold and thus increase the popular privatization kitty for individual citizens; and imposing capitalist disciplines so that consumers get a better service and society suffers less waste of resources.

I would privatize all government services, including education, health care, and ultimately even areas that have been thought unprivatizable, like the judiciary, the armed forces, and the police [7]. For social services like education and health care, the main reason to privatize is not to generate funds for popular privatization, but rather to increase standards and extend the ideal of the active and liberated individual. Education is discussed, as an illustration, in the next chapter.

Popular privatization will provide funds for individuals to help themselves become active participants in the capitalist economy, as skilled workers, entrepreneurs, or shareholders in the companies where they work. It will allow all young people, and perhaps everyone, to learn the habits of capital appreciation from investment in equities. It will include everyone in the wonderful game of capitalism.

After a time, however, the benefits of popular privatization will diminish. After 5, 10, or at the most 20 years, there will be nothing left to privatize. The privatization funds should continue to grow, through reinvestment of dividends and through capital growth; and the benefit of the funds used for education or direct investment in the individuals' businesses should continue to be felt. But the direct value of the funds will decrease, as withdrawals for approved purposes exceed the value of capital growth and dividends. At this stage, privatization funds cannot be relied upon to kick-start active capitalism for individuals. We will need other means to ensure that ordinary people have a starting capital base and are able to continue accumulating capital.

Capital start

Capital Start is an asset redistribution program to ensure that each citizen has an asset base when starting economic life, at age 16 or 18 or whatever age each society sees as appropriate. Capital Start could be funded by Popular Privatization and/or by general taxation. As with a variant of Popular Privatization we have just discussed, Capital Start funds would go into earmarked accounts and only be used for generating a useful professional start in life, for education, training or starting a business. Capital Start funds would be invested in equities until required, managed by a fund management firm selected by the individual. As with the privatization funds, all investment income would be free of tax and rolled up into the fund. Unlike most privatization funds, Capital Start funds would have to be used within a finite period for self-development or investment in the individual's business.

One attractive policy might be to link decreases in overall government expenditure – brought about by lower subsidies and reductions in social security payments – to increases in the Capital Start dividends. The state would thus be investing in the future, laying the foundations for each citizen to become active, liberated and economically independent of future state subsidy. As Capital Start raises economic activity from the new businesses it funds, and reduces unemployment, it would lead to a virtuous circle – more business wealth, lower government expenditure, reduced taxation, lower crime, greater business and personal wealth, and so on.

One neglected point is the leverage from investing in our young people. The ability or inability of each young person to establish himself or herself as an economically independent unit is a crucial determinant of the individual's future happiness and value to society. Will the young person develop into a fully active and liberated individual? Will she enrich society? Or will she impoverish it?

If the young person becomes economically independent, ceasing to be subsidized by the state or the family, all kinds of good results follow. The individual is likely to be happier, more self confident, and more responsible. The individual stops being an economic drain on others, and starts adding to social wealth. She does not cause trouble, engage in crime, require medical care or commit suicide. She is much more likely to make others happy, provide security for children and help other family members or friends. The most important points are non-economic, but the economic difference, over the life of the individual, were we but able to compute it, would be phenomenal.

Imagine the difference between a hundred people who become economically independent early in life and another 100 who do not. Imagine the wealth and happiness created by the first group. For the second group, imagine the aggregate cost to society of 100 such lifetimes, all being subsidized by society, and many imposing other heavy costs on society: some causing crime or road accidents and the huge costs of dealing with them, some becoming alcoholics or drug addicts, many causing unhappiness in others, and all the other social costs that derive, entirely or in part, from people not having the dignity and pride that follow from being able to take care of themselves economically.

If we could accurately measure the difference, or even guestimate it, the economic return on investment in Capital Start over the next 50 or 70 years would prove enormous, quite apart from the return in terms of happiness and social cohesion.

How do we make Capital Start effective? Our answer, like our answer to most policy issues, is to use the market and to experiment. How do we use the market? By paying specialized firms to supervise the administration of Capital Start, to provide advice to the individuals, and help them get established in skilled employment or their own business or one with a few similar partners. (The specialist firms would employ educationalists, industrial psychologists, venture capitalists, or communications experts – or whatever mix of personnel proved most cost-effective.) By measuring the success rate of Capital Start administered by each specialized firm and rewarding it – or firing it – accordingly. How do we maximize experimentation? By administering Capital Start on a decentralized, local basis, and by having many specialist firms provide the advice. Then the firms that are most effective can increase their business, based on demonstrated performance.

Capital renewal

Rather than provide all assistance in one splurge to young people, it would probably be sensible to also provide some help, at a reduced level, a bit later in life. Capital Renewal would provide additional funds for education, training or starting a business at specific ages, for example, on the 21st, 25th or 30th birthdays. Otherwise, the principles are the same as for Capital Start. The effectiveness of the different programs could be monitored and funds rebalanced toward the age of maximum average effectiveness. Nonetheless, because people do not mature and develop equally, and many people will need a second or third chance to establish themselves in a new career or enterprise, it will be sensible to provide Capital Renewal. The principle should be that everyone becomes economically independent, active and liberated.

The capitalist employee collective (CEC)

Not everyone will want or be able to start their own business. But there is another way for workers to become capitalists.

This is the CEC, the Capitalist Employee Collective – a new class of company where all employees are shareholders and where their shareholding increases over time, provided the firm performs well for all shareholders. My proposals for CECs can be found in Chapter 10.

Everyone an active capitalist

We have suggested new funds – Popular Privatization, Capital Start, and Capital Renewal – that will be owned by individuals but constrained by certain rules and run by professional fund management firms. But besides these funds, which are necessarily to a degree paternalistic, society should encourage direct investment in the stock market by individuals.

Why? The best way to understand something is to do it. If investment remains a black box, it will not be thought about much. Investment requires saving. Saving requires effort and discipline. For most people, saving is less fun than spending. If investment becomes a hobby as well as a means of building capital, there is likely to be more saving and investment.

Also, someone who is a capitalist through investment is more likely to become a capitalist – or at least have a capitalist mentality – at work, and more likely to vote for measures to deepen democratic capitalism.

Remember the ideal of the active and liberated individual. It is one thing for the ordinary person to own the major share of the country's business via her pension fund or her insurance policy. This is quite an indirect link, and the individual may not perceive any connection between the stock exchange hitting a new peak and her prosperity. It is quite another thing for the individual to have picked a portfolio of shares and check their prices every week or every day.

Making money through investment is a skill, but it is hardly rocket science. There are a few basic principles that any intelligent person can learn in a few hours [8]. Actually, an individual who bought, at random, 15 out of the top 30 or top 100 shares, and held them indefinitely, would be very likely to exceed the performance of most fund managers. If the person sold any share that went down by 15 per cent, and invested the proceeds in the share that had done best, the chances of beating the professional fund managers would be even better.

Most countries today discriminate against the individual investor and in favor of collective, managed funds. The individual investor usually pays high taxes on the sale of shares, even if the money is reinvested. The institutional fund usually does not. In order to encourage personal investment, the rules should be slanted the other way. Possible means include tax exemption for share dealings by individuals, no transfer tax on buying or selling shares, no tax on reinvested dividends, and no capital gains tax. States could also impose a very small tax on investment institutions in order to fund a marketing campaign to encourage individual share ownership.

Facilitating financial independence

Read a small selection of 19th century novels and you will notice a recurrent dream: that of financial independence – securing sufficient capital so that the hero or heroine can live off the income, without dependence on other people or uncongenial work [9]. It is time to revive the dream, not for the few, but for the many.

Individuals in all advanced countries in the next century will have, as a realistic objective, the attainment of financial independence before, and preferably long before, working life is over. Far from leading to greater materialism, such independence will focus people on what matters in life: using the only truly exhaustible resource we have, time, to explore one's potential, build and deepen personal relationship, and help others to be happy.

This is a matter not just of individual dreams, but of collective policy. It requires a reversal of 20th century tax policy.

A tax policy to facilitate becoming wealthy

Milton Friedman pointed out in 1962 [10] that taxes are 'much less taxes on being wealthy than on becoming wealthy. While they limit the use of the income from existing wealth, they impede even more strikingly – so far as they are effective – the accumulation of wealth.' Income taxes, he suggested, 'protect existing holders of wealth from the competition of newcomers.' This is still true a generation or two later. Despite significant reductions in average income tax rates around the world, income remains far more heavily taxed than wealth. The logic of taxing the income from wealth, while not taxing wealth itself, is perplexing. Such a policy penalizes productive wealth and subsidizes unproductive wealth. It is against basic market principles and lowers the wealth of nations.

I advocate low and flat rate income taxes reducing over time as government expenditure falls (see Chapter 11), zero taxation of reinvested investment income, zero taxation of wealth while it is accumulating up to a certain level (to be determined by each democracy according to what it can afford, with the level of zero taxation being set as high as possible, and progressively higher over time, as the need for tax reduces), modest taxation of wealth beyond this certain level, and heavy taxation of spending. This policy cocktail will encourage individual saving, individual enterprise, and individual wealth accumulation.

Pensions

Lastly, pensions. Pensions have been one of the great and unwitting forces moving society toward democratic capitalism. There is much further to go.

First, the benefits from pensions should all go to the employee, not to the firm. This would seem self evident, but pensions legislation and practice in many countries fails to deliver this basic right. Often, the pension is merely a contractual obligation to provide a certain future income based on years of service and/or final compensation, regardless of investment performance. Because of the startling increase in equity values in the past 20 years, many pension funds are 'over-funded'. This is a misnomer. A fund for the benefit of specific individuals can only be funded; it is what it is, and can never be properly under- or over- funded. What over-funding means is that the employer can legally appropriate some or all of the excess funds that were meant for the benefit of the employee. This practice is unethical – in effect it is stealing from past and present employees in order to give to shareholders – and it should stop.

Second, pensions should be administered, as far as possible, by employees themselves. This will both stop legal stealing of pension benefits by employers and also give employees closer control of their own money, and a more accurate fix on how close they are to realizing the dream of financial independence.

Third, we should make it easier for pensions to be used by the individual to increase his own productive wealth, so that the capital can be levered into more capital through the individual's direct efforts. One way of doing this is for the person working in a large corporation to be able to invest a portion of the pension capital, on favorable terms, in the corporation itself. Though this increases risk for the individual, it could also dramatically raise returns if linked to the concept of the CEC, the Capitalist Employee Collective (see above and Chapter 10). Another way, with even higher risk and potential returns, is to use part of the accumulated pension money as seed capital for a new enterprise to be pursued by the individual. Pension rules currently discourage or prohibit such use of funds.

But what is the point of a pension? Historically, the point has been to provide a cushion of funds for retirement and old age. The state usually provides some level of pension and so has a vested interest in preventing dissipation of private pension funds. In the next century, however, the point of a pension will change. It will be to provide financial independence as early as possible in life. To do this at acceptable risk, to preserve the fall-back option that the pension will prevent destitution in old age, will require skilful financial engineering. This should be a challenge to be accepted, not a devil to be avoided. Given that capital begets capital, to remove any control of the individual over her own pension capital is an act of undemocratic paternalism, stopping ordinary people from becoming wealthy and awarding a monopoly of wealth to those who are already wealthy.

Conclusion

Capitalist society only works really well if there is capital for everyone. Otherwise, society unfairly rewards the rich, restricts social mobility, and encourages ordinary people, as workers and voters, to fetter and reduce the power of capital.

Today we have some capital for most people. But the capital is mainly inaccessible and often invisible. It is trapped within pension funds, insurance policies and other opaque instruments of wealth. Making people's wealth obscure makes it less powerful, both as a means of leverage and as an incentive to save more. Even worse, those who control the wealth, employers and pension funds, sometimes abuse their control to enrich themselves at the expense of the ordinary employee. That such abuse is nearly always legal, and often just skimming at the edges – via unjustified charges by fund managers – should not obscure its unethical and undemocratic character.

Tomorrow we need capital for everyone. Capital accumulation for the people and by the people. Universal participation in society's amazing capacity to generate wealth. Universal capitalism to match universal suffrage.

The rules of today's society discourage capital accumulation by ordinary people. Taxes do not restrict wealth; they restrict becoming wealthy. Knowledge, culture and popular attitudes do the rest. Elsewhere, society properly outlaws monopoly. The rich are different. They are allowed to preserve their monopoly of wealth.

The rules preventing wealth accumulation must be removed. But that will not be enough. We need to move from restricting wealth accumulation. But we also need to facilitate it. Happily, popular privatization – selling government businesses and property assets – can give us a head start.

Giving every young person a capital start is essential. The cost will be high. The benefit will be astronomical.

Capital is one part of the equation. Talent, motivation and the opportunity to work is the other essential part. To this we now turn.

Endnotes

1   Lester Thurow (1996) *The Future of Capitalism*, New York, William Morrow/London, Nicholas Brealey, p. 243.

2   Karl Marx (1867) *Capital*, Volume One, first English translation of 1887, section headed Results of the Immediate Process of Production, Oxford University Press edition of 1995.

3   See Lowell Bryan and Diana Farrell (1996) *Market Unbound*, New York, John Wiley & Sons, p. 237. They report that from 1925 to 1994 inclusive, US equities earned a real rate of return of 6.9 per cent, long-term Treasury bonds a real return of 1.7 per cent per annum, and 3-month Treasury bonds only 0.5 per cent per annum. Total returns by 1994 for one US dollar invested in 1925 were $3.10 in real dollars ($26 nominal) for long-term Treasury bonds, but $97 in real dollars (a stunning $810 in nominal dollars) for stocks – that is, over 30 times higher for the stocks compared to the bonds. Since 1994, the performance of equities has been even more stunningly favorable.

4   Peter F. Drucker (1993) *Post-Capitalist Society*, New York, Harper-Collins.

5   Adolf A. Berle Jr and Gardiner C. Means (1932) *The Modern Corporation and Private Property*, New York, The Macmillan Company.

6   There are some objections to using fund managers rather than having the individuals themselves invest the money. In future democratic capitalist society, fund managers will be largely or totally unnecessary, because individuals will have the knowledge to invest their own funds. Also, the concentration of power in the hands of fund managers goes against the Democratic Principle, even though the fund managers are selected by the individual beneficiaries. It should be a high priority to train the latter to use capital effectively, and at this stage – which is easier to attain than is generally imagined – we can dispense with the paternalistic but initially essential requirement to have experts invest the peoples' funds.

7   This may seem controversial, but I firmly believe that the public good,

both in terms of value of money and quality of service, and perhaps even more importantly in terms of civil rights, will best be served by having the greatest possible number of functions run either by accountable commercial organizations or by accountable non-profit organizations. The key is to create a large number of local, specialist organizations that are subject to periodic removal by local voters if they do not perform. Already this principle has been partially applied, successfully, for a long time in the United States, where some law and police offices are subject to local popular election. No one has seriously tried to test out how far this principle could be pushed in practice. There is still a great deal of practical thinking to be done, but there can be no doubt which direction best serves liberty and prosperity.

8   Richard Koch (1994, 1997) *The Investor's Guide to Selecting Shares That Perform*, London, Pitman.

9   Most of the novels of Jane Austen, William Makepeace Thackeray, Charles Dickens, Charlotte Brontë and George Eliot make great play of the interplay between love and financial calculation, where characters are divided clearly into those who already have financial independence, and those who do not, but hope via work (if they are men) or marriage (if they are women) to attain it. See for example Thackeray's *Vanity Fair* (1848), where the scheming Becky Sharp, an orphan and penniless governess, sets about making herself invaluable to the rich Crawley family. In contrast to modern novels, where much often revolves around the relentless search for upward mobility, where those who are well off always want more money, the 19th century aspiration is to have enough capital to live off its income without work or worry. This is a more sensible goal, and one that is undergoing a revival and also being stripped of its more gross materialism. The very recent concept of *downward mobility* is that personal success lies in establishing independence as a worker, and that beyond this point spending has little value, and conspicuous consumption none at all.

10   Milton Friedman (1962) *Capitalism and Freedom*, Chicago, The University of Chicago Press, p. 173.

Chapter Nine

Knowledge and Jobs for Everyone

The first, and perhaps crucial, evidence that capitalism is not going to continue much longer is the continuous presence within the capitalist nations of mass unemployment *and the failure of all means tried of getting rid of [it].*

— James Burnham in 1941 [1]

Summary

- Knowledge is the key to valuable work. To diffuse knowledge and skill universally requires market-based education for all.
- We will turn all schools into autonomous and competing educational corporations, some for-profit and some not.
- Educational experiments reveal that some educational methods are thousands of times better than others. To experiment and copy successful experiments requires a system with many different methods and in-built incentives to adopt the best methods.
- Full employment is quite possible. Instead of restricting markets, we will use markets to engineer full employment. Experimentation will reveal the best market mechanisms. Probably, micro-credit, franchising and marketized jobs will prove key ingredients. If all else fails, marketized workfare will not.

Introduction

The Market Principle suggests that we organize education and job provision along market lines; this is the only way to achieve the best possible results.

The Democratic Principle states that society should be run for the benefit of everyone and by everyone, and that we must look to the common good. The Principle of Inclusion requires that everyone feels part of the same society. These two Principles are incompatible with a division of society into those who are well educated and have jobs, and those who are not well educated and experience long periods of unemployment.

The Knowledge Principle states that society must raise the skill level of all citizens and ensure that everybody attains a certain minimum level of useful skill.

Taken together therefore the Principles of Progress require market-based solutions to provide education and jobs for everyone who wants to work. Can we think of ways to attain these? The ideas here represent a start. Readers are asked to test, refine, and add to them.

Providing knowledge and work are related imperatives

In developed economies today, roughly four out of every ten workers are (and soon five out of ten will be) knowledge workers, people who use knowledge to produce goods or services. This 40 or 50 per cent of the workforce produce perhaps 80 or 90 per cent of valued output, and are increasingly paid accordingly. The other half or so in developed countries, and the overwhelming majority in developing ones, are unskilled laborers: blue collar workers, menial service providers, domestic servants, and, in agricultural countries, peasants. Both real equality in society, and the creation of greater wealth, require the continued elimination of unskilled jobs – which, when wages reach civilized levels, machines can do better and cheaper – and the extension of knowledge work to virtually all workers. Creating this knowledge and this work is the only way to a rich and fully democratic society, and only the market – liberated as never before – can create the knowledge and the work.

Being a knowledge worker plainly requires two things: knowledge and work. It also requires specialization. Outside of quiz programs, there is no such thing as the general knowledge worker. Specialization requires knowing where to specialize. So we need to create huge quantities of three things: knowledge, work, and insight for individuals so they know where to specialize. If we look back at the past three centuries there has been a vast explosion in knowledge, work, and specialization. It is still not enough. We need much more of all three, much more extensively and democratically spread throughout society.

The potential for improvement is enormous. We have not yet deployed the phenomenal power of the market to proliferate knowledge, jobs and specialization.

The really difficult part in creating knowledge and knowledge work is not for the first fifth, two fifths or even three fifths of the relevant population. It is making knowledge and knowledge work prevalent throughout society – in making 80, 90 or 95 per cent of workers knowledge workers. At root this is not a problem of creating useful knowledge work. It is a problem of creating useful knowledge workers, of extending knowledge and the wish to deploy marketable knowledge throughout the population. This means that we must pay particular attention to the losers and potential losers in society.

Historically, capitalism has been very poor at this, and democratic capitalism requires social engineering – a new type of social engineering, based on the market – to correct capitalism's natural tendency to leave the unlucky behind. Interestingly enough, Friedrich Hayek, incorrectly thought of as a heartless advocate of laissez-faire capitalism, recognized the need to help capitalism's casualties: [2]

> ... in a system of free enterprise chances are not equal, since such a system
> is necessarily based on private property and (though not perhaps with the
> same necessity) on inheritance, with the differences in opportunity which
> these create. There is indeed a strong case for reducing this inequality of
> opportunity as fast as congenital differences permit and as it is possible to

do so without destroying the impersonal character of the process by which everybody has to take his chance and no person's view about what is right and desirable overrules that of others.

Hayek did not say how. I will provide some clues.

Knowledge and skills for everyone

Market-based education

If we want knowledge and skills for everyone, the only way to realize this is by market-based education available to everyone.

Everyone knows that standards of education vary enormously. What is needed is this: first, identify the reasons and the key levers to pull to get exceptional results; second, decentralization, and third, competition. Only a market system can pull the key levers, decentralize, and enforce competition.

Research has proved that different schools and different teaching methods can have enormously different results. A Brookings Institute study [3] of 500 US high schools found that some schools were dramatically better. The difference was not found in the usual suspects: teacher salaries, spend per student, class size, or graduation requirements. What mattered were parental control of the school, the clarity of its mission, its leadership, the freedom and respect enjoyed by the teachers, and its autonomy.

Very few schools aim to maximize, or even encourage, these desiderata. In fact, most state school systems largely rule them out: autonomy for the school and control by teachers and parents are impossible. Yet decentralization is imperative if we are to get the best possible results in each school. Each country should have thousands or even hundreds of thousands of autonomous educational establishments, each a local democracy under control of parents, students and teachers.

The autonomous educational corporation – competing against others

Imagine this. Each state school or college becomes a separate, autonomous, democratic corporation, controlled by its teachers, students and/or parents. Teachers vote on whether to incorporate as a for-profit or non-profit corporation. In either case, the school competes for students. These are funded by vouchers from the state, either issued free or as soft loans, and by private 'topping-up'. Good schools attract many students, and have the funds to expand. Bad schools cannot continue. They either have to improve, agree to takeover, or close. Good schools expand by mutual agreement or on the vote of parents and students.

Competition shakes up teachers and their teaching methods. As Milton Friedman says [4], under non-market systems, good teachers are grossly underpaid and bad teachers grossly overpaid. The market now corrects this. Good teachers are in great demand and schools are forced to pay them what they are worth. New and more entrepreneurial teachers come into the market. Poor teachers raise their game or retire.

Decentralization and competition lead to experimentation and new teaching methods. Already, there are stunning differences in performance with different techniques. As we deploy best teaching practice, we quickly transform not just education but society too.

Some existing teaching techniques are documented and celebrated in a terrific book, *The Learning Revolution*, by Gordon Dryden and Jeannette Vos. For example: [5]

- in Flaxmere, New Zealand, backward 11-year-olds, up to five years behind their peers, are catching up within ten weeks, using a tape-assisted reading program
- in a US army trial, soldiers using techniques explained in the book learned German over six times as easily as normal, achieving more than twice the results in one-third of the time
- Bridley Moor High School in England uses accelerated learning techniques for foreign languages. Under normal methods, only 11 per cent of stu-

dents score at least 80 out of 100. Under the new methods, 65 per cent did. Under normal methods, only 3 per cent got 90 out of 100 or better; under the new methods, 38 per cent scored 90+ – ten times as many!

Increasingly inexpensive and seductive technology makes learning easier and cheaper, more accessible for those with learning disabilities and for students who are simply behind their peers. Techniques are tailored to individual students who are increasingly liberated from the need for constant supervision by a teacher or even for a class room.

Schools today have a vested interest to *resist* the spread of these techniques, which threaten not just traditional and comfortable routines but also teachers' jobs. They even threaten the institution of the school itself. Given new technology – and even old technology, like the television – why should the school or college be the exclusive, or even the main, center of education?

The history of business has shown that creating markets and competition is the only way to get new technology developed, diffused, and very widely used. Without competition, there will be small islands of excellence and vast continents of mediocrity. Competition alone can get demonstrated techniques used widely. A market education system alone can generate the funds for investing in new techniques, and ensure the best mix of buildings, capital equipment, software, teachers, educationalists, psychologists and leaders, whose job is to unlock the motivation to learn.

Education must excite

The education industry is unique in the extent to which it depends for its output on the ability to capture the imagination and commitment of its consumers. To transport goods does not require the collaboration of the packages transported. To transport people requires some low level of collaboration: the passengers must board the train or plane, sit in their seats, fasten their seatbelts, and get off when required. In education, the collaboration between student and instructor is pivotal. This is not primarily a matter of social conditioning or behavior. It is mainly a question of excitement. Someone who wants to learn and is excited by the subject and the way it is communicated will not just learn 10 or 20 per cent easier, faster or cheaper than a student who is conscientious but unexcited. The difference will be measured in the hundreds or thousands of per cent.

Competition will focus much more attention – hundreds or thousands of times more attention – on how to excite each type of student for each type of study. Marketing will enter education, not just in the gross sense of advertising results (though there is a place for this), but mainly to make learning exciting and relevant to students who have hitherto reserved their creativity and energy for non-scholastic pursuits. The same skills that sell McDonald's hamburgers and Sega computer games to children everywhere around the world will be used to redirect imagination and effort into expanding the mind.

Specialization

Many more decentralized learning units will mean much greater specialization. Successful consumer product markets, where goods have constantly become better and cheaper, have left standardization behind long ago. New niches have arisen, tailored products grown, cheap distinctiveness flourished. Education, not being thought of as a consumer product, and not being organized into markets, has lagged behind. Yet nowhere is specialization, niching, fragmentation and customization so appropriate as in education. We know now that there are many different types of intelligence and many different ways to make individuals motivated, proud, productive and useful to others.

We cannot create a society of free and equal citizens unless each individual has the dignity and usefulness that comes from having a marketable skill, from having useful knowledge. Everyone can achieve something significant. The key is not effort, but finding the right thing to achieve. You know that you are hugely more productive at some things than at others. The same is true of your neighbor. If we had 15 or 30 different types of school (and infinite gradations or mixes from the 15 or 30 basic types) there is a much greater probability that each individual would be able to develop into a knowledge worker of some variety.

Market-based education facilitates so many other links between the individual, the school (or whatever learning establishment replaces the school) and the world of business. At one level, this is simply the vested interest that exists between for-profit schools and employers. As with American business schools, which are more and more commercial in their marketing and operation, great effort will be put into out-placement and cultivating links with employers. The real payoff comes, however, when there is a close and continuous relationship between local schools and local businesses.

If the purpose of an educational establishment is to make people specialized knowledge workers, then the imperative and opportunity to link up with the right sort of specialized business becomes so much more apparent and available. If the system is lubricated by market demand and rewards, the links and their value are likely to multiply. There may come a time when certain businesses, great and small, become as a matter of course not just benefactors of schools but also, and more usefully, shareholders in them, not for the investment benefit, but for access to skilled and enthusiastic knowledge workers.

Vocational guidance – early and often

Few people know what they are really good at doing. At almost any age it is a good investment, both for the individual and society, to undertake psychological tests that help point them in the right direction. The tests are only signposts. Introspection and experienced advice are necessary too. But how much more valuable at an early stage, so that the young student can go to a specialized school to obtain specialized knowledge? Along with educational vouchers, it will be an excellent investment for the state to issue vocational guidance vouchers.

Helping the losers

Democracy is only successful if there is no underclass. This is not primarily a matter of having jobs available. The jobs must be there. But the key thing is to have the skills to fill them. Wealth and dignity require skill even more than they require jobs.

In South Africa, the ANC government faces a huge unemployment problem. But education, not jobs, is the root issue. A large part of the population, deprived during the apartheid years of proper education, does not have the skills necessary for any but the most menial forms of employment. Education and skill development are necessary first steps. There have been major moves toward so-called 'black empowerment', which in practice means transferring nominal ownership of parts of South African business to a very small (and now very rich) black elite. Any real empowerment of the non-white population must await massive training and education initiatives.

How do we empower the unempowered? There is only one way to do it properly. It is to use the market. If there is a social task to be performed, create buying power among the people who need help, and leave the market to fill the consumers' needs.

In developed societies with a small but recalcitrant minority of losers, we need specialist enterprises who get paid for results, in retraining and endowing the losers, in giving them marketable skills. The cost per individual will be high. The benefit for society will be even higher. The firms should be rewarded on a geometric sliding scale, where a 90 per cent success rate, for example, merits twice the return of 80 per cent success, and a 95 per cent rate twice the 90 per cent level. The test both of the compassion and the viability of democratic-capitalist society is making useful and proud knowledge workers out of those previously written off as losers.

Jobs for everyone

The democratic-capitalist society will return to the earlier ideal of full employment and make it work in changed circumstances by doing something new: using the market to the fullest possible extent to remove unemployment. The market allows and thrives on local experimentation. Experiments in different countries and in a huge number of places within each country – in states or shires, in cities and towns – will indicate the best solutions. The market will ensure the diffusion of those solutions, providing some entrepreneurs and corporations with incentives to create and deploy the best solutions.

The state will be responsible for setting up the market arrangements and ensuring that they reach the goal of full employment without raising inflation. Such is the ingenuity of entrepreneurs and the surprise inherent in the market, that the suggestions made below may bear little resemblance to the policies eventually adopted. But here are some ideas, offered as illustrations of possible market solutions.

Employment Creation Co-ordinators (ECCs)

What if, everywhere around the world, countries appoint a large number of Employment Creation Co-ordinators (ECCs)? These are commercial firms under contract to improve the level of employment in a particular region, each contract covering a few hundred thousand people up to a million.

The firms (the ECCs) which compete for contracts could be very small, comprising a few professionals working on just one project, or very large, winning many contracts – the market will decide the most appropriate size and type of contractor. Each local government unit puts the first Employment Creation Co-ordination contract out to tender and appoints the firm with the best proposal. The ECC may or may not be paid a small retainer – this is up to the local government unit offering the contract – but the ECC makes its profit out of the results. If employment hits certain agreed targets, the firm is paid progressively more. The contract lasts for five years but either side, the local authority or the firm, may withdraw from the contract with six months' notice. After five years, or whenever the contract is terminated, a new tender is issued. Any firm can tender for the new contract, and, over time, the most effective firms gain a high market share of contracts nationally or internationally.

The role of the Employment Creation Co-ordinator is not to employ people itself, but to find ways that will create employment, either by direct initiatives itself – such as launching an inward investment program ('inward' here meaning into the small area covered, attracting firms perhaps from around the world, but perhaps also from down the road, the adjacent region covered by another Employment Creation Co-ordinator – free competition will be encouraged!) – or by acting as a catalyst for initiatives by the local authority, local voluntary groups, and local free enterprise.

Local entrepreneurship and the Good Banker

A key plank of any local employment creation campaign is the creation of new entrepreneurial ventures. Instead of being a welfare recipient, the unemployed person becomes an entrepreneur or partner in a new business. The key is to encourage micro-business, where it would not normally arise.

It so happens that this is not as difficult as one might imagine. There is already a wonderful model that works.

To eliminate poverty from the developing world, rather than to stimulate employment, Muhammad Yunus, an economics professor from Bangladesh, invented the idea of 'micro-credit' [6]. Micro-credit means lending very small amounts of money to very poor people so that they can start a micro-business. Over the past 25 years, Yunus has built the largest rural bank, the Grameen Bank, in Bangladesh, which now has over 2 million borrowers and lends around $1 billion a year. The World Bank has assessed Grameen favorably, and verified that within five years Grameen helped about half its borrowers, a million people, pull themselves out of poverty.

The idea is terribly simple. Loans from as little as $40 are made to the destitute. The typical borrower is a divorced or widowed woman, forced to beg to feed her family, who may never have handled money before. With the loan she buys an asset – cotton to weave, raw materials for bangles, a calf for fattening, a small rice field, or goats, ducks or chickens – anything that can be used to generate income. This is necessary, because loans have to start being repaid from the second week. Eventually, she repays the loan and becomes a self-sufficient micro-capitalist.

It is all based on self-help and mutual help, the landless, assetless rural poor and downtrodden helping themselves and each other to become active and liberated individuals. Though he does not express it this way, Yunus has proved that even the very poor want to, and can, become entrepreneurs and capitalists, bootstrapping their way to economic independence. His bank provides no training or education; it relies on releasing the spark of creativity inherent in everyone. Says Yunus:

I firmly believe that all human beings have an innate skill. The fact that the poor are alive is proof of their ability. We do not need to teach them how to survive: they know this already. Giving the poor credit allows them to put into practice the skills they already know. And the cash they earn is then a tool, a key that unlocks a host of other problems.

Poverty covers people in a thick crust and makes the poor appear stupid and without initiative. Yet if you give them credit, they will slowly come back to life. Even those who seemingly have no conceptual thought, no ability to think of yesterday or tomorrow, are in fact quite intelligent and expert at survival. Credit is the key that unlocks their humanity.

Yunus' formative experience was field work in 1975–76 when he interviewed 42 women villagers who made bamboo stools. They had to borrow the equivalent of 25 US cents to buy the bamboo for each stool and ended up receiving less than 2 cents net for each stool because nearly all the value added went in interest. Yunus again:

Their poverty was not a personal problem due to laziness or lack of intelligence, but a structural one: lack of capital. The existing system made it certain that the poor could not save a penny and could not invest in bettering themselves. Some money-lenders set interest rates as high as 10 per cent a month, some 10 per cent a week. So, no matter how hard these people worked, they would never raise themselves above subsistence level. What was needed was to link their work to capital to allow them to amass an economic cushion and earn a ready income.

Grameen's lending works like this. Only the destitute can apply, and men are discouraged. Women comprise 94 per cent of the borrowers because Grameen found they are more careful about their debts and the benefit to whole families is greater; interestingly, women in Bangladesh are also the most oppressed and have the least economic opportunity. The borrowers must join up with four fellow borrowers, each from a separate family, to form a 'group', which is then liable for each others' debts. Each borrower must take an oral test to show that she understands the principles of Grameen, and must pledge to abide by 'the 16 decisions', such as sending her children to school. Loans and repayments are made weekly at 'center meetings', comprising eight or ten groups (40 or 50 borrowers). Loans are at 20 per cent simple interest for a year. Bad debts are low because of the peer pressure and support, and the bank now makes a small profit. The bank follows democratic–capitalist principles in that it is almost wholly owned by its borrowers, who receive a share along with their loan.

Can micro-credit work in developed countries?

Grameen is being replicated in over 50 countries, including the United States, where there are more than 500 similar banks. Bill Clinton has hailed Yunus as worthy of a Nobel Peace Prize and the micro-credit model as a way to rebuild America's inner cities. In Englewood, a crack-ridden Chicago ghetto, the South Shore Bank runs the Full Circle Fund, lending to welfare mothers. Taking out loans from $400, they make jewelry, rehabilitate buildings, open daycare centers, bookstores or beauty salons, anything to generate a return. It is said that the women weep for joy when they inform the authorities that they no longer need welfare.

If given the chance, poor people make very good capitalists. This is how it was in the Great Depression of the 1930s in the United States; even when capital was least available, those poor people who obtained it were able to escape unemployment and many of today's successful businesses were founded then. The problem of the underclass within capitalist countries like the United States, Britain or France is not that capitalism requires the poor or makes people poor; it is that the poor have been excluded from capitalism. To be a capitalist requires capital. Capital, even more than education, is the vital ingredient denied to the poor. This is true in America, true in Europe, true in Africa, true in Asia.

Of course, the evidence is not universally favorable. Grameen–type schemes have worked in American black ghettos, on Indian reservations, in rural Arkansas, in Albania and Bosnia – wherever there is enough group solidarity to provide mutual support among borrowers. They have not worked very well in

Paris and some Asian and African cities, where there does not appear to be enough social fabric left, where the homeless have no neighbors or group identity.

Grameen-type banks have probably suffered from an excess of idealism and a deficit of market mentality. There would probably be more, and even more successful, micro-credit banks if they were run to generate ever-increasing profits for shareholders. Doing good is good business in more than one sense.

Credit as a means to the universal entrepreneur

Micro-credit or not-so-micro-credit need not necessarily be constrained within the Grameen model. Micro-credit need not just be for the very poor and the most downtrodden. The entrepreneurial model has always provided opportunity for the relatively affluent: the skilled, the educated, those who already have some capital, the downsized or retired executive, the middle-class housewife who sets up a hairdressing business, the smart and well-educated drop-out nerd like Bill Gates who turns his enthusiasm for software into a business. In the last generation, Grameen has proved that the very poor can become entrepreneurs.

There is still a lot of middle ground between the extremes of Grameen and Gates. The principles of entrepreneurship – individuals' desire to become economically independent, the liberating role of capital, the suppressed creativity and business sense of almost everyone – apply everywhere along the spectrum from destitution to affluence. The best way of dealing with unemployment is to make the unemployed entrepreneurs. This is best for the individuals, best for the economy, best for taxpayers, best for democracy, best for a cohesive society. There are two ways to ensure that the unemployed become entrepreneurs. One is to provide capital. The other is to reduce or remove welfare. This may sound harsh, but remember what Yunus says: the poor are survivors.

Franchising can make millions of entrepreneurs

How do we do this? There are many ways, not all of them obvious, but all of them deriving from the same principles of decentralization and descaling of big business. For instance, take a concept like franchising. Franchising is not a new idea, but will be one of the most important ways of unlocking wealth and improving service over the next 25 years. I have seen unprofitable retail outlets – in this case, supermarkets in South Africa – turned into very profitable businesses by being handed over to individuals and families who become franchisees. Everyone benefits. The company with the brand and the infrastructure liberates capital and turns its losses into profits. The individual entrepreneur ceases to be unemployed or under-employed by a big company. The customers get better service and longer shopping hours. The investors make good returns. Wealth is created because individuals are liberated and working for themselves.

Now, throughout Africa, basic supermarkets are being set up where none existed before. Many are franchised to blacks who were previously employees or even unemployed. Distribution and availability of food is improved, groceries are cheaper, new businesses are created, wealth proliferates. Some of the benefit would exist even if the stores were not franchised. But much greater benefit, for individuals and society, is created with franchising. The habits of capitalism become spread throughout the population; the energies of people are released for the benefit of their families and their customers.

Franchising, incidentally, is one of the great business secrets of our time. Almost every retail business, every bank, and every restaurant chain, that has a good brand and business formula, could raise its profits and reduce the capital base needed to support the profits by franchising. Entrepreneurial energy is released. Large company structures implode. Franchising is real decentralization and (a very rare phenomenon) real empowerment. Franchising is often resisted by senior executives because it takes power away from them; their 'own' operations contract; they own less and directly control less. But large organizations that decide to franchise some or all of their retail outlets generally see a profit explosion. In Australia, Colonial State Bank started in 1997 to franchise 60 of its branches [7]. If all the world's banks followed suit, as they may be forced to do by competition, think how many new entrepreneurs would be created. There must be hundred of thousands or even millions of bank branches in the world. Branded retail outlets of all sorts certainly run into millions and probably tens of millions.

Providing capital not welfare

Starting capital can be provided by Grameen-ish banks. But there is also a role for the state, to switch funds from welfare or to use other taxes or assets in order to provide every individual with starting capital.

The great thing about capital is that it is not jealous of other capital. Any venture capitalist will tell you that commitment and results are greatest when the budding entrepreneur puts up some of her own capital, even if this is a small proportion of the total, as long as its loss is enough to hurt her. It is therefore important that everyone, especially poor people, have some capital to contribute towards their own new business. *Capital Start* and *Capital Renewal* programs have been described in the last chapter, the principle being that the state sells its assets or levies taxes to fund the provision of seed capital to every young person.

The capital will often, perhaps usually, need supplementing, which is where commercial banks and venture capitalists come in. It may be sensible for these providers sometimes to provide capital only where groups of individuals guarantee each others' obligations, along the lines used by Grameen. What is likely is that we will need new financial institutions to provide debt and equity finance to new entrepreneurs. What happens if these institutions do not spring up spontaneously, or if they cannot make a good return on their capital?

The Republic of Demos conquers unemployment – and lowers taxes

The answer, as always, is to use the market. Let's assume that there is a small country or community of ten million people. Let's call it Demos. Assume further that Demos has an unemployment rate of ten per cent, one million people. Demos privatizes its state industry and sells state land to raise 30 billion dollars, and it gives all citizens $3000. Average earnings in Demos are $20,000 per annum and the unemployed each receive $10,000 per annum in welfare benefits, costing the Demos treasury $10 billion per annum.

The unemployed, and those coming fresh to the employment market, each have, like everyone else in Demos, $3000 in earmarked funds that can only be used as seed capital or for retraining. But let us assume that it takes an average of $5000 to start a new business. Then $2 billion is required in venture capital for businesses started by the unemployed. Is this forthcoming from the private sector? Because of the risk, the venture capitalists in Demos require an annual average return on their money, after taking account of the cost of default, of 30 per cent per annum. They calculate that the business they can write will return only 15 per cent. They sit on their money, or use it to develop businesses that already exist. There are still ten million unemployed.

What should the government of Demos, a most enlightened state, do? It should use the market to remove unemployment. Assume the only way to do this is by making the unemployed entrepreneurs. Then they should invite venture capitalists to tender for the lowest possible subsidy in providing capital to the unemployed. The market clears, on average, at a 15 per cent subsidy, to give the venture capitalists their required 30 per cent rate of return. This costs Demos $300m per annum. But, assuming that just 75 per cent of the freshly self-employed remain, on average at any time, employed rather than unemployed (because many of the new businesses will fail), the Demos exchequer will be saving $7.5 billion per annum in welfare payments. The arithmetic demonstrates, that at almost any subsidy required by the venture capitalists, and any reasonable rate at which the newly self-employed become unemployed again through the failure of their business, the state saves money through making the unemployed capitalists.

Of course, there are difficulties. Not all the unemployed will think of new businesses they can create (though, if unemployment pay is phased out, most probably will eventually). Even more of a problem, we do not have venture capital organizations that are interested or experienced in providing small amounts of capital to a large number of individuals. The cost of evaluating and monitoring the investments would be very high relative to the potential returns. Venture capitalists know, or think they know, that there is no profit in this. This just means that there need to be innovative means to reduce both risk and administrative costs. Grameen Bank does not assess the business proposition or creditworthiness of its applicants. It uses the group structure and mutual liability for debts amongst the small group, which produces a very high rate of repayment. In developed countries, unemployment is so expensive for the state, that there are plenty of funds available to lubricate the market. The key is to use the market in two ways: to make the unemployed entrepreneurs, and to make it worthwhile for profit-maximizing fund providers to provide any gap between seed capital and necessary total capital.

So far, we have focussed purely on making the unemployed entrepreneurs. We have argued for a mass campaign to provide capital and self-employment. But this won't remove all unemployment. We'll need other market-based solutions, like marketized jobs.

Marketized jobs

In a market economy, unemployment means that there are too few jobs at the prevailing pay level. Classical theory would suggest that the price of jobs should fall until the market clears. This does not happen, because employers are not able to reduce the pay of existing jobs, and because job seekers in receipt of welfare will not take wages below a certain level. So we have the absurd position that the unemployed are robbed of dignity and see their skills and marketability atrophy further, while society pays heavily for zero output. Social capital is dissipated.

There is a way round this impasse, and that is to lower the price of jobs another way: by 'marketizing' jobs.

If there are too few jobs, we should lower the price of jobs by having the state pay subsidies to employers. This has been done, with mixed results, at the fringes of the employment market, for example for school-leavers, whom employers have sometimes been able to hire at very low cost. The trouble with these schemes is that they are usually opportunistic and short-term on both sides. Properly marketized jobs should involve more substantial commitments from both employer and employee.

Unemployed people should be able to *buy employment* from companies. In place of unemployment benefit, the state provides a substantial lump sum or an annuity to the unemployed individual enabling her to buy a long term employment contract from an employer. Here's the bargain. The prospective employee and employer agree an initial job specification and they both agree to be flexible if the role needs to change. The employee then hands over the lump sum or the annuity (let's call it the dowry) to the employer. In return, the employer guarantees employment for five or ten years, subject to satisfactory performance by the employee. If later the firm no longer needs the particular job for which the individual was originally engaged, it would have to provide an alternative job and appropriate training. If the firm later dismissed the employee, the relevant portion of the dowry would have to be returned.

Clearly there would have to be safeguards, to ensure, for example, that companies teetering on the edge of bankruptcy did not use the dowries to stay afloat. And some firms would go out of business during the period anyway, so the state would have wasted part of the dowry. But marketized jobs use the market to adjust the price of jobs without disturbing existing relationships. If unemployment quickly receded towards vanishing point, the marketized job scheme could be suspended or the dowry reduced. If unemployment fell but then persisted at a certain level, the dowry would need to be increased. There might also need to be higher dowries for those with no qualifications or skills; but this investment by society would be justified. Clearly, if unemployment pay is reallocated to buying jobs, the total amount of production in society can be greater – and capital further accumulated – with no extra spending.

Changes in tax policy to encourage employment

Most new jobs now come from small companies. Democratic–capitalist governments would therefore encourage small businesses to the extent necessary, together with other policies, to reduce unemployment to negligible levels. If necessary, businesses below a certain size could be exempted from all taxes, from corporation tax and sales tax. Capital and loans to start small businesses could also be exempted from taxes, so that investment income and capital gains from the new business would be tax free for the initial investors. Small business should also be exempted from all but the most necessary regulations.

The taxman could also encourage employment by encouraging *Sabbatical years off*, so that every fifth or seventh year employees had a year free to do whatever they wanted. Measures to encourage Sabbaticals include a lower rate of corporate tax for Sabbatical employers and tax refunds to employees (for example, by refunding one fifth or one seventh of taxes).

Removing rigidities that depress employment

Democratic capitalism will also raise the number of jobs over time by phasing out the institutional rigidities that depress employment. Unemployment and welfare benefits will be lowered and eventually removed. Social on-costs – the amount employers must pay to the state or insurance companies for employees' social security – will also be reduced and/or abolished. Trade union privileges will be removed as soon as they are no longer necessary to protect individuals. Corporation tax will be cut.

City-based projects

Cities are typically centers of great employment and great unemployment, serious wealth and serious deprivation. City government typically has considerable powers of patronage, the right to allow or prohibit development, to grant licences, and a whole variety of other powers. Local businesses, especially those involved in retailing and distribution, and all residents, have a strong vested interest in the quality of city life, in keeping crime, drugs and homelessness at bay. Local government should therefore co-opt local businesses and volunteers, and use its powers of patronage, to provide training and work experience in the private sector for the unemployed.

Marketized workfare

A final new policy is marketized workfare. Imagine that people who are still unemployed and don't take advantage of any other scheme are invited to join one of a number of approved workfare projects organized by private sector firms. Each individual is free to refuse, but then forfeits unemployment pay and other welfare benefits.

Each local government unit – on as decentralized a basis as possible, with the unit being the same one that appoints the Employment Creation Co-ordinator (see above, p. 199) – licences a small number of competing Work Organizer companies. The companies tender for a subsidy of so much per person to be taken on to their books, and each local authority appoints between two and five firms, based on the lowest tenders and their track records in providing good work.

The Work Organizer companies either act as agencies, hiring out temporary or permanent manpower, or as direct providers of products or services themselves. Each Work Organizer company has to pay its clients (the previously unemployed) a minimum wage set by the local authority, for the period of the contract (usually annual), regardless of demand for their services. But each Work Organizer company is free to pay above the minimum level and to introduce whatever incentive schemes it wants to provide extra income for employees in return for high productivity.

Some Work Organizer companies are divisions of the big employment agencies; others specialize in particular industries; others again are generalists. Some are small and local, others large and global. Those who perform best and make the most profit naturally expand the fastest.

Conceptually, marketized workfare is not far removed from marketized jobs. Marketized workfare is the wholesale provider of jobs and also the provider of last resort. The subsidies required for employing each individual would tend to be higher under marketized workfare than marketized jobs, and therefore it would be in the interests of the local authorities and their Employment Creation Co-ordinators to have more employment provided via marketized jobs than marketized workfare.

Back to full employment

All of these moves will generate a virtuous circle in which the natural rate of unemployment can be reduced to the very low levels observed in the 1950s, while (as then) also maintaining very low inflation. Individuals will have dignity, choice, security and money; there will be far more entrepreneurs; employers will have an incentive to invest in retraining and developing their long term employees; output will go up; society will waste no more money on encouraging idleness; and the total cost for society in subsidies will fall.

The key is using the market to clear unemployment, so that the ideal of the active and liberated individual can be universal throughout society. From the very poor to the not so poor, everyone must be given a chance to make capitalism work for them at work.

Conclusion

The four Principles of Progress require a revolution in our thinking about education and employment. The Democratic Principle and the Principle of Inclusion require that everyone in society has a good education and the availability of a fulfilling job. The Knowledge Principle points out that useful knowledge is the route to a wealthy and happy society. The Market Principle says that we will only achieve these results by setting up new markets in education and jobs.

When we go from the Principles to specific policies, we find that the Principles open up a whole new range of ideas that should be tested in the market by experience.

Market-based education can provide knowledge and skills for everyone. By giving teachers and educationalists the incentive to perform, by changing the composition of the teaching profession, by giving each school and college autonomy and accountability to their consumers, by empowering all the consumers with purchasing power, by using teaching methods which are several times as effective as traditional methods, by exciting and enlisting the active collaboration of all those who learn, by encouraging specialization in useful skills, by providing vocational guidance early and often, and above all by helping the losers, we ensure that all citizens of working age become fulfilled knowledge workers.

Market-based employment policies ensure jobs for everyone, pathological cases only excepted. By organizing employment provision locally, by appointing Employment Creation Co-ordinators who are paid by results, by providing capital through Capital Start and Capital Renewal, and providing microcredit to make the poor and unemployed into entrepreneurs, by providing marketized jobs, by changing tax and social security policies to encourage employment, and by organizing marketized workfare, by all these routes we use the power of the market to end the divisive and debilitating scourge of unemployment. In the future democratic capitalist society, only the rich and the successful will ever be unemployed.

Endnotes

1   James Burnham (1941) *The Managerial Revolution: What is Happening in the World*, New York, The John Day Company, p. 31.

2   F.A. Hayek (1944) *The Road to Serfdom*, London, Routledge, p. 76.

3   Quoted in David Osborne and Ted Gaebler (1992) *Reinventing Government*, New York, Plume, pp. 93–107.

4   Milton Friedman (1962) *Capitalism and Freedom*, Chicago, The University of Chicago Press.

5   Gordon Dryden and Jeanette Vos (1994) *The Learning Revolution*, Aylesbury, Accelerated Learning Systems, pp. 330–33 and 378–81.

6   See Alan Jolis (1996) article titled 'The good banker', in *The Independent on Sunday*, London, 5 May 1996, pp. 15–16. I have drawn heavily on this excellent article in this section.

7   Ian Rogers (1997) article titled 'Colonial to speed franchise plan', Sydney, *The Australian Financial Review*, 5 June 1997.

Chapter Ten

The Democratic Corporation

If there is a single assumption that pervades conventional organizational theory it is that authority is the central, indispensable means of managerial control ... this behavior is not a consequence of man's inherent nature. It is a consequence rather of the nature of industrial organizations
...

– Douglas McGregor [1]

Summary

- Organizations today violate the Democratic Principle. They are based on hierarchy and authority and take power away from individuals.
- This is not necessary for markets to work well. Markets will work better with democratic organizations.
- Corporate democracy is already making slow headway. Under pressure from economic forces, though resisted by corporate hierarchies, firms are becoming smaller and simpler, and hence less undemocratic.
- But new catalysts for democracy at work are urgently needed. Two are proposed here. One, the Capitalist Employee Collective (CEC), gives employees the incentive to own a large chunk of their firm. The other, the Democratic Corporation, gives owners incentives to make firms democratic. Top management is elected by employees at large.

Introduction

The Democratic Principle states that society must be run for the benefit of everybody and by everybody. The Democratic Principle is that power should be decentralized wherever possible: that power should be given to people as individuals, unless power is necessarily concentrated in more aggregate forms as a result of market forces.

When we consider organizations, the most powerful and pervasive institution of our days, and especially our largest and most powerful business institutions, it is evident that the Democratic Principle is not being followed. Organizations are generally neither democratic nor decentralized. Nor is the current degree of autocracy, oligarchy and centralization at all necessary in order to satisfy the Market Principle.

We will see in this chapter, that our large organizations can be decentralized and made democratic, without violating the Market Principle at all. In fact, radical changes in the way we run our corporations will actually reinforce the Market Principle, which is often violated by large corporations when they insulate massive amounts of their internal resources from market processes and pressures. In reforming our large organizations we can serve the Democratic Principle and the Market Principle simultaneously.

Democracy at work?

It is not enough that everyone in society has capital, knowledge, and, if they want it, a job. It is not enough that consumers have freedom of choice, or that voters can overturn governments. For society to be fully democratic, democracy must extend to the workplace. For both individuals and society, the nature of work is of paramount importance: it defines whether life is harsh or pleasant, dull or stimulating, liberating or enslaving, hierarchical or collaborative, cynical or service-driven, grasping or ethical, in short, whether life is more than blood, sweat and tears.

It has been argued since at least the 1930s that business corporations are the dominant form of social institution in society. When people argue this, they generally have in mind the large, publicly quoted enterprise.

Even taking this rather narrow definition, there is a lot of truth in the argument. From their skyscrapers to their local factories, sales offices and distribution outlets, from their brand names to their advertisements and products, from the reports of their activities and their rising or falling profits on the news and in the papers, and from their collective representation in the world's stock markets, whose gyrations affect both the individual wealth of hundreds of millions of people and the performance of the world's economies, quoted corporations are the most visible, vibrant, pervasive and dynamic institutions we have. Governments and entertainers may make more headlines, churches may still in some places have more authority, but the modern business corporation has more success, more money and more control of resources. The corporations provide employment. They provide popular products and services. They are the great paymasters, both of those they employ, and, via taxes, of those they do not. They make the world go round. Very few families in the developed world are not dependent, directly or indirectly, on one or more business corporations. They provide jobs, vital products and services, and, for most people, they organize their savings, insurance and other financial affairs.

If we widen the definition, as we should, to include *all* organizations, not just big business but small business, state corporations, and charities and other non-profit organizations, it is absolutely clear that they collectively set the tone for our society and are far more powerful than individuals or government.

We live in a democratic society. But are our dominant institutions, our corporations, democratic? If not, is there something wrong?

No and yes.

Corporations are subject to the law, and society can therefore in theory control corporations through legal mechanisms. But there are problems with this, not only the well-flagged issue of multinational corporations and global markets overriding national governments, but more importantly sheer lack of public interest.

Does this mean that most people think corporations run well in society's interests and can be trusted to regulate their own affairs? Absolutely not! Opinion polls consistently show mistrust and suspicion of big business and its motivations.

So we have a very curious paradox. Business sets the tone for society, but in a democratic society, business is not democratic, and not greatly trusted. People are dependent on corporations for their products and services, for their jobs, and often for the organization of the most important things in their lives (like their savings). In general, people as consumers are satisfied with these arrangements; the democratic mechanism of the market sees to this. But in so far as people are employees, or citizens, they are often critical of corporations or even cynical about the elites who run them.

But fear not, help is at hand. There have already been two great, and generally successful, revolutions in the world in the past century or two. One has been the struggle for political democracy. The other has been capitalist consumer revolution, whereby mass market goods have been made affordable and attractive, and living standards transformed for the great bulk of people (in developed countries), partly by passing purchasing power to these people (a task shared by government and business), and partly through the wonderfully democratic mechanism of the market. Great progress has been made through these two revolutions, yet democracy and capitalism have not yet converged. They will. The third revolution will see to it.

The third revolution will democratize the dominant institution in our society: the business corporation. Though little heralded, the third revolution is already underway. Some of the new institutions, laws and practices, and ideas for transforming the way that business organizes itself already exist. The rest are well within our reach. The third revolution will make our organizations democratic. This chapter explores how.

The idea of the democratic corporation

It is very simple. We already have democracy in politics. Everyone can choose their government, constrained only by other peoples' choices. We already have democracy in and through our consumer markets. Everyone can choose which products and services to buy, constrained only by the amount of money they have and the choices available (the extent of competition). Also, everyone can choose which firm to work for, constrained only by their skills and the jobs available. We do not have direction of labor and the state as employer of last resort, the essential means by which socialism and Nazism ensured full employment. In these three regards – politics, consumer markets and the labor market – we have democracy.

But there democracy stops. Democracy has not yet made much headway into the corporation. The most successful institution of our society, some would say the most dominant institution, the most powerful institution, the richest institution – this remains largely impervious to democracy. In a democratic world, the corporation is the last, and hugely important, redoubt of hierarchy. Corporations and other organizations may be controlled by one person, by a small clique, or by a broader elite. Very few, either in form or in practice, are democratic.

So, we are free as citizens. We are free as consumers. We are not free as producers. For two thirds of our life, we are free. For a third, and often the defining third, we are not. Karl Marx called the proletariat 'wage slaves'. Today, some very highly paid professionals use the same epithet to describe themselves.

Recall the closing words of the 1848 Communist Manifesto: 'The proletarians have nothing to lose but their chains. They have a world to win. WORKING MEN OF ALL COUNTRIES, UNITE!' Some 150 years later, we still have some freedoms to win at work. Yet the signs of progress are suddenly more evident.

The slow advance of corporate democracy

Simple is beautiful

In a market economy, what works best tends to get done. (It takes longer than those who believe in perfect competition would expect – because competition is never perfect, and usually highly imperfect. Competition works through humans, implying inefficiency.) Increasingly, what works best economically is decentralization, focus, and simplicity. Increasingly, this is becoming better understood. Therefore, vested interests notwithstanding, capitalism is becoming increasingly decentralized, focussed, and simple [2].

Something odd, and quite new, is happening to our industrial structure.

Since the industrial revolution started rumbling, firms have become bigger and more complex. They have grown. They have diversified. Before about 1850, all firms were in one business only; and this remained overwhelmingly true before 1900 and predominantly true up to 1950. Before 1850, nearly all firms had a mere handful of employees: the McLane Report of 1832, covering ten US states, showed that the overwhelming majority of enterprises had a payroll in single figures. Between 1850 and 1900 the numbers on the payroll of a very small number of pacemaking companies, notably the railroads, grew enormously. In 1891, the Pennsylvania Railroad employed over 110,000 workers, at a time when the US armed services – soldiers, sailors and marines combined – numbered only 39,492. After 1900, employee numbers in the largest companies multiplied off the chart.

Along with the proliferation of products and employees went all manner of increasingly complex operations: assembly lines; new management disciplines like finance, 'scientific management' (productivity enhancement), marketing, research and development, market research, data processing, 'human resources', PR, even strategy and 'investor relations'. Then came the multinational enterprise, conglomerates, and the hostile takeover. Finally, in the last 40 years, the profitable cult of market share and the burgeoning of exceptional (nay, unreasonable) rewards for the biggest fat cats, have given the final push to the movement to corporate size. Bigger, it was believed, was better. Indeed, from the boardroom chair, bigger is better. And bigger means more complex.

The 19th century, and the first three quarters of the 20th, saw progressive and accelerating expansion in the average size and complexity of enterprise.

But now this seemingly unstoppable trend has gone into sharp reverse. In 1979, Fortune 500 firms comprised nearly 60 per cent of the US gross national product. By the early 1990s this had slumped to just over 40 per cent. Now it is below 40 per cent. In less than 20 years the large firms have lost one-third of their share of the pie.

Why? Because the costs of complexity are becoming ever greater, and ever more evident. When a firm grows big, it grows complex. Internal complexity has huge hidden costs. Complexity makes market signals more difficult to detect and very difficult to interpret accurately. Even if the signals are heard, complexity multiplies the response time. Study after study has shown that the most profitable and fastest expanding firms are less complex than their competitors: the winners have fewer products, fewer customers, fewer suppliers, fewer operations, and fewer employees relative to their revenues [3].

The movement to simplicity takes many forms and has many results, all of which – and here we finally get to the punchline – move in the direction of corporate democracy.

Outsourcing

Large corporations are reviewing and increasing the extent to which they buy in goods and services from outside suppliers. Outsourcing may involve dispensing with whole departments at head office or other centers of overhead – the property department, the strategy department, the security department, the training department, whatever. Beyond this, firms may decide to focus on just one part of what is momentously called the 'value chain' – for example, *just* on production, or marketing, or research and development, or distribution, or retailing – on whatever the company does best. Other firms then provide the non-core activities. Outsourcing is a wonderful way to cut complexity, cut cost, and raise profits. Sometimes, whole departments become new autonomous firms, with a contract to provide services for a time to the old company, and the freedom (and necessity) to develop new business for themselves.

Some 30 per cent of large US industrial firms now outsource more than half their production. Outsourcing reduces the average size and complexity of firms. It creates and supports new, small, focussed concerns.

The network corporation

Also known as the 'virtual' corporation, the network(ed) corporation has very few employees and an extremely high ratio of revenues and profits to employees. The network corporation carries outsourcing to its logical conclusion: it is in just one business, and even in that business makes great use of outside suppliers, who are friends, allies and often erstwhile colleagues. The outside suppliers are themselves usually other network corporations, partnerships, or single-person enterprises ('SPEs'), and may have cross-shareholdings with other network corporations.

Capstone, this book's publisher, is a typical network business. Capstone is one of the smallest multinationals in the world. It has three partners and one employee, yet has a high share of its small niche in America, Asia and Europe. It could not operate without its network, without having most of its work done by other firms, with whom there are informal but clearly understood alliances: with authors, academics, sales forces, designers, editors, printers, retailers, book clubs, translators and other publishers. In the largest publishing firms, most of these functions are (or were until very recently) undertaken in-house.

The network corporation also relies upon new or newly cheap technology – PCs, modems, faxes, phones – to facilitate communication and avoid the expense and complexity of property. The invisibility and lack of physical substance has led some to call them 'virtual corporations'.

Network or virtual corporations are small and focussed and don't have head offices (sometimes they don't have offices at all!). They are another reason for the decreasing size and complexity of business today.

The single-person business ('SPC'), the entrepreneur-led business, the partnership

There are other forms reflecting the revival of small and micro enterprise, as they take market share from big business. *The partnership* is one of the most venerable business forms, known to Adam Smith as the 'co-partnery'. Partnerships – which are democratic in the sense that all partners have a right to a designated share of profits, and because all partners elect the senior, managing partner – are becoming more numerous, despite ancient laws imposing unlimited personal liability on each individual partner for the actions or debts of the partnership.

The SPC or single-person corporation, also known as a sole tradership, is growing as former employees set themselves up as contractors, consultants and individual entrepreneurs. The SPC clearly does away with the problem of alienation; the individual controls her own destiny. The technology that helps the virtual corporation is making the isolation of the SPC progressively less costly, less isolated, and more splendid. Downsizing and delayering are doing their bit too, increasing the supply of potential SPCs. Many former corporate hacks have found economic and spiritual salvation in becoming SPCs.

Thus Adam Smith's entrepreneurial prototypes – where ownership and management are not separated – are enjoying a late 20th century surge. The rewards for successful *entrepreneurship* have never been higher, as public markets beckon with high valuations and taxmen are forced to become less inordinately greedy. The supply of well trained entrepreneurs, well educated in business, and with specific skills in one micro-industry, has also probably never been higher. And finance, once the great constraint in an era when individuals could no longer fund the necessary capital from family and friends, is now more readily available too. In 1970, venture capital in the United States was a small and exotic cottage industry. Now it is a well organized, major branch of finance, still doubling every decade, but now from a serious base. In the rest of the world, venture capital is where it was a generation ago in the US: very high growth, immature, about to repeat the American experience. Nothing is going to stop the advance of small business.

The only important difference between Adam Smith's small business and that of today is that the owners tend to be teams of individuals rather than families. Where venture capital is involved, there will nearly always be several owners of each corporation, each of whom can hope to get rich if the business performs well.

The late 1980s and 1990s have spawned a new species of more democratic business: the *public sector entrepreneur* within newly privatized state agencies.

First in New Zealand, and now replicated in many other countries, the privatized state agency is a small and focussed administrative corporation serving government. Previously civil service departments, the new agencies are owned by their management teams, or in some cases fully democratic – owned by all the employees. This marriage of syndicalism and capitalism has made an auspicious start, and provides a model capable of much more widespread, and varied, application.

The focused business corporation ('FBC')

Up to the 1980s, successful companies sought further growth by increasing the number of things that they did. They became unfocused. They offered too many products and services at too many price levels in too many markets. General Motors in the 1960s. Sears in the 1970s. IBM in the 1980s. Very often, the corporations concerned went in for major diversifications into hot areas about which they knew little or nothing. Financial Services was a particular flytrap. Not only Sears, but also American Express, Prudential Insurance, Westinghouse Electric, and Xerox got caught in this web. Some other diversifications by major corporations, all reversed within a decade [4]:

Diversifier	Diversification	Bought	Sold
IBM	Rolm	1984	1989
Coca-Cola	Columbia Pictures	1982	1989
Metropolitan Life	Century 21 Real Estate	1985	1995
Chrysler	Gulfstream Aerospace	1985	1990
Eastman Kodak	Sterling Drug	1988	1994
Dow Chemical	Marion Merrell Dow	1989	1995
Matsushita	MCA	1990	1995

In some cases, industry leaders made the same mistake together. Exxon, Shell and British Petroleum all bought profitable minerals companies in the 1980s. They then made them unprofitable. Now oil companies are retreating from minerals. They are returning to what they know.

In the 1990s, American firms were twice as focussed as the late 1970s – the average number of Standard Industrial Classifications (SIC codes) in which firms participate has plummeted from 4.35 in 1979 to around 2. Behind these dry statistics lies the whole Focus Movement, tirelessly championed by marketing expert Al Ries. In a recent book, David Sadtler, Andrew Campbell and I described what we called the *focused business corporation (FBC)* [5]:

> *The FBC is a multi-business organization, but it is focussed. An FBC is not focussed on one business like a single business corporation [or 'SBC', for example McDonald's or Intel]; it is focussed on one set of corporate center skills. In an FBC, the corporate center has a set of skills or resources that add value to each of its businesses. Procter & Gamble is an FBC. Disney is an FBC. 3M ... is [now] an FBC. Each has earned its FBC credentials; each has built a company around a set of central skills and capabilities that can create value across the portfolio of businesses.*

The Breakup! movement

The 1990s has seen an explosion of breakups, whereby companies split themselves into two, three or more new autonomous corporations. The Americans call it spinoff; the British, demerger; the South Africans unbundling. This breakup movement is great news, for business and for democracy. It leads to greater simplicity, smaller corporations, lower alienation and higher profits [6]:

> *Corporate America and corporate Britain [and we could now add, much of the rest of the world] are in the midst of an epidemic that will change the face of capitalism. In an unprecedented whirlwind of self-dismemberment, companies that used to believe that big is beautiful are splitting into two, three or more separate smaller companies ...*
>
> *The epidemic is good news. It will be the greatest wealth-producing change in management attitudes in our lifetimes. It will create enormous improvements in company performance and ... vastly improved shareholder wealth. Companies will produce better products, will serve their*

markets more responsively, and will be better places to work … In the long run, everyone will win.

The movement is in its early stages, but has already reached the 'tipping point'. It has rapidly accelerated to a point where its importance cannot be in doubt, and from where it will grow relentlessly…

There has been a sudden and startling explosion of breakups! In 1993 the total value of companies spun off in the US and UK was $17.5 billion; in 1994 it rose to $30 billion; and in 1995 shot up to a staggering $80 billion. It is already clear that the total for 1996 will exceed $100 billion. This contrasts with an average during the 1980s of less than $5 billion per year.

Breaking up corporations raises profits and market value. A comprehensive study in 1995 [7] showed that spinoffs performed 25 per cent better than the stock market during the first 18 months after Breakup! Among the smaller (and therefore more focussed) spinoffs, most of which were now SBCs (single business corporations), the out-performance was a stunning 45 per cent, all just in the first 18 months of independence.

The importance of the Breakup! movement to corporate democracy is that in decreasing the size and complexity of corporations, Breakup! takes power away from head offices and corporate hierarchies and restores it to those running individual businesses. Breakup! decentralizes and devolves power, releasing huge value along the way, simply by cancelling out the value destruction inherent in distant hierarchy. The logical conclusion of the Breakup! movement will be that most quoted corporations become SBCs, single business corporations, with no head offices.

Certainly, Breakup! does not, in and of itself, create democratic corporations. But it does markedly raise executives' control over their own destiny and it does provide the preconditions for corporate democracy: simple and focussed corporations, responsible for their own performance, with no insulation or barriers between the executives and their capital and customer markets. Breakup! is the single most important cause of the decreasing size and complexity of modern big business, and powerful evidence that the trend works – that it produces better economic results – and will continue accelerating.

Smaller and simpler corporations pave the way for democracy

All the trends we have discussed mean smaller, simpler and more focussed corporations. But are they trends toward more democratic corporations?

Imagine you are a lowly employee, a foot soldier in a giant, hierarchical corporation. You feel alienated. Why?

There are two distinct problems, entirely analogous to the problem of the citizen living under a non-democratic political regime. One problem relates directly to not being an owner or a voter. If you are not an owner, the place where you work does not belong, even in part, to you. However much effort you put in, and however much value you create, you are not really part of the company, and will get your reward, if at all, indirectly: you have no real stake in the company. This is similar to the position of the citizen who has no vote, who has no stake in his society's governance or its success. This problem can only be corrected, in society, by giving all citizens the vote (and, I would add, access to capital); and in business, by giving all employees rights of ownership that carry with them the same rights that other owners have: the rights to a share of profits and to a say in who runs the company. This is what democracy means in an economic organization. And the question is clear-cut, digital, either-or, black or white, yes or no. Just as you are either a voter or you aren't, so too you are either an owner or you aren't.

But there is a second, more muted and less black or white aspect to industrial or political democracy. This is the dimension of the citizen's or employee's control over her daily life, the extent to which she identifies with what is being done in her name by government or top management, the extent to which business or society is governed by consensus, the emotional identification between citizen and state, employee and corporation, what is sometimes confusingly called 'psychological ownership'. This is a matter of degree and opinion rather than hard fact.

Two countries may both have universal suffrage, but one may *feel* more 'democratic' to its citizens than the other country does to *its* citizens. The more democratic country may have any number of mechanisms that facilitate the sense of true democracy – it may have very frequent elections, proportional representation, frequent referenda, decentralized local government, a bill of rights, an elected judiciary, and restrictions on the power of the executive – but of equal or greater importance may be cultural factors: the extent of trust between strangers in the society; the density of its intermediate institutions like social clubs and voluntary organizations, churches, professional bodies, charities, or universities [8]; the cultural homogeneity of the people and their predisposition toward tolerance, compromise and consensus; and a whole host of other elusive and subjective factors that go to make up the quality of life and the cohesiveness – one might almost say, the democracy – of a democracy.

Similarly, two firms may have negligible employee ownership (or both have 100 per cent employee ownership), and yet a markedly different perception of psychological ownership – and in this vague but important sense, be more or less democratic. One firm may have had a founder who encouraged participation in wide debate about important decisions for the firm; another a secretive autocrat. One firm may have employees who are naturally assertive and self-possessed; another a set of timid time-servers. One firm may have had the good or bad fortune to have had a chief executive who set a bunch of industrial psychologists loose within his domain; another firm may be firmly in the grip of authoritarian, rule-bound accountants. All these are accidents of history and location that lead to a firm feeling more or less democratic, quite regardless of legal ownership. These are like the cultural factors in a country that make it seem more or less democratic. If we want to make industry more democratic, we can work on the cultural factors, but it is a slow process.

In business, perhaps more than in society at large, the sense of psychological ownership is affected by structural factors, particularly the size and complexity of the firm. Put the other way, the sense of alienation is likely to be greater, the larger and more complex the firm. There will of course be exceptions – because of the accidents of history and location – but it should be evident why size and complexity encourage alienation and subvert the sense of belonging. If a business is small, the individual is more important and more noticed, the gap between action and feedback is smaller, and the typical individual employee will be closer both to the boss and the customer. Regardless of ownership, small companies are likely to feel more democratic, and less alienating, than large companies.

Likewise, simple companies. At the extreme of simplicity, if a firm does just one thing, it will be easier for everyone to identify with that one activity, that one skill set, that customer base, that purpose. There will be no rivalry between sister divisions, because there will be no sister divisions. It should be transparent what everyone is doing and why. There will be no favored cliques based on product or activity. Certainly, we cannot guarantee that there will be little or no alienation even in the simplest of companies. But there should be a great deal less than in more complex ones. The simpler the corporation, the more democratic it is likely to feel.

Small business is inherently more democratic, or at least less undemocratic, than large business, both because the proportion of ownership to total employees is likely to be higher, and because the small business is likely to feel more democratic and less alienating. Even more so if the business is not only smaller, but more simple too. The trends away from diversification towards focus, and in particular the Breakup! movement, and the gains smaller companies are making at the expense of larger ones, all point in the same direction. At last, business is becoming smaller, simpler and more democratic.

But we can do more for democracy.

A new blueprint for the democratic corporation

Here are two ways to democratize corporations. Both apply to all corporations, regardless of size. They will work in small companies and in big ones. One is an ownership device, pure and simple. The other gives voting rights to employees. And neither device threatens the interests of owners, who will remain free to adopt the devices, or not, as they choose. But it will be in owners' interests to choose democracy.

The Capitalist Employee Collective (CEC)

I propose a new class of company, with two distinctive characteristics. One, that all employees (after a qualifying period) are shareholders. And two, that under certain conditions, the employees can, over time, come to own collectively one quarter of the total share capital.

All employees who pass their probationary period are granted a certain number of shares in the company, as a sort of delayed signing-on bonus or 'golden hello'. Firms would be free to decide how many shares to grant, but the legislation setting up the CEC as a separate class of company would specify the minimum number of shares to be granted, as a fixed minimum proportion of the total number of shares in issue. In practice, in a firm with 1,000 employees, earning an average of $20,000 each, and with a total market value of $100 million, the minimum value of shares to be held by all employees as the golden hello might be set at one per cent of the market value, giving a value of $1000 for each person's starting share stake. The shares would rank the same as all other shares in all respects – including the right to vote and to receive dividends – but could not be sold until at least five years after they were issued. If the employee left the firm before this five year cut-off, one half of the shares would be forfeited and the other half be 'unfrozen' and able to be sold.

This would be just for starters. Employees would be entitled to receive more shares each year, but *only* if the company was performing very well. Individual firms would be entitled to set their own criteria for what constituted very good performance, but one requirement might be that earnings per share grow by at least 20 per cent for at least five years, properly audited. If so, employees would receive extra shares constituting a given proportion of the surplus value over the 20 per cent earnings per share hurdle. For example, one firm might decide to allocate a flat rate of a quarter of the surplus value to employees in the form of shares. Thus, if earnings per share rose by 30 per cent, the initial non-employee shareholders would receive all of the first 20 per cent of benefit, but only three quarters of the rest; their earnings per share would thus advance by 27.5 per cent, the other 2.5 per cent being taken by the allocation of new shares to employees, thus adding to the number of shares and constraining the increase in earnings per share to 27.5 per cent.

Other firms might experiment with more sharply graded ratchets, so that, for example, above a 30 per cent earnings per share increase, one third of the surplus value went to the employees, and above 40 per cent, one half. The market would soon determine which schemes were most effective in producing the desired result: the highest earnings per share increase for all shareholders.

Why would owners want their firms to become CECs? Clearly, the incentive effect on employees. Employee-owners will strive to maximize earnings per share because this would have a dramatic effect on their wealth (more so than for other owners), and because it is now *their* firm. For more than 30 years, venture capitalists have used this type of incentive device, including a ratchet of shareholding based on performance, very successfully, though usually for a small group of top employees.

If all colleagues had a common interest in the firm, four benefits would flow. First, the CEC would be able to attract talent and ambition to a greater degree than non-CECs. Second, all employees would have the incentive to reduce waste, increase sales, and expand the sales especially of the most profitable products to the most profitable customers. Third, the universality of the common shareholding interest should create a greater bond and identity of interest between all employees, between non-managers and managers, and between employees and other shareholders. Fourth, there would be incentives for staff to stay rather than defect to other firms.

For the non-working owners, there is only a small sacrifice at the beginning, with the golden share hello – and perhaps none at all, if it is argued that the employee would compare the total package, including the shares, and value it accordingly. Thereafter, the only sacrifice would be in the context of rapidly rising earnings and, normally, share price. At worst, even if the shares had zero motivational effect, a small slice of the surplus disappears to employees. At best – and we believe this would happen more often – the employees would add more to earnings per share increases than they take away in shares. It would take time to establish whether CECs worked better, on average, than comparable non–CECs, in delivering value to the non–employee shareholders. If they did, one would expect self-interest to lead to nearly all firms becoming CECs. If it did not work, one would expect the CEC experiment to peter out, and, absent the gains to society from increased democracy, one could argue that the experiment should end.

Given, however, the gain to society from increased democracy, one might argue that CECs should be given a head start by being given a concessionary rate of corporate taxation – not enough to cancel out the earnings dilution, but enough to go part way toward this. For example, if non–CECs are taxed at 30 per cent, CECs might be taxed at 25 per cent. Each country would decide whether to grant this concession and how big to make it.

Over time, employees would, in most corporations, become the largest single bloc of owners. Perhaps in some cases the restriction on employee shareholding benefits to 25 per cent of total shares would be lifted, if it was clear that the talent attraction and motivational benefits exceeded the costs. Within a generation or two, direct employee ownership could conceivably become the dominant type. This would transform the character of capitalism; and also create a huge amount of extra wealth in society.

The Democratic Corporation (DC)

At the risk of confusing our terminology, we propose to reserve the term Democratic Corporation (DC) for another new class of firm. The DC would be a firm where the shareholders and board of directors had agreed to let the employees vote, every few years, for the top management. At the moment, top management is nominally selected by the shareholders; they have the right to hire and fire the CEO and all top officers of their firm. In practice, most large quoted corporations everywhere around the world are self-perpetuating oligopolies, where senior management is only thrown out after the most egregious errors, and, absent disaster, is able to select its own successors, from inside or outside the company. In the DC, instead of delegating the *de facto* right to select top management to top management itself, the shareholders would give the right to elect the top management to all employees as voters. The board, and the shareholders, would have the right to veto the slate of top management elected, but would only do so under exceptional circumstances. If the system worked well, this right might never be exercised.

Imagine this. Every four years the top management team of DCs formally announce, in July, their resignation, to take effect at the end of the year. The resignation triggers the election process, the start of the democratic campaign.

Resources are then made available to qualifying groups of executives (and, if the rules allow, outside buy-in teams) who run for office. They present their manifestos – their strategies, their target markets, their internal policies, their way of executing their designs. The manifestos are presented to the full body of employees in a series of campaign meetings, in leaflets, in videos, or in even more creative media. At the end of August, a vote is taken and one team emerges victorious. The team leader becomes the CEO and has a four year term to implement the vision.

Difficult to imagine? Are the top dogs going to voluntarily give up their hard-won positions? We can be sure top management in general is not going to like the proposition. But hang on. Though managers are *de facto* in charge – James Burnham got this right – the owners, the shareholders, still have the right to decide how top management should be selected. Suppose they see advantage, from their selfish viewpoint, in the DC. Suppose the owners think it might lead to better strategies, to more cohesive team work, to less complacent top management, to corporations more like the consensus-run Japanese or German ones, but without the cost in excess bureaucracy? Suppose the owners like the idea of opening up management to competition? Suppose it works? Employees and shareholders would both benefit, at the expense of incumbent management. Is management really so entrenched as to prevent the possibility, if it's a good idea? No.

And is it a good idea, for the owners? I can't be sure. Whether such a democratic corporation would be efficient enough to survive short term competition from the more conventional dictatorship or oligopolistic organization is unclear. But if it could, surely the DC would clean up in the long term. Talent would gravitate there. Maybe the true long term survivors in the new democratic-capitalist economy will be single-person businesses, partnerships and large organizations that follow the partnerships' ethos. These democracies may be able to show us the way forward.

Conclusion

In our democracy, the most dominant and successful institutions we have – corporations – are far from democratic. Yet help is at hand.

At long last, capitalism has uncoupled itself from the treadmill of ever greater size and complexity. This has helped to make business less undemocratic. But it is a slow process that has not yet changed the face of business, or taken it very close to anything that can be recognized as generally democratic.

The answer lies in owners realizing that they have an incentive to create two new classes of corporation. One is the CEC, the Capitalist Employee Collective, where employees are all shareholders and can become large and rich shareholders if the firms do exceptionally well for their owners. The other is the DC, the Democratic Corporation, where employees at large, rather than top management, have the right to select the top management. Both mechanisms can be encouraged by government, by giving a concessionary rate of taxation to CECs and DCs. But the main reason why CECs and DCs are likely to spread is their advantages for owners. All that owners have to realize is that their interests lie more with democracy, with the whole body of employees, than with the narrower interests of incumbent senior management. Under democracy, employees and owners are united in releasing the demon of competition into the boardroom. Only then will capitalism and democracy, the lion and the lamb, lie down together in perfect harmony.

Endnotes

1   Douglas McGregor (1960) *The Human Side of Enterprise*, New York, McGraw Hill. McGregor characterized these assumptions as 'Theory

X' and advocated instead a more optimistic and democratic 'Theory Y' which assumed instead that individuals wanted to work, and would, if trusted, work creatively and without supervision.

2   These themes are explored more fully in two earlier books:
Richard Koch and Ian Godden (1996) *Managing Without Management*, London, Nicholas Brealey.
Richard Koch (1997) *The 80/20 Principle*, London, Nicholas Brealey.

3   See Richard Koch (1997), *ibid.*, especially Chapter 5, where the study by Gunter Rommel of middle-size German companies is of particular interest. For the full story, see Gunter Rommel (1996) *Simplicity Wins*, Cambridge, Mass: Harvard Business School Press.

4   I am indebted here to the pioneering work of Al Ries, the brilliant champion of the focus concept. See Al Ries (1996) *Focus*, New York, HarperCollins, especially pp. 4–5, and Al Ries and Theodore B. Kinni (1998) *Future Focus*, Oxford, Capstone.

5   David Sadtler, Andrew Campbell and Richard Koch (1997) *Breakup!*, Oxford, Capstone, p. 11.

6   *Ibid*, pp. 3–5.

7   Unpublished study by global investment bank JP Morgan (1995) *Spinoffs*, quoted with permission in Sadtler, Campbell and Koch (1997), pp. 33–35.

8   See Francis Fukuyama (1995) *Trust*, New York, The Free Press, especially pp. 6–12 and 24–32.

Chapter Eleven

The Good State

Has the Megastate worked? In its most extreme manifestation, in totalitarianism, whether of the Nazi or of the Communist variety, it has surely been a total failure — without a single redeeming feature ... But has the Megastate worked in its much more moderate form ... in the developed countries of Western Europe and in the United States? The answer is: hardly any better. By and large, it has been almost as great a fiasco there as in Hitler's Germany or in Stalin's Russia.

— Peter Drucker [1]

An open society ... is a complicated, sophisticated structure, and deliberate effort is required to bring it into existence ... our global open society lacks the institutions and mechanisms necessary for its preservation.

— George Soros [2]

Summary

- The state has never been so powerful as in this century, nor done so much harm.
- Despite the reduction of the state's economic power in the past 25 years, the state is still doing the wrong things. Most of its existing activities and assets should be made subject to markets.
- Yet, the idea that the state should stand aside and allow full rein to *laissez-faire* capitalism is utterly wrong. Our society and in particular our economic system is not sufficiently democratic and will not take care of the common good or the positive liberties of individuals without positive intervention by the state.
- The good state of the future will use new methods, and in particular new market mechanisms, in order to achieve its social objectives and create a fully democratic, open society.
- In the third revolution, the state will transform itself and its policies, both nationally and internationally. Democratic capitalist states will co-operate internationally to encourage all countries to embrace democracy and markets. If good states play their role, the 21st century can be one of unprecedented peace and prosperity.

The state and human happiness

Throughout history, the state has been an instrument of oppression, taking from the many and giving to the few, seeking to expand its boundaries by conquest, exacting tribute from foreigners, and, with rare exceptions, subtracting more from human happiness than it has added.

When modern democracy came, democratic states, while driven by noble ideals, contrived to practise, often in more terrible and thorough ways, the state's traditional oppressive role. The French Revolution, the Russian communist state and its affiliates, the German Nazi state, the Chinese communist state and its imitators – all these states, acting in the name of the people, created the worst tyrannies history has known.

When democracy eschewed oppression, and sought to create a more fair and equal society, as in most advanced Western states and Japan after World War II, there were major gains in aggregate individual happiness. But the state as a direct economic power, seeking to replace or seriously restrict markets, has proved a near-universal failure.

In the past ten years, we have seen a total reaction against the power and role of the state. The prevailing intellectual winds have favored markets against the state, and a smaller and smaller role for the state. Untrammeled laissez-faire capitalism has raised its head in practical ways too. Global markets threaten to render nation states powerless.

The third revolution rejects both the traditional social and economic powers of the state, and also the view that the state has had its day. The state is essential to create and maintain a civilized and open society, one in which democracy and markets are in total harmony. The bad state *has* had its day. But the day of the good state is only just dawning.

The new good state

The good state follows the four Principles of Progress. It ensures that all economic activity, including the provision of social services, occurs through a market, so as to maximize wealth, growth and choice: the Market Principle.

The good state divests itself and all other institutions of power, so that power returns to the people; the good state sees that society is run for and by the people; the good state protects and enhances the common good. This is the Democratic Principle.

The good state sets up mechanisms to include all citizens in the good life: the Principle of Inclusion.

The good state fosters useful knowledge and skill amongst all its citizens: the Knowledge Principle.

The good state is also the astute state: it ensures that none of the four Principles of Progress conflict with each other.

The good state has proved elusive. Now we can see it coming.

Good news for the state

Our century has witnessed unprecedented state power, unprecedented democracy, and unprecedented market power. Nearly all the bad things that have happened this century have been down to the state. Nearly all the good things have been due to democracy and the market. Though the worst excesses of the megastate have been mercifully expunged from most of the globe, the state remains a failure. The only coherent theories of what the state should be and do have been: the liberal-capitalist theory (answer: as little as possible); socialism (answer: as much as possible); and social democracy (answer: as much as is consistent with letting the market economy still function). All of these solutions, all of these roles for the state, have been tried. All have failed. We need a new theory for the role of the state and a new way of *turning around* the state, so that it can add value rather than subtract it. The third revolution provides this new theory and practice: a positive role for the state which can get it off the hook on which it currently wriggles.

It is noteworthy that neither Bill Clinton, a popular, reforming President, nor Tony Blair, a popular, reforming Prime Minister of Britain, has a clear or new view of the state's role. In so far as they have a view, it is simply warmed-over social democracy. They believe that government can have a positive role in creating a better society, but they do not want to do so at the expense of interfering too much with the private sector. Ask them whether they want to extend or contract the power of the state, or fundamentally change its nature, and they have no answer. They want a nicer and more compassionate version of the status quo. Without a new paradigm they will achieve nothing worthwhile or lasting.

The state is not a paper tiger. The state has great residual power and presence. In most countries, it is still the largest employer, the largest landowner, the largest property company, the largest investor, the largest spender, and the greatest influence on the economy.

In the United States, the state employs 20 per cent and spends 30 per cent of GDP. In Britain and continental Europe, public expenditure in 1979 was around 45 per cent. Since then the continental state has grown to account for half of GDP and in Britain all the reforms of Margaret Thatcher and John Major managed to do was to drag the state's share down to 40 per cent. Even after major privatizations, the British state – central and local – still employs 30 per cent of all workers!

Except in Asia, where the state accounts for a much lower share of national spending, government spends 30–50 per cent of society's output. And yet, the state is clearly by far the least productive sector of our economy. The experiences of privatization show that over a period productivity can be roughly doubled by shifting companies and assets from the state to the private sector. On this basis, if we virtually eliminated state spending, we could expect to see a 15–25 per cent addition to wealth in society. This is probably an underestimate, because a virtuous circle would be created.

The third revolution will make this change. But removing the state's spending power and executive role is a necessary first step towards a more active and crucial role for the state. This is not a return to the liberal-capitalist 'nightwatchman' theory of the state, to *laissez-faire*.

No. The state will become more effective and more powerful, in making individuals more active, more liberated and happier. The state will play the key role in social engineering to reform our economy and society. The difference is that for the first time, the state will use the market rather than ignore it or restrict it. But it will not be any old market. It will be the markets that conduce toward the best society for everyone, toward the greatest good of the greatest number. The result will be that for the first time ever, democracy, the state and capitalism will all be pulling together in the same direction. Both at home and, more importantly, abroad, in catalyzing the creation of wealth and democracy throughout the world, government will be able to do a tremendous amount of good.

How the state can make individuals active, free and wealthy

The state should help to make all individuals in its own society, and throughout the world, more active, more liberated, and more wealthy. How? Let's illustrate changes in four areas: knowledge, wealth and well-being; freedom; community; and transnational. In all four areas, creative new government uses the Market Principle as fully as possible.

Knowledge, wealth and well-being

Creating the knowledge society

The new state must ensure that every citizen has useful and marketable knowledge. It does this through the market. It ensures that every citizen has the right to receive a good education, perhaps even including a university education. But the state has no schools, no colleges, no universities. The new, active state does two things to produce a knowledge society.

One, it revolutionizes schooling, by ensuring that all educational units are autonomous, self-determining corporations that must respond to consumer power – in this case, the power of students and (where relevant) their parents.

The state ensures that all educational units compete and that therefore good units grow and bad units die. This does not require an army (or even a battalion) of inspectors. It simply requires setting up the educational system on market grounds.

Teachers will not have to become entrepreneurs, but they will have the opportunity to do so. Like parents and students, teachers will be able to choose: in their case, whether to form for-profit or non-profit schools. But both will have to compete in the market and offer value for money.

Every citizen has the right to a good education and to acquire marketable skills. The state has the responsibility to ensure that this happens.

And two, the state pays. Ideally, in a wealthy society, some or eventually all of the cost of education should be paid by consumers themselves. But in every large country, for the state to withdraw as educational paymaster would lead to greater inequality and blighted lives. Whether the state maintains its current expenditure levels on education, raises them or is able to lower them depends on local conditions. Competitive education will multiply value for money, but whether this will be sufficient to ensure a good education and marketable skills for everyone at current expenditure levels is indeterminate. If necessary, more money must be spent by the state. The right of each individual to good education and marketable skills is absolute and sovereign.

The state pays of course, by giving the consumers vouchers, so that the students can spend their educational funds where they want. The state pays and the consumers spend. In this sense, the state *does* absolutely nothing. The market does everything.

Making all citizens capitalists

Through a combination of privatization, Capital Start and Capital Renewal programs [3], the state ensures that every citizen starts economic life with a useful amount of capital. The state also ensures that there are market providers of micro-credit, both debt and equity for starting new businesses. If the commercial market will not clear by providing sufficient funds, the state must subsidize the market providers, through the market, until sufficient funds are available [4].

Making everyone productively employed

The democratic-capitalist state ensures that everyone who wants a job can have one.

Historically, the state has done this by providing vast amounts of employment itself, and by various other full employment policies. These no longer work. The more the state does to stimulate employment, the less productive employment there is, because the cost to society greatly exceeds the benefit. The evidence is crystal clear. During the 1950s and 1960s, unemployment in Europe was roughly half that in the United States. By the mid-1990s, the ratio had reversed: unemployment in Europe was roughly double that of the United States (for example, in March 1995, 10.8 per cent and 5.4 per cent, respectively). The paradox is that European governments took active steps to provide and encourage employment, whereas the United States did so on a much more limited scale. Within Europe, countries like France, Spain and Finland that had the most interventionist governments also have the highest unemployment [5]. It is true that the attempt to stimulate employment is not the only reason for these higher levels of unemployment; the social democratic states of Europe have also artificially raised the price of labor and reduced the demand for it through payroll taxes and lowered the supply of labor by generous unemployment benefits. In theory it might be possible to eschew the latter policies and still have the state intervene to reduce unemployment. Whether more narrow interference with the labor market would lower rather than raise unemployment, except in the very short term, is dubious. In any case, there is a better way: to use rather than abuse the market.

The democratic-capitalist state therefore uses the market to provide full employment. The state does this through a whole host of market mechanisms: private-sector Employment Creation Co-ordinators, stimulating local entrepreneurship, micro-credit (providing funds to individuals to start businesses) through the market, marketized jobs, changes in tax policy, removing institutional rigidities that depress employment, and marketized workfare [6].

These are all market solutions, many of them brand new. The state does nothing, except that it sets up the market solutions and ensures that they are working. If they are insufficient to ensure the right of each individual to meaningful and productive employment, the state must augment the market measures or find new ones. The state, at least initially, pays a great deal, so that if the market will not clear without state assistance, then the state provides anonymous funds to lubricate the market. The market does everything. The state sets up the right markets, and ensures that they deliver.

Putting democracy into the workplace

The state encourages the injection and extension of democracy at work. Here, the state cannot compel, since this is incompatible both with free markets and with freedom. The owners of companies must decide how to run them. But the state has enormous and benign power to nudge companies towards democracy, without in any way detracting from – in fact, while adding to – the power of markets.

We have shown how in the previous chapter. The state provides a new blueprint for the democratic corporation, and lower taxation for firms that incorporate in this way. The state similarly encourages companies and individuals to set up a special type of company, where the employees, over time, become the largest shareholder. These corporations are likely to be more successful anyway. Over time, the tax breaks can be phased out. But the democratic-capitalist state will have changed the nature of work, increased wealth, increased autonomy, increased freedom, and increased equality.

Privatization

Democratic-capitalist government will privatize everything. Up to 1914, no government on earth was able to spend more than 5–6 per cent of national wealth, because it was not able to tax more than 5–6 per cent, and large government deficits between income and expenditure were a desperate expedient only used in wartime. Democratic-capitalist government may still tax and spend around a quarter of national income (at least initially – though there should be a program to reduce the expenditure progressively over time, with an ultimate target of getting back to 5–10 per cent). But the demo-cratic-capitalist state will spend the vast majority of its money in creating and subsidizing market solutions to national needs, like education and employ-ment. The democratic-capitalist state will own as few assets and do as little directly as is possible. Private enterprise and non-profit market-based corpo-rations will do everything, always in competition with each other and with other organizations of their own species.

Clearly, public services need to be provided. We need police, judges, even prison services and armies. We need public funding of education and health care. We need collective sanitation, street cleaning, and protection of the envi-ronment. We need all these services to be better and more effective. Private enterprise, left alone, is not going to provide all of these services in sufficient volumes and to sufficient quality, to ensure an attractive, free, and egalitarian society. The state has a role, a role that has never been more important, to ensure that excellent public services are provided. Democratic-capitalist soci-ety has no truck with private affluence and public squalor.

The solution is neither for the state to withdraw nor for the state to do. It is for the state to provide, to underwrite, to guarantee, to supervise, and to moni-tor – *but to do it all through the market.* This will require a new and sweeping wave of creative and liberating privatization.

To date, privatization has meant mainly selling state-run businesses to the private sector. The businesses should never have been run by the state. The transfer was not revolutionary. No new organizations were formed, and in most cases the new corporations were run by the same people as the old ones. The market, when allowed to work (that is, when public monopolies were not simply made into private monopolies), ensured that efficiency and customer service shot up. This first wave of privatization was extremely beneficial: to customers, to taxpayers, to society as a whole, even to most executives and employees (though not to the many people who lost their jobs).

The second wave of privatization will be different and much more revolu-tionary. It will replace huge tranches of state-run or state-subsidized social or-ganizations, that are not inside the market economy, not subject to competi-tion, and not providing choice to their users, with many more completely new organizations, generally much smaller, all subject to the market and to competition. State schools and hospitals will cease to be part of enormous well-intentioned bureaucracies; they will become autonomous corporations, either for-profit or non-profit, that have to stand or fall by the quality and value of the services provided. Prisons will be privatized and compete to serve socially useful functions (and they will cease eventually to be recognizable as prisons as we have known them since Antiquity). Civil service departments will become employee collectives, delivering service to governments on a contractual basis as close as possible to normal market conditions. Local government services like street cleaning will all be provided by competing contractors. Transportation services will be run by competing private companies. With ingenuity and, where necessary, state subsidy, all public services can be turned into market-based services, raising value, effectiveness, service and choice for consumers; and choice, autonomy, rewards and job satisfaction for employees too.

Democratic taxation

Democratic-capitalist government has very clear views on tax policy. All taxes reduce individual wealth and choice. From this perspective, they are bad. (Taxes have also been bad for society in that they have been highly correlated with state spending and state doing, which has always wasted money and restricted consumers' choice. This is not, however, a necessary correlation or a necessary fact of life. If governments spend but markets do, there is no inherent inefficiency or consumer disbenefit. If I am taxed to give my neighbor choice and value in education, I suffer and she benefits, but as long as she spends what used to be my money in a competitive market, there is no net loss of efficiency or choice). On the other hand, taxation is necessary to support democracy, to create a tolerably equal society *and* to provide a minority of citizens with decent live chances and a civilized existence. Taxes are justified if they add to the greatest happiness of the greatest number, provided they do not interfere with the essential liberty of any individual.

Taxation also restricts choice in that centralized decisions are made, by government, on where and how to spend money. Governments, it is true, are elected from time to time, and voters can choose between different packages of expenditure and taxation. But there are currently very clear limits on the extent to which I can choose how my tax money is spent.

It is wrong to view taxation and redistribution of wealth as a necessary evil. If we are aiming for the greatest happiness of the greatest number, it makes more sense to view taxation as a necessary good. It is just that most taxation has been extremely inefficient in achieving its intentions. For example, we have had progressive income taxes for a century, and income still ends up being extremely unequally distributed. Taxation also has second- and third- order effects that are difficult to unravel and quantify. Some taxes, though, clearly mess up markets badly (for example, very high rates of personal taxation), while others (for example, wealth taxes) seem to have little negative effect on the economy.

Here are some ideas on tax, derived from the four Principles of Progress:

- There must be sufficient taxation to ensure that decent public services are provided through the market, specifically in education, health care, and crime prevention.
- There must be sufficient taxation to ensure that everyone starts economic life with a useful amount of capital.

Once these two requirements have been met, the less taxation the better.

Wherever possible, the individual taxpayer should have the choice of where her tax money is spent. This is called 'hypothecation' – taxes raised and spent on specific purposes. If hypothecation is extended to allow, within limits, each individual to allocate her taxes to whatever purposes she wants, the money taken from the taxpayer ceases to have little or no utility to her. It becomes much more like money freely donated to a charity, which has a wonderful multiplier effect: it gives pleasure to the giver and the receiver. In practice, hypothecation is likely to expand the amounts allocated to education and health care, and decrease the amounts allocated to military budgets and infrastructure projects. There will be limits to how much hypothecation can be allowed, but it is inherently a democratic practice and also one that increases utility.

Redistribution of wealth will be expanded and that of income decreased. Income taxes are much less taxes on being wealthy than on becoming wealthy. Income taxes can therefore decrease rather than increase equality, and protect those already rich from competition. Democratic-capitalist government wants people to become rich, implying a lowering of personal income taxes to encourage accumulation of capital by working. Once people are already wealthy, it makes no sense to discourage them from using their wealth as productively as possible. There will therefore be no taxes on investment, low taxes on investment income, but high taxes on spending and on unproductive wealth (perhaps by having a flat rate annual wealth tax above a certain level, set perhaps at 2–5 per cent of wealth).

There will be *tax exemption for savings invested in businesses or in equity accounts* (that is, in savings accounts and instruments invested in the stock market), both to encourage investment in equities by ordinary people and to facilitate capital accumulation. Money put into banks and the equivalent will continue to be taxed, to discourage the state of affairs that has prevailed everywhere this century where the bottom half of society lends its money to the top half for no real return, while the top half compounds its wealth through the stock market. Since most people would rather avoid tax, it is to be hoped that this will change behavior (if it did not, of course, the taxation would worsen rather than ameliorate the inequality, and should be ended).

All personal income reinvested in small businesses will be totally tax free. The individual will avoid paying any income tax on the initial investment, and any subsequent dividends and capital gains will be tax free, subject only to:

Savings withdrawal tax. Any savings withdrawn from any investment account in order to fund personal expenditure (rather than qualifying reinvestment) will be subject to a flat rate tax, probably around 15–30 per cent, in lieu of taxation during the period of investment.

There will be *progressive taxation of spending.* The bulk of personal taxation will be indirect, but focussed on higher-ticket and discretionary items, on what used to be called luxuries. These taxes will need to be increased carefully and only gradually, to avoid stoking up inflation. Capital accumulation will be encouraged by taking as little in tax as possible until money is actually spent on personal consumption. Millionaires with modest lifestyles – who are in fact increasing capital on behalf of the community – will therefore escape much taxation. Yuppies who spend everything they earn or more, who are subtracting from social capital (often via obnoxious conspicuous consumption), will be conspicuously taxed. Their freedom will be reduced by their own profligacy.

Anything that imposes social costs on society – what economists call *externalities*, because the cost is external to the person or corporation that creates it – will be heavily taxed, up to or beyond the imputed cost to society. Drugs that create illness like tobacco, or products such as oil derivatives that harm the environment, will be hard hit. Though travel increases personal freedom, the side-effects for society are still not adequately compensated for in tax.

Corporate taxation will be progressively reduced, because corporate taxes often destroy more wealth than other equivalent taxes. At all times *small firms and democratic corporations* will be taxed at lower rates than large and non-democratic corporations.

Notwithstanding the bias toward lower taxation, if essential market-based public services of high quality cannot be provided to everyone, taxes will be raised until they are. Also, it is not democratic to borrow from the future to fund the present. Democratic-capitalist governments will therefore balance budgets over the business cycle, if necessary cutting government spending or raising taxes to do so.

Welfare and well-being

There is a tremendous opportunity in welfare policy. The democratic-capitalist state is interested in the well-being of every individual in society, but, more than this, wants every individual to be active, free and independent. Changing our welfare policies by using the market will do an enormous amount of good, some of it very quickly.

The cost of welfare can be reduced, or the quality of service improved, by obtaining better value for money. The state as paymaster must ensure that the real value delivered increases, by at least 5 per cent per annum. For 200 years, the market system has delivered productivity increases averaging around

3 per cent compound per annum [7]. For the past 50 years, the real productivity of welfare payments has actually *declined*. This means that there is a huge backlog of productivity to be delivered (a similar phenomenon explains why the productivity increases when state corporations are privatized are always underestimated). Therefore the government should stop delivering any services at all via state mechanisms and insist that the *new free enterprise social services deliver productivity increases of at least 5 per cent per annum compounded. Competition should be introduced as quickly and thoroughly as possible in order to further drive up productivity*.

Yet, there is a deeper problem, a greater opportunity. Welfare itself is self-defeating. It leads to dependency and quashes the spirit of self-confidence and individual achievement. It divides society into the active and the passive, the doers and the done-to. Therefore, all welfare programs of whatever sort should be phased out, or transformed into something more useful and sustainable, provided that this can be done – and it can – without increasing human misery.

Insurance against ill-health, economic misfortune and old age should be taken out of the state sphere as quickly as possible and restored to friendly societies and insurance companies paid for by individuals. This is, of course, a tremendously difficult project; but the sooner it is faced the better. At all levels the state should seek to withdraw but to foster and encourage intermediate institutions, as specific, focussed, small and local as possible, to ensure that real need is met with constructive action to remove both the need and its cause, economic incompetence.

But what happens in the meantime? We cannot invoke the democratic-capitalist mantra, slash welfare budgets, and leave the poor and deprived to fend for themselves. When the homeless or the single mother who cannot feed her baby approach us in the street, do we simply tell them to get a job? Do we want to see our once-great cities to continue sliding into centers of squalor, crime and misery? Do we pass by on the other side?

Of course not. Nor do we leave private charity, useful and efficient as it is, to patch up the fabric of our civilization as best we can. Instead, we use the magic of the market.

Take single mothers on welfare. We want to end welfare. But we don't want babies suffering. So we find a civilized, market-based solution. What do we want to achieve? Mothers off welfare, mothers with dignity and skills, mothers being useful to the rest of society, mothers with independence and self-respect. So we invite organizations, whether for-profit or non-profit, to tender for what we want, and we pay by results. We want the single mothers that they serve to be well cared for, but to become independent (or if this cannot be achieved, at least able to contribute to their upkeep as far as possible, and to do the rest of society some good) as soon as possible. We want excellent service and results at the lowest possible cost. This the market can deliver.

Peter Drucker [8] tells a moving story about the Judson Center in Detroit. It's a charity that recruits and trains welfare mothers to raise two or three emotionally disturbed or handicapped children. The welfare mothers are paid a modest wage. Drucker:

> *The rehabilitation rate for the welfare mothers is close to 100 per cent, with many of them in five years or so moving into employment as rehabilitation workers. The rehabilitation rate for the children, who otherwise would be condemned to lifetime institutional confinement, is about 50 per cent: and every one of these kids had been given up as hopeless.*

Now, the Judson Center exists outside the market. It is extremely cost-effective. It could compete in the market. But it doesn't, because the market for what it does doesn't exist, except via personal charity. So the Judson Center, a tremendous force for good, remains extremely small, and relatively uninfluential. Drucker notwithstanding, its light is hidden beneath a non-market bushel.

The great thing about markets is that good practice gets replicated, copied, extended, and improved. So we need a market in the rehabilitation of welfare mothers. Perhaps the Judson Center would care to compete in this market, and do much more good. Perhaps it would not. But even if it didn't, entrepreneurs would step in to learn from Judson and extend its practices. The money taken from welfare would do more good, alleviate more poverty, and create more independence.

There is nothing unique about welfare mothers. The same principles apply to the homeless, or to any other sad group. Allow commercial or voluntary organizations to tender to remove homelessness in New York or London or even Delhi, and pay by results, and there would be cost-effective solutions. How long will it be before we adopt the method proven in all other fields, the method of the market?

Freedom

The usual libertarian suspects

The democratic-capitalist state wants to maximize the freedom of individuals, subject only to their not decreasing the freedom of others. There is no new principle here: it is the tradition of liberalism espoused by John Locke, David Hume, John Stuart Mill and more recently restated by libertarians of the right like Friedrich August von Hayek and Milton Friedman.

Though the principles of liberalism are venerable and now once again intellectually in vogue, the state has been very slow to implement very obvious measures to maximize freedom. Though it should not need to do so therefore my manifesto must round up the usual suspects. I favor all libertarian reforms, including:

- the removal of all civil disabilities for individuals, to ensure equal treatment, regardless of race, religion, creed, sex, or sexual orientation
- a bill of rights for individuals
- freedom of the individual under the law, including freedom from surveillance by the state or its agencies, freedom of property, freedom from retrospective legislation, and freedom from interrogation by the police or other authorities, unless specifically authorized by an independent court
- the removal of all regulations and restrictions (e.g. limitation of shopping hours) that restrict freedom and choice, without clear and direct and equivalent value to increasing the freedom of others

- the legalization of drugs (except poisons), gambling, prostitution and pornography
- the end of the draft.

But personal freedom is not maximized just by permissiveness. Freedom also requires active steps by the state to liberate the individual. Some of these, like education, capital provision and employment, have been discussed. But one other area requiring social engineering, and use of the market, remains to be covered: crime.

Ending endemic crime

Liberals have always asserted that protection of the individual against crime is a necessary function of the state. Despite the vastly increased power of the modern state, however, crime has remained an intractable problem for liberal societies (and, actually, though it is not so visible, for non-liberal ones too. It is not often realized how serious a problem crime was, for example, under the authoritarian rule of the National Party before the South African revolution of 1994, or in the Soviet Empire. This is because the state suppressed information about crime). Crime, perhaps more than any other social problem, restricts the freedom of vast numbers of citizens: the freedom to walk without fear, the freedom to quiet enjoyment of property. The democratic-capitalist state needs to use market principles to do better on crime than social-democracy has managed.

Crime is an excellent example of a thriving market economy. The market for crime is buoyant, and crime is expanding its market share of GDP in most places around the world. Not all markets, of course, are good. And the only way to defeat a market, outside of a dictatorship, is through the market. The market share of crime must be rolled back, by competing against crime more effectively.

We can start with the police. Crime is an unequal battle. The criminals use private enterprise, and the state uses a bureaucratic organization. If we could compose a league table of organizations ranked by inefficiency, it is a safe bet that everywhere around the world the police would feature in the top ten (probably alongside the armed forces, a few remaining state enterprises, social work, and state education). Nearly every police force in the world is organized into large, unfocused national forces, with a network of police stations run on hierarchical and even quasi-military principles, and primitive information technology. About the only place in the developed world that you can still find working typewriters is police stations. The principles of cost-effectiveness have permeated even most state organizations, but not the police. Everywhere, huge amounts of crime are unsolved. The odds heavily favor the criminal.

Applying market principles to the police is easy. The police should be broken down into a large number of autonomous, specialized forces, focussed by location or function or both. Effectiveness should be measured and compared by an outside auditing body [9]. Police work should be opened up to competition, allowing existing police units to become autonomous commercial firms. The state should pay by results, and allow police forces to charge for their services too, provided minimum standards provided free for everyone are reached.

Reforming the police is just a start in the war against crime. The profitability of crime must be reduced, so that far fewer criminals enter or remain in the market. By far the most important way to reduce the profitability of crime is to raise the probability of detection and conviction. (By comparison, the severity of punishment is of marginal importance.) If every crime stood an eight in ten chance of being detected, rather than a two in ten chance, the volume of crime would plummet [10].

To raise detection rates to high levels requires privatizing the police but also, initially, spending far more money to ensure that all crime, especially serious crime, professional crime, has a high probability of being detected. Where is the money to come from? One answer is via general taxation, since it can be demonstrated that the benefit of stamping out crime greatly exceeds the cost. But assume that taxes cannot be raised further for the time being, or other state budgets cut. What then? One elegant answer is to *raise the price of crime*. This means that any crime on which a monetary sum can be put automatically receives a tax of several times that amount. For example, if a company is caught evading tax of $1 million, it automatically becomes subject to a tax of $50 million. If a robber steals goods worth $1000, he automatically has to pay a tax on conviction of $50,000, and the state has the right to sell all his assets to recover as much of the $50,000 as possible. It this is not possible, the robber will have an obligation to society to pay the $50,000, perhaps at a minimum rate of $5000 per annum. All funds will then be used to fight crime.

Another source of funds to fight crime is to cut the cost of imprisonment. All prisons should be handed over to private enterprise, with the joint objective of lowering their cost through using prisoners to generate revenue (via, of course, non-criminal enterprise!), and of preventing repeat offending (again, the 'prisons' – which would rapidly evolve into institutions offering greater dignity and training, and providing large amounts of marketed goods and services – would be paid by results).

Not all crime is a matter of combating individual criminals. A lot of crime is effectively 'social' crime, non-professional crime, one might almost say 'neighborhood' or 'community' crime. Some of this can be very serious. For example, up to 1993, New York City had crime-infested neighborhoods where criminality, ranging from public urination to homicide, was rampant. The solution adopted in New York under police commissioner William Bratton, was to set targets for crime reduction by precinct, to empower the local teams to deal with their targets, and to monitor and reward results. The concept of the 'tipping-point' helps to explain what happened. Up to a certain point, effort seems to produce little return. Then, suddenly, the tipping-point is reached, and results pour out. Take the homely case of extracting tomato sauce from a bottle by tipping it up:

> *Tomato ketchup*
> *In a bottle*
> *None'll come*
> *Then a lot'll*

While a certain amount of crime existed in the worst areas of New York City, even in apparently innocuous forms such as public drinking, urination or graffiti, behavior sank towards the lowest common denominator. Cars were vandalized, moderately law-abiding citizens committed minor misdemeanors, and the elderly and affluent stayed out the way. But once the police effort reached the point where crime was sufficiently rare, and the neighborhood had become tolerably civilized, attitudes and behavior suddenly shifted. The area became transformed. In Brooklyn North, murders fell from 126 in 1993 to 44 in 1995, down by 65 per cent. Putting in more and more effort, so that the tipping point is reached, produces a terrific payback.

Going local

The essence of good government is that it centralizes only where this is absolutely necessary. Decentralization should give power to local communities so that the market can be used to revive local economies and so that individuals feel part of the process [11]. 'Going local' is also good because it allows much more innovation and experimentation. The market, to the extent that it is allowed to operate, will then ensure that good local models are replicated elsewhere. Decentralization also makes it easier to realize a new moral basis for society, through an enhanced sense of community [12].

Community

The democratic-capitalist state aims for the active and liberated individual, and the greatest good of the greatest number. One important component of this is a sense of community, at local, national and regional level. The state has a unique role in creating and maintaining community spirit. There are enormously valuable free, or almost free, goods to be created here.

The active and liberated individual is not just an economic animal. She is also a social animal. She is a neighbor, a member of the local community, a citizen. Making money and becoming independent is not enough. Contributing to friends, family, neighbors and society, through the market and outside of it, is necessary for happiness.

The ideal of citizenship is central to democratic-capitalist society. A good citizen used to be willing to die for his country. Exceptional acts of heroism apart, the good citizen of tomorrow must be willing to live for his or her community or country. This means helping other people, directly and indirectly, and making society a better place for everyone. Why? Because each person makes a difference to others, and therefore if society is to be set up to maximize aggregate individual happiness, we need everyone to be aware of the impact they have on collective happiness. And because we all, pathological cases only excepted, appear to have altruistic as well as selfish genes. We derive happiness from making others happy, and from pride in our citizenship.

Peter Drucker has celebrated the citizen as volunteer. He points out, only slightly perversely, that voluntary organizations have become America's biggest employer. He points out that 90 million US citizens – one in two adults – work at least three hours a week as unpaid volunteers, and he comments with great insight:

> *What the US non-profits do for their volunteers may well be more important than what they do for the recipients of their services.* [13]

Yet citizenship can be latent or fully fleshed. Good citizenship does not happen automatically. It needs to be cultivated, nurtured, magnified, celebrated and reinforced. Individuals can do this themselves. But the state can do it most effectively, most powerfully, and only the collective state can do it symbolically on behalf of all citizens.

The symbolic role of the state requires a different breed of politician. In the age of reticence, deference or (let us call a spade a shovel) an unfree press, flawed men like Abraham Lincoln, Winston Churchill or John F. Kennedy could appear saints, or, if not quite saints, symbolic leaders able to manufacture vast quantities of community spirit with no raw material save their own eloquence (or in Kennedy's case, that of his speech-writers). In an age where the press and television leave no peccadillo unrevealed (or at least unrumored), symbolic leadership is much tougher for politicians.

It seems that the pursuit of political power nearly always goes with venality, vanity or sexual vampirism. Yet society has not suddenly become unpopulated by decent, admirable, articulate and relatively unflawed people. They just do not go into politics. We need put a few of these people into the positions of symbolic state leadership. This can be best done by separating the business of governing from the business of leadership. The Republic of Ireland may have had some of the most corrupt chief ministers in the developed world in recent years. But it now elects a President who is above politics. Mary Robinson, the recently retired Irish President, had long been a universal focus of pride and citizenship for her people. Similarly, President Nelson Mandela is almost certainly not the most powerful politician in South Africa, but he is a universally admired icon, a symbol of peace and reconciliation.

All countries need a 'good person' as model citizen, spokesperson and symbolic leader. The democratic-capitalist state will separate this role from the messy business of governing. This is increasingly important because the most vital functions of the state now transcend national borders.

Going global

Happiness requires internationalism

What are the most important things that individual governments can do or contribute toward? Try this for a list: establishing democracy and capitalism, and therefore stability, wealth and a decent life for all citizens, in the Third World; extending and maintaining free international trade; protecting and repairing the environment; maintaining peace; eliminating or at least containing international terrorism, crime and drug-dealing; preventing nuclear war or accident.

All of these things are vital for widespread happiness in the next century. Each of these is necessary: six out of six is a great score, five out of six a disaster. Has government ever had such important tasks?

Yet all six require international collaboration and a spirit of internationalism that is unprecedented in the history of the world.

Fortunately, the third revolution creates extremely favorable conditions for such internationalism. Only the fusion of capitalism and democracy can create such favorable conditions. In this sense, one could say that the third revolution is historically necessary. Otherwise, human history will have been pointless, and cold, cruel, indifferent nature will once again reign supreme.

Why and how does the third revolution create the requisite degree of internationalism?

Capitalism has created world civilization

Capitalism has, since 1750, created a cohesive world economy and world society. Once capitalism became central to the economies of the world's most developed countries, initially to Britain and America, then to Germany, then to the rest of Europe, then to Japan, then to most of Asia, these countries and regions have become part of one seamless and interdependent world economy. Though a large part of world production and consumption is not yet subject to effective international competition, and though national market shares of any product tend to be still surprisingly divergent, knowledge and technology are shared to an amazing degree through the workings of the market. The benefits are transmitted to consumers very quickly.

By the 1970s, the Japanese had learned how to make much better and cheaper motorcycles than the British or anyone else. By 1980, they had virtually wiped out the British motorcycle industry. By the 1980s, Japanese car makers had learned how to make autos that were much safer, more reliable and better value. By 1990, surviving car makers around the world had learned how to do the same. Increasingly, there is convergence of taste, exchange of knowledge, transnational production and distribution, and interdependence of national economies.

The world's currencies are now freely traded. A currency is not worth what its government says it is worth. It is what the international currency traders and speculators bet that it is worth. The world's debt markets are glomming together. The world's stock markets are increasingly priced by the flow of footloose capital across national borders. Capital is becoming more mobile. A global capital market is emerging. These trends in the money economy are dragging the real economy rapidly down the global path. The power of governments to control their own economy has diminished, is diminishing, and will continue to diminish, not toward vanishing point, but well beyond the point where national economic independence is a viable option. The whole process, barring disaster, is irreversible.

A globalizing economy requires international collaboration and international attitudes. There is no other defensible or realistic approach.

But we have more than a globalizing economy. We have a globalizing society.

Everywhere, aspirations and lifestyles are converging. For the first time ever, the top ten per cent of society everywhere regards foreign travel as a natural part of life. An international plane trip is less of an event, less expensive, less uncomfortable, less risky and less time consuming than a trip to another distant national city would have been at the turn of the century. What is true now for the top ten per cent will become true in the next century for almost everyone in developed countries. Until then, television, movies and whatever new technology replaces them will do the rest to internationalize culture and community.

All this capitalism has done. It has created a world economy and a world civilization. This makes internationalism possible and easier, though not automatic.

Democracy: the only viable international value system

Sustainable and heartfelt internationalism requires a common set of values and a commitment to nurture the values and all national communities subscribing to the values. Democracy is the only set of common values that can come close to meeting this need.

Yet, capitalism is not enough and democracy is not enough. We have had capitalism and democracy for a long time and we have, at best, gone only half way to creating the quality, depth and resonance of internationalism needed to guarantee peace and prosperity throughout the next century.

The third revolution is necessary to unite nations

I bring glad tidings of great joy. The third revolution, by fusing democracy and capitalism, can create the concert of interest required between nations.

The third revolution brings a new quality of commitment to the well-being of all democratic-capitalist nations, and a series of practical steps to make democracy and capitalism central to all developing nations.

The 19th century invented the Socialist International. The 21st century will invent the Democratic-Capitalist International ('DCI'). Like the earlier International, the DCI will be a virtual organization, with no headquarters, no employees and very little solid infrastructure. But the DCI will take over from the United Nations as the repository of the hopes of mankind.

The DCI will comprise national governments that describe themselves as democratic-capitalist and follow democratic-capitalist policies. One of these policies will be a commitment to nurture other democratic-capitalist governments around the world, especially in developing countries. To give substance to this sentiment, DCI members who are developed countries will commit to three policies.

First, they will pledge to redistribute capital from the First to the Third world. They will do this by allocating two per cent of their country's GDP, or ten per cent of their taxation, whichever is greater, to capital redistribution direct to the citizens of developing countries who are members of the DCI (to qualify as members, they must be fully democratic-capitalist). The capital will go directly to individuals in the Third World countries and may be used only to fund the individuals' education or micro-business ('Capital Start').

Second, each First world DCI nation will 'twin' with a Third world DCI nation, normally after a referendum to decide between competing 'twin' nations. Thus, for example, the United States might twin with a newly democratic-capitalist China; Britain might twin with Russia; the Netherlands might twin with South Africa, and so on. Twinning will spawn a whole host of official and unofficial links between the two countries and their peoples.

Third, all DCI nations will pool their military forces and seek to keep the world free from terrorism and international drug dealing. All DCI nations would defend the territorial integrity of any individual DCI nation.

Conclusion

The state is innocent. The state is necessary. Only now do we have a model for the good state.

The third revolution saves and dignifies the state, and enables the state to add to, rather than subtract from, the sum of human happiness.

The state has a pivotal role in making individuals active, free and wealthy. It does this by setting up benign market mechanisms. It does this by active social intervention. It does this by mobilizing the innate potential and desire of individuals to collaborate to create a great community.

The national democratic-capitalist state will create the community of international democratic-capitalist states that alone can provide peace and prosperity for the next century. It will do this not with seductive semantics, but with acute actions to bind together nations that have abundant capital with those that have little. The developed democratic-capitalist state will put its money where its mouth is. It will create a virtuous circle. At last, we have the theory and practice to make international democratic capitalism the world's prevalent reality. Finally, the state is a force for good.

Endnotes

1   Peter F. Drucker (1993) *Post-capitalist Society*, Oxford, Butterworth-Heinemann, p. 119.
2   George Soros (1997) 'The Capitalist Threat', in *The Atlantic Monthly*, February 1997, Volume 279, no. 2, pp. 45–58.
3   See Chapter 8.
4   See Chapter 9.
5   The figures are quoted from Lester Thurow (1996) *The Future of Capitalism*, New York, William Morrow & Co/London, Nicholas Brealey, p. 36.
6   See Chapter 9.

7   This is my own estimate derived from many sources. It is important to define productivity as output per worker hour, since the benefit to workers is taken not just in higher real wages but also in reduced working hours and greater leisure. Peter Drucker estimates that from 1881, productivity thus defined has risen 3–4 per cent per annum (Peter F. Drucker (1995) *Managing in a Time of Great Change*, Oxford, Butterworth-Heinemann, p. 196). Joseph Schumpeter recorded that the Day-Persons index of total production rose by an average annual rate of 3.7 per cent between 1870 and 1930 (Joseph A. Schumpeter (1942) *Capitalism, Socialism and Democracy*, New York, Harper & Row, pp. 63–64). Taking France, Germany, Japan, the UK, and the USA as benchmarks, GDP per annum rose by an average of 1.8 per cent between 1913 and 1950, a staggering 5.4 per cent per annum between 1950 and 1973, and 2.5 per cent between 1973 and 1992. These numbers, which produce a long run average of 3.2 per cent, do not take account of decreases in working hours or increases in quality, which are not measured (source: Nicholas Crafts (1997) *Britain's Relative Economic Decline 1870–1995: A Quantitative Perspective*, London, The Social Market Foundation, p. 36).

8   Peter F. Drucker (1995) *Managing in a Time of Great Change*, Oxford, Butterworth-Heinemann, pp. 239–40.

9   The Audit Commission in the UK has conducted a series of excellent studies into the performance of local police forces in the UK. Reading between the lines, the studies are a powerful indictment of police inefficiency and a very helpful blueprint for replicating best practice.

10 In South Africa, admittedly an extreme example, the Nedcor Project in 1996 revealed that on average criminals stand only an 8 per cent chance of being punished for a crime. The murder rate in South Africa is around 50 per 100,000, compared to 14 in the USA, an international average of 5.5, and a rate under 1 in Britain and Japan. The main difference between South Africa and other countries is not the severity of the punishment, but the probability of avoiding it. See Lester Venter (1997) *When Mandela Goes*, Johannesburg, Transworld, pp. 210–13.

11   There have been many promising local experiments in the United States, including community corporations, localized banks, and community-friendly industry – reinventing private economics as a tool for public good. See the encouraging survey by Michael Shuman (1997) *Going Local: Creating Self-Reliant Communities in a Global Age*, New York, The Free Press.

12   There is an important current debate about the importance of community, and the 'communitarian' school of thought is particularly critical of the way that market values have undermined community feeling. One of the best recent discussions is Geoff Mulgan (1997) *Connexity: How to Live in a Connected World*, London, Chatto & Windus. Mulgan suggests that governments should have more authority through becoming more democratic, more open, and less hierarchical. Unlike some communitarians, Mulgan wisely seeks to retain liberty while also searching for fraternity.

13   Peter F. Drucker (1993), *Post-capitalist Society*, Oxford, Butterworth-Heinemann, p. 159.

Parting Shot

Chapter Twelve

All Hands to the Revolution

Politics are made up of two elements – utopia and reality – belonging to two different planes that can never meet.

— E.H. Carr [1]

Elites, no matter how enlightened, cannot by themselves make a new civilization. The energies of whole peoples will be required.

— Alvin Toffler [2]

Imagine ... I wonder if you can.

— John Lennon

Summary

- There have only been two revolutions that have turned the course of history and that are still increasing in power today.
- Capitalism is one of these revolutions. The move to market-based societies and now a market-based world has transformed social relations and turned poverty into plenty.
- Democracy is the other lasting revolution. For this first time in history, most of the earth's inhabitants enjoy civil liberties and are able to set up and set aside their governments.
- The reason why history is not complete is that capitalism and democracy do not fully share the same values. While in some ways reinforcing democracy, capitalism also leads to levels of inequality that are unfair and inconsistent with democracy's objectives: happiness and freedom for all. Large corporations, the distinguishing characteristic of capitalism for over a century, are not very democratic either.
- Democracy has not found an economic program that works well. Socialism failed spectacularly. Social democracy has had its successes, but has faltered. Laissez-faire capitalism, once thought the enemy of democracy, is now being tried by some democracies, with mixed results. None of these are viable solutions.
- The right answer is to use and engineer markets to achieve democracy's goals. This requires a third revolution, the democratization of capitalism. Instead of restricting markets, they are carefully set up to deliver maximum individual happiness and enhance the common good.
- Though this is a genuinely new solution, we can be confident that it will work very well. Markets work. Democracies work. A democratic system based on markets deliberately engineered to raise happiness will work extremely well. All that is required is your constructive energy to hasten the third revolution.

Just two important and sustained world revolutions

Revolutionaries have always believed that they have history on their side, and that the coming of their creed – Christianity, Islam, capitalism, Enlightenment, democracy, Jacobinism, communism, anarchism, National Socialism or whatever – was inevitable. Though decidedly useful, the belief is not usually correct. Typically, history is more fickle.

To date, there have only been two revolutions in the history of the world that have proved to be global, irrevocable, permanent, and progressively more important – and that we may be reasonably confident will continue to be so [3].

The first revolution was capitalism, the organization of life around markets. Since capitalism started its successful takeover bid for society, some 250 years ago, it has transformed individual lives and the world as a whole. No-one before 1800 would have been able to imagine the wealth and technology that capitalism has created, the complex yet relatively homogeneous world it has created, or the extent to which it has allowed the population to grow in the capitalist world while also removing hunger from it.

Capitalism today has many flaws. The worst are galloping inequality and capitalism's inability to supply a vision of the common good are the most important. What cannot be doubted, however, are the strength, the vitality and the sheer global power of capitalism.

Democracy is the second and only other revolution of comparable importance and staying power. The world's richest and most developed countries are democracies; the world's most stable and free societies are democracies. The extent of democracy, defined as societies under popular control, where individuals have a high degree of personal liberty, individual rights are systematically protected and where the state is under control of individuals rather than the other way round, has dramatically increased since 1776, when the United States formed the world's first real democracy [4].

As Francis Fukuyama has shown convincingly [5], since 1776 there has been a clear secular trend toward democracy. He counts three liberal democracies in the world in 1790 – the United States, Switzerland, and (perhaps eccentrically) France; five in 1848 (deleting France, and adding Belgium, the Netherlands, and, generously, Great Britain); 13 in 1900; 25 in 1919; a relapse back to 13 in 1940; a surge to 36 in 1960; a minor fall to 30 in 1975; and then a near doubling to 61 in 1990. Moreover, he does not count any of the many countries of the former Soviet Union as democracies in 1990; a revised list today would add several. If China eventually democratizes, this would bring into the democratic orbit the only really populous or powerful country still bucking the trend.

What is significant is that liberal democracy has recently made headway in many areas of the world that, it used to be argued, were culturally resistant to the idea and 'preferred' or were naturally prey to strong, illiberal government – Spain and Portugal, Latin America, Asia and Russia. Liberal democracy, like capitalism, can now claim to be a universal phenomenon rather than a peculiar and particular expression of Protestantism or 'Western' values.

Accepting that nothing is certain except death and taxes, it seems a very good bet that at the end of the 21st century, democracy and capitalism will continue to the most powerful and important revolutions ever. The odds are that both capitalism and democracy will continue to extend their power and influence. Their staying power is a happy prospect, making it likely that aggregate world wealth and happiness will be higher in a hundred years' time than today.

★ ★ ★

But what is the relationship of capitalism to democracy? Are they really one revolution – part of the same phenomenon? Or are they fundamentally different and antagonistic in terms of their values? Or is their relationship altogether more complex and indeterminate?

Is there only one revolution?

There is a high correlation between countries that have had or have liberal democracy, and those that have had or have capitalism. Arguably therefore they are part of the same historical process of modernization. Modern natural science produces industrialization and capitalism, and also produces liberal democracy. Capitalism – a liberal economic system – is by far the best, and perhaps the only viable, economic system for the 'post-industrial' world; while liberal democracy is the best, and the only sustainable, way of integrating individual needs with the complexity of modern society. This argument would lead us to talk, not about the two revolutions of capitalism and democracy, but about one revolution, perhaps best encapsulated as 'the modern, liberal revolution', encompassing both trends.

Though this argument is tempting, and may from the vantage point of the late 21st century prove to be historically correct, we regard it as unproven and, from where we stand today, as a confusing simplification. The picture we can see is altogether more complex, and justifies our presentation of two quite distinct historical revolutions, capitalism and democracy.

Democracy can arise without capitalism. Indeed, the first clear example of liberal democracy, and the model for all other democracies, was the American Revolution of 1776, which arose in an agricultural, pre-capitalist society. Similarly, Switzerland became a democracy before it evolved a capitalist economy. Nonetheless, it is difficult to find any example of a contemporary democracy which is not capitalist.

On the other hand, it is clearly possible to have capitalism without democracy. Examples of countries that industrialized rapidly and successfully – that moved over to a capitalist economy – under authoritarian, non-democratic regimes include Germany under the Kaisers (1870–1918), Meiji Japan, pre-revolutionary Russia, Brazil after the military coup of 1964, Pinochet's Chile, and many of the recent Asian so-called economic miracles, including Singapore, South Korea, Taiwan and Thailand.

Authoritarian regimes are able to move to capitalism faster than democracies because they do not have to take so much account of public opinion: the non–democratic regimes can therefore squeeze out inflation, avoid large welfare bills, keep unions in check, institute free trade, and allow unemployment to rise, while allowing sufficient economic freedom, encouraging entrepreneurs and importing the most modern technology.

Once the transition to capitalism has been made, it *may* be a different story; there are few examples today of countries that have been capitalist for several decades, but which are not democracies. But this may well be coincidental. There is no absolute necessity for a capitalist country to be democratic, and it is quite possible to imagine many ex-socialist third world countries successfully adopting markets while continuing to remain dictatorships or ruled by tribal or other elites, perhaps for generations. Many countries today, especially towards the East, are largely market-based but not very democratic – Iraq, Iran, Saudi Arabia, Kuwait, Singapore, Malaysia, South Korea, Indonesia, and Hong Kong. China itself is increasingly market-based but not at all democratic. There is a danger that China may become the prototype for a new kind of market-based tyranny incompatible with both democracy and capitalism as commonly understood.

Though we can observe a correlation between the incidence of capitalism and democracy, and even a convergence whereby democratic countries tend to become capitalist, and capitalist countries tend to become democratic, there is no historical inevitability in the convergence.

Are capitalism and democracy natural antagonists?

There is an opposite argument: that far from being part of the same trend, or natural bedfellows, capitalism and democracy are fundamentally incongruent.

This argument has been advanced most recently and persuasively by the American economist Lester Thurow. His argument is not historical, but relates to the different values that he sees espoused by capitalism and democracy [6]:

> Democracy and capitalism have very different beliefs about the proper
> distribution of power. One believes in a completely equal distribution of

political power, 'one man, one vote,' while the other believes that it is the duty of the economically fit to drive the unfit out of business and into economic extinction. 'Survival of the fittest' and inequalities in purchasing power are what capitalistic efficiency is all about. Individuals and firms become efficient to become rich. To put it in its starkest terms, capitalism is perfectly compatible with slavery. The American South had such a system for more than two centuries. Democracy is not compatible with slavery ...

Democracy holds out beliefs and reference groups that are not compatible with great inequalities. Capitalism also has a hard time defending the inequalities that it generates with a contrary set of beliefs as to why those inequalities are right and fair ...

Capitalism postulates only one goal – an individual interest in maximizing personal consumption. But individual greed isn't a goal that can hold any society together in the long run.

Thurow's comments are provocative and useful. He is right that democracy is inherently egalitarian. He is also right that capitalism can lead to inequality, and, as we have seen, that the most capitalist societies today, especially the United States, are also more unequal than the more moderately capitalist societies of Europe and are also rapidly increasing in inequality, as the constraints on capitalism are increasingly removed. Thurow is also right in saying that the inequalities of capitalism cannot be justified on logical grounds of fairness. The inequalities of wealth that contemporary capitalism generates are far greater than can be justified by differences in intelligence or effort, and rely heavily on inherited chances and luck as well as skill.

Nonetheless, it is unbalanced to claim that capitalism and democracy have incompatible values.

Capitalism, as we have seen, has a strong element of value neutrality: it can survive and thrive under societies that are both inegalitarian and egalitarian, authoritarian and democratic. Capitalism is very elastic, and has distinct chameleon characteristics. It has evolved tremendously since the 19th century, and as society has become more democratic, so too has capitalism. Capitalism would not have survived the 1930s if it had not been able to adapt to, and play a large part in creating, the humanitarian–democratic Western world after World War II. The capitalism Marx – and many honest capitalists – denounced is not the capitalism of today. Capitalism today happily accepts social responsibility and is in fact the willing paymaster of all the systems that redistribute cash to the poorer elements of society.

Moreover, capitalism demonstrates many values highly compatible with democracy.

Some values shared by democracy and capitalism

Capitalism is extremely decentralized. So is democracy.

Capitalism centers around the individual, as producer and consumer. Democracy centers around the individual, as citizen, voter and as the ultimate repository of rights and value.

Capitalism requires and enhances the active and educated individual, as entrepreneur and knowledge worker. Democracy requires and nurtures the educated individual as a responsible citizen.

Capitalism avoids compulsion, leaving the individual free to respond to society's needs and constraints through the market. Democracy also limits the extent to which the state or other corporate bodies may oppress the individual or constrain her liberty.

Capitalism requires a substantial number of individuals who are eccentric, maverick thinkers, risk-takers, and who will pursue new and unconventional ways. Democracy also allows the heretic to be tolerated and prosper.

Capitalism socializes behavior, channeling egotism and ambition into socially useful actions, that enrich the individual precisely because they are useful to others. Democracy forces everyone to allow everyone else dignity and respect, and recognizes and encourages socially useful acts by individual citizens.

Capitalism is no respecter of rank, privilege or social convention. Neither is democracy.

Capitalism is restless and dynamic, catalyzing social mobility, spotting, encouraging and rewarding talent, making the best possible use of human re-

sources, regardless of background, beliefs, sex, religion, race or any other taboo. Democracy also breaks down hierarchy, class, and irrational prejudice.
Private enterprise has been the most meritocratic and progressive force for liberating individuals that the world has ever seen.

It is also historically inaccurate to associate capitalism with inequality. While
it is true that the greater freedom given to individualistic capitalism in the late
20th century is leading to greater inequality, it is also true that, taken as a whole,
capitalist society has tended to be much more egalitarian than non-capitalist
society. In the broad sweep of history, capitalist society replaced feudal or agricultural society, increasing social mobility and greatly levelling the distribution
of wealth. In this century, non-capitalist societies such as communist Russia or
Nazi Germany had considerably greater inequalities of wealth than contemporary capitalist countries. For example, James Burnham [7] showed in 1941,
using communist Russian data, that the top 11–12 per cent of Soviet society
received 50 per cent of national income, whereas in the United States, the top
10 per cent received 35 per cent. It is also difficult to measure inequality in a
quantitative way that reflects the tenor of society. Most people are willing to
accept, and even delight in, a small proportion of society being extremely rich,
provided three conditions apply: (1) that it is possible, even if very unlikely,
that they could become very rich themselves; (2) that the richest and poorest
citizens are treated fairly and have equal dignity; and (3) that the poorest citizen
is well fed and housed.

Capitalism has shown remarkable flexibility in adapting some of its less egalitarian values toward those of democracy, while in many other respects capitalism and democracy have very congruent values.

★ ★ ★

Capitalism and democracy are distinct revolutions: the most powerful in history, with the greatest staying power; the most benevolent too.

Capitalism is the best economic system. Democracy is the best political system. Capitalism and democracy shared common roots, yet initially saw each
other as enemies. In the 1930s democracy nearly killed capitalism. Since 1945

the two systems have been more allies than enemies. Capitalism has moved its values closer to those of democracy. The issues of inequality, and social purpose, remain stumbling blocks between capitalism and democracy.

For the future, capitalism and democracy can either fight each other, as they did up to 1945; cohabit without making common cause, as they have since 1945; or sink their differences and merge into a new and even more powerful force.

It is clearly in the interests of mankind to see the third of these options: to combine capitalism and democracy, so that capitalism is democratized and democracy is marketized; to see a third revolution consolidate the advances of the first two revolutions and to create new gains.

Already, capitalism and democracy have moved toward each other.

Democracy has discovered the virtues of markets. In the 1980s, state businesses valued at $185 billion, and worth a great deal more, were transferred to the market economy, in the biggest ever redrawing of the public-private boundary. More important still is the shift in the intellectual consensus. The left and the center have become enthusiastic privatizers. The market is no longer a demon, but a useful ally. Governments around the world are deregulating and opening up global markets, aware that the benefit to their citizens is greater than the loss to their own power.

Capitalism has slowly but surely become more democratic. Industry is now owned mainly by ordinary employees and citizens. Business has cheerfully funded welfare. Firms today are unlikely to order their employees or manipulate their customers in the way they did in the first half of the century. Firms are more likely to engage their employees and serve their customers. Class divisions have diminished; modern capitalism has delivered the middle class, consumer society. Recently, small business has gained at the expense of big business, and over-diversified big business has begun to dismantle itself into smaller, more focussed, less alienating units.

These are disparate beginnings, early stirrings. They do not yet amount to a coherent movement. Until now, they have lacked a name, a common purpose, a coherent blueprint, a body of supporters. Now, these trends have a name – the third revolution – four Principles of Progress, and an illustrative blueprint of some possible policies.

But these are not enough. No revolution has yet succeeded without powerful economic and non-economic forces driving it, without an ideology, and a mass of enthusiastic revolutionaries. Does our putative third revolution have these?

What forces are driving the third revolution?

The initial force driving the third revolution is the power behind the first two revolutions, and the increasing realization that capitalism and democracy will waste much of their energy unless they join forces.

Every political movement needs an economic ideology. Democracy has tried several. None has stuck. First there were the various shades of socialism, communism, fascism, Nazism, all centered around the masterly state as economic supremo. For a time there was economic success, as the state ruthlessly enforced industrial modernization on backward agricultural economies (or, in the case of Nazi Germany, conscripted the workforce to provide for war). Thereafter, state-centered economics faltered, unable to decentralize or motivate. Throughout, however, the state subordinated the individual; democracy had created undemocratic systems, incompatible both with individual rights and social equality.

Then democracy tried social democracy: full employment, the mixed economy, welfare. Again, social democratic economics initially worked miracles, as labor gained purchasing power and sought collaboration rather than confrontation. And social democracy worked in the political sphere too: individual liberty and freedom of opportunity were enhanced simultaneously. Then, the golden age of social democracy (1945–65) began to falter. Welfare (and, in the United States, war) raised government spending beyond what taxpayers would finance. Governments borrowed from the future and stoked up inflation. The oil crises of 1973 and 1980 did the rest. In Europe, the home *par excellence* of social democracy, organized labor acquired too much power, and centralized decision making by the state, unions and employers stoke up inflation and constipated market forces. It appeared that there was a trade-off between inflation and unemployment, and a worsening one at that. Social democratic economics started to seize up.

Politically and socially, too, social democracy flattered only to deceive. Welfare not only harmed the economy, but also harmed the recipients. Dignity gave way to dependency. As it became more difficult, and less necessary, to obtain a job, society became divided into the majority and the underclass. Denied the discipline and satisfaction of work, whole tranches of youth turned to alcohol and drug abuse.

Increasingly, democrats of the center and left, not much later than those of the right, began to question the effects of social democracy. The general population did likewise. The 1980s saw a general move away from social demo-economics, toward market-based solutions, of which privatization was just the most conspicuous.

Yet, the results were mixed. As we stand in the late 1990s, there is confusion. From the 1980s, market economics were allowed the greatest freedom in the United States, and the greatest proportionate *movement* from social demo-economics to market economics occurred in Great Britain. In both Anglo-Saxon countries, unemployment, inflation and taxation fell dramatically, and international competitiveness rose, benefitting the bulk of the electorate; but inequality and the number of citizens slipping into the underclass soared. By contrast, the Continental European governments moved much less away from social democracy. Their peoples suffered relatively high unemployment and taxation, and deteriorating competitiveness, but no increase in inequality.

Two things should be clear. Social democracy has failed. But rampant capitalism, without constructive political and social intervention, will not work either. However much free markets raise wealth, they will not be accepted if they threaten the social fabric.

The solution is evident. We cannot go back to the non-market intervention of social democracy. But we should go forward to the market intervention of democratic-capitalism (if you still dislike the 'c' word, call it democratic-marketism). We should use markets to accomplish what we collectively, democrats and the world's electorates, want to achieve. If we want education and skills for everyone, we should set the market up to deliver it. If we want full employment, we must set up the right market to provide it. The good state must not try to deliver these services. The good state should finance them and use the market to deliver them. The same is true of all other public services. In every sphere we must give the maximum possible autonomy and force to decentralized market forces; but we must insist on democratic and civilized objectives and results.

Markets do not have to lead to greater inequality or a diminished sense of community. Since marketism first became powerful, in the late 18th century, marketism has greatly expanded its force and has *lowered* inequality and *raised* social cohesion. The way that markets are set up, and the framework set by government for them to operate in, determine whether they will increase or lower equality and fraternity.

The natural destiny of democracy is with a reformed capitalism; conversely, capitalism can only become truly unfettered if it is popular and delivers results for all of the people. Democratic-capitalism will not replace either democracy or capitalism, which will remain glorious parallel pillars of a civilized society. What democratic-capitalism will do is provide the arch linking the two pillars, so that all citizens can admire and pass through the arch to a better, more fraternal future.

The forces driving democratic-capitalism therefore are precisely the forces driving democracy and driving capitalism: the desire for dignity and fairness for all, the power of the people; and the delivery of ever greater wealth through creation, exploitation and dissemination of science and technology. What democratic-capitalism does is remove the negative energy that democracy and capitalism have spent fighting each other, and reinforce the power of democracy and capitalism to deliver more for everyone.

Democracy needs markets, to raise wealth and solve social problems.

Capitalism needs democracy, to allow it to be popular, legitimate and autonomous.

The unresolved issues of society – inequality, the underclass, unemployment, and social purpose – can only be resolved by democratic-capitalism.

The poor need democratic-capitalism to gain education, jobs, and capital, and in the process to become full members of society, with the same dignity and status as everyone else.

The rich need democratic-capitalism, to make their gains sustainable and constructive for all, and to preserve all their liberties.

Everyone in between needs democratic-capitalism, so that society can advance both in new wealth creation faster than before, and so that it can serve a worthy purpose: the enhancement of human health, liberty and happiness at home and throughout the world.

The global vision of democratic capitalism

There is a great prize available, to turn the 21st century into the richest, fairest and happiest century in history.

The way to do this is not easy, but it is clear. It is to turn every single government around the world into a democratic-capitalist community. The vision is that all countries become democratic, and all countries adopt democratic-market economies. If we manage this by the end of the century, we will finally have banished hunger and war to the barbaric dustbin of history.

The vision is demanding in the extreme, but not unattainable. We must start by turning every country of the world that is a democracy and capitalist into a democratic-capitalist state. Some existing political parties may turn themselves into democratic-capitalist ones (ideally, if confusingly, in some countries both the main parties may do so; the electorate should then judge which party is more truly democratic-capitalist); if not, a new democratic-capitalist party should arise in each country, and be swept to power.

By the year 2010 therefore most or all of the existing capitalist-democracies, comprising a clear majority of the world's economic power, could be democratic-capitalist.

The democratic-capitalist countries can then form an alliance, perhaps called the Democratic Capitalist International (the DCI), with the explicit purpose of turning all other nations democratic-capitalist. The means to be used, of course, will be both diplomatic and market-related. Since the DCI nations will be rich, and most of the non-DCI nations poorer, there will be considerable leverage. Capital and technology will be transferred – on a decentralized, market basis, not involving money passing through state coffers – to countries that join the international community of democratic-capitalist nations.

DCI nations will also pledge not to go to war with other DCI nations, and would form a collective security pact to protect each other against other nations and terrorism.

Over time – and it may take the whole century – DCI nations will combine into a common trading bloc, with no tariffs or restrictions on the movement of people and goods within the DCI. Along the way, groups within the DCI may combine first. For example, if the North American Free Trade Area (NAFTA) and the European Community (EC) both became exclusively democratic-capitalist groups by the year 2020, they might decide to merge into one Northern DCI (NDCI) trading bloc.

★ ★ ★

Join the revolution!

Utopia and reality are only different planes if we allow them to be so. Today's society is in any case an 18th century utopia. But we do much better. It is within our grasp to ensure that peace and prosperity are in everyone's hands, throughout the world, within the next century.

Do you share the vision? Do you believe that markets deliver the best economic results? Do you also believe in community, fairness, liberty, and a decent life for everyone? Can you believe that the demands of markets and the demands of democracy can be reconciled? If so, join the third revolution!

What can you do? The first task is to publicize the idea. Talk about it to your colleagues and friends. If you are involved in any media, give the idea exposure and the oxygen of publicity. If you are in the communications industry, tell me how to promote the idea.

The third revolution needs the best possible manifesto. Test the ideas. Refine and improve them. Add new ones. Publicize them. Let the market decide which ideas go forward and which fall by the wayside.

If you are a member of a political party, see if you can convert it, even if only on a local basis, to democratic-capitalism. Form a pressure group. If necessary, form a new local party. Link up to other local groups. Run for office in local elections.

Those who have never become involved in politics before should have a go now. You will bring new energy and commitment to the process.

Be ready to vote for democratic–capitalist parties. Tell opinion pollsters that you intend to do so. Create a bandwagon. When you have the opportunity, be sure to use the political market: vote!

Do whatever you can. The cause is right and just: for you and for every-one else. Create the third revolution. Citizens of the world, unite! We have nothing to lose but our poverty or our guilt. We have a wonderful world to win.

Endnotes

1   E.H. Carr (1966) *The 20 Years Crisis, 1919–39*, London, Macmillan, p. 93.
2   Alvin Toffler (1980) *The Third Wave*, London, William Collins Sons & Co., p. 451.
3   Apart from capitalism and democracy, the only revolutions that come anywhere close to satisfying my criteria are Christianity and Islam. Both are growing now but neither can demonstrate steady and consistent growth over time, nor the ability to take root in all types of culture. Nor can Christianity demonstrate the ability to organize society in an important way around its principles; Christianity has always been most effective as a minority, 'opposition' movement and has been uncom-fortable, and ultimately self-diluting, as an official creed. It is difficult to imagine that the 21st or 22nd century world will be organized around the principles of either Islam or Christianity, except to the extent that they (and other religions) have contributed to the ideals of democracy.
4   To date democracy in the United States from 1776 is actually prema-ture, as explained in the Preface. But for brevity, and because the mile-stone is the best available, I use the normal convention here.
5   Francis Fukuyama (1992) *The End of History and the Last Man*, New York, Free Press. My Preface explains why Fukuyama is premature in

calling Great Britain democratic in 1848; 1884 would be a much better (and the earliest arguable) date. Throughout, Fukuyama calls states democratic when they introduce universal (or substantial) white male suffrage, which is an undemanding and increasingly incongruous criterion. A more rigorous definition of democracy would not, however, affect his argument, which is simply that the extent of democracy has dramatically grown over time, especially this century.

6   Lester Thurow (1996) *The Future of Capitalism*, New York, William Morrow/London, Nicholas Brealey, pp. 248 and 257. Charles Handy (1997) *The Hungry Spirit*, London, Hutchinson, makes similar points in a more personal and visceral vein.

7   James Burnham (1941) *The Managerial Revolution: What is Happening in the World*, New York, The John Day Company, p. 46.

Index

Christianity 282
Christie, A. 7
Churchill, W.S. 63, 256
classical theory 118
Communist Manifesto xi–xiii
community, and citizenship 255–7,
    263
complexity theory 27
crime 252–5
Cuba 79, 174
customers
    and complaints procedure 79, 81
    and manipulation of markets 88
Czech Republic 175

death, corporate 118–19
decentralization 119–20
democracy
    at work 215–17
    as best way 128
    and capitalism 73–4, 122, 128–
        32, 139–40
    dark side of xxv–xxvii
    defined xxiv–xxv, 137
    history of xxiii–xxviii
    as only viable international value
        system 259
    as second revolution xx–xxi,
        269–70
    social 47
    versus managerialism 92–3
    in the workplace 243
    see also capitalism/democracy
        relationship

Democratic-Capitalist International
    (DCI) 260, 281
democratic corporation
    idea of 217–18, 231–2
    new blueprint 228
        capitalist employee collective
            (CEC) 229–31
        Decmocratic Corporation
            (DC) 231–3
    slow advance
        Breakup! movement 224–5
        entrepreneur-led 222–3
        focused business corporation
            (FBC) 223–4
        network (virtual) corporation
            221
        outsourcing 220
        partnership 221–2
        simple is beautiful 218–20
        single-person business (SPC)
            222
        smaller and simpler 226–8
    see also organizations; state
        organizations
Democratic Corporation (DC)
    231–2, 233
democratic principle 150–52, 191,
    211, 215
    and capitalism 152–3
    and the common good 168
    as incompatible with market
        principle 153–4
democrats, and implications of free
    market 120–21